The Civil War in the Northwest

THE CIVIL WAR
IN THE NORTHWEST

Nebraska, Wisconsin, Iowa, Minnesota,

and the Dakotas

ROBERT HUHN JONES

UNIVERSITY OF OKLAHOMA PRESS : NORMAN

The publication of this volume has been aided by
a grant from the Ford Foundation

To Estelle

Contents

Illustrations

Maps

Preface

THERE HAVE BEEN AT LEAST 34,000 volumes written on the Civil War, and the approaching centennial of that awesome event will insure the outpouring of many more. In this most explored facet of American history, it is curious that there still remain areas to examine, and people and events to reconsider, re-evaluate, and reinterpret. One of the neglected areas is the northwestern frontier. The problem is unusual, for there two turbulent streams of history, the frontier and the rebellion, converge and flow together until the newer ends in a muddy backwash as the older flows on. It is far too arbitrary to paddle one stream without the other, yet most often this has been done. The Civil War has been forgotten as historians probed the Indian massacre, or vice versa.

In a military sense, the northwestern frontier was administered by the Department of the Northwest, which included the states of Minnesota, Wisconsin, and Iowa, and the territories of Dakota and Nebraska (for a time). This unit was not strategically concerned with crushing the rebellion in the South. Its military necessity was derived from Indian troubles, but it also had considerable value as a source of men and bread in the larger war. The total population of Minnesota, Wisconsin, and Dakota Territory in 1860 was over 1,500,000, and this area sent enough men into the field to compose an army more than twice as large as that McClellan had before Richmond.[1] In the commissary de-

---

[1] Figures given in this paragraph from Joseph C. G. Kennedy, comp., *Population of the United States in 1860 Compiled from the Original Returns of the Eighth Census,* 137, 253, 531, 551, 597; Kennedy, comp., *Agriculture in the United States in 1860 Compiled from the Original Returns of the Eighth Census,* xxix, xlvi, cviii–cix; Frederick Phisterer, *Statistical Record of the Armies of the United States,* 10; *Statistical Atlas of the United States,* 1924, 5.

partment, this region furnished 7 per cent of the nation's wheat, 16 per cent of the corn, and every twenty-third beef animal or milch cow, and every thirty-third hog. Important also was the fact that this geographic domain included 17 per cent of the total land area of the United States.

THE TERRITORIES IN 1862

During the period the gold mining region of western Montana grew prodigiously, as did the other areas. Dakota Territory, which boasted a population of nearly 5,000 in 1860, could itself be proud of more than tripling the number of its settlers in a decade, even though the territory had been shorn of its western reaches, which became Montana Territory and most of Wyoming Territory. These sections, by 1870, claimed over 29,000 inhabitants, which, added to the 15,000 in Dakota, totaled slightly fewer than 45,000, or an increase of over ten times the population of 1860. The states of Iowa, Minnesota, and Wisconsin experienced similar, if not such spectacular, booms: by 1870 the population of Iowa had increased 77 per cent, Wisconsin, 36 per cent, and Minnesota, 156 per cent.[2] From these facts, then, it is not

[2] Francis A. Walker, comp., *The Statistics of the Population of the United*

far-fetched to assume that the military commander had a relatively significant area to preserve and administer, even if the
latter was not actively engaged in the rebellion.

Another facet of the Civil War open to exploration is the study
of military administration. Such a project could acquaint us with
the variety and complexity of the problems that an army must
face. Many accounts include, either by design or implication,
the problems of various administrative levels. Biographies and
memoirs of general officers and government officials touch the
subject; histories of army groups, such as the Army of the Potomac, and of various other units, usually regiments, but sometimes divisions, or brigades, or battalions, also show an occasional tentative approach. A study of the Union army, from the
aspect of general problems facing the nation, can be found
in Fred A. Shannon's *Organization and Administration of the
Union Army, 1861–1865,* and of non-military problems to a lesser extent in other works. But few seem to comprehend the magnitude and scope (and thus the tremendous responsibility) of
directing an army in all its activities, such as strategy, supply,
and organization, and in all its relations, such as civil, political,
and legal, and also in the organization's entirety, in the South,
on the frontier, in reserve. In the present volume an attempt has
been made to present the day-to-day workings of a military department on the frontier in time of war, intended to help illustrate the interplay of complexities on the departmental level.

It might be well at this point to define a military department.
It was a geographical area, often arbitrarily and artificially ruled
off on orders from the War Department, for purely administrative purposes. Officers commanding such areas "exercise supervision and command over all the military forces of the United
States within their territorial limits . . . where special exception
is not made by the War Department." The commander of such

States . . . *The Ninth Census,* Vol. I, p. xvii; Kennedy, *Eighth Census, Population,* 551. No reliable data can be found for the population in 1865. Hence, the
only basis of comparison can be the census of 1870, not too accurate for such a
purpose since it includes the post-war exodus to the West, but does not show the
population of the gold area at its height.

MILITARY DEPARTMENTS OF THE UNITED STATES,
DECEMBER 31, 1862

a unit regulated the establishment of military districts and posts, and originated and directed all military operations within the area. A geographical military division could consist of a number of military departments, in which case the officer in division command exercised the above powers.[3]

The United States was innocent of this military administrative area until March, 1815, when the country was divided into nine such units, all of which fell in either the Northern Division or the Southern Division. Prior to 1815 the country had been split into military districts. After 1815 the organization fluctuated until on October 31, 1853, the United States was divided into seven departments, one of which sufficed for the whole area east of the Mississippi. This organization continued until the outbreak of hostilities in 1861 rendered it impractical. By June 30, 1861, the number of departments doubled. During the war, department lines changed with considerable frequency, particularly in the East. By 1865, however, order began to emerge from

[3] Edward S. Farrow, *Farrow's Military Encyclopedia* (3 vols.), Vol. I, 759. A geographical department does not refer to the organizational department such as the Adjutant General's, the Inspector General's, the Commissary, etc.

the helter-skelter arrangement of departments, by resort to the division level. Four geographical divisions contained ten of the eighteen departments. After the war, the division unit again was dropped, and by 1866, with considerable redrawing of lines, thirteen departments emerged, and this area remained the standard administrative unit until after the army reorganization of 1903–1904. The Department of the Northwest was created in time of hostility because of necessity and convenience, as were Eastern departments following the outbreak of the war.

A consideration of the first of the Sioux wars also is a result of any effort to understand army affairs in the Northwest during the Civil War. There is no dearth of histories of the Sioux outbreak, or massacre, or war of 1862, but there is no comprehensive view of it. Most common are Minnesota accounts, logical since the brunt of the outburst was felt there, but accounts that include the Siouan impact all along the frontier are nonexistent. Since the Department of the Northwest, as created, embraced nearly the whole Sioux area, the picture of this important Indian action can be seen better from that perspective. The first of the great Sioux wars is considered as the framework on which the theme of military administration rests.

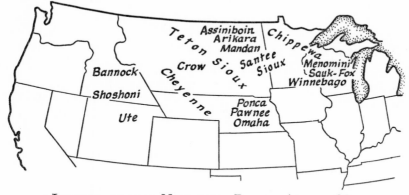

INDIANS OF THE NORTHERN PLAINS AREA, 1862

Note: "Teton Sioux" include the Brulé, Blackfoot, Minneconjou, Oglala, Sans-Arc, Two Kettles, and Uncpapa tribes. "Santee Sioux" include primarily the Mdewakanton, Sisseton, Wahpeton, and Yanktonai tribes.

Another result is a second look at John Pope. In most histories Pope is the windbag who apparently fought well in the West then fumbled to Lee in a humiliating defeat at second Bull Run. After that, Pope is dismissed as "sent to the Northwest" and not heard of again. He did not resume the fight against Johnny Reb, or lead troops in the field after that, but in the Northwest he was important both to the frontier and the nation. He was valuable to the frontier because of the campaigns he conceived and directed from a desk in St. Paul or Milwaukee, and because he honestly tried to do something about the Indian problem, and notable to the nation because of his level-headed handling of civil affairs at a time when civil affairs were not always well handled.

The responsibility of naming the campaigns of 1863 and 1864 is mine, as it is for judgments and evaluations here presented. I alone am to blame for any and all errors in these pages. I owe a tremendous debt of gratitude to Professor Fred A. Shannon of the University of Illinois, without whose encouragement and guidance this study would have been impossible. To Professor Frank Freidel of Harvard for his encouragement, and to my colleagues at Kent State, especially Professor William F. Zornow, who read portions of the manuscript, must go many thanks. The University of Illinois Library opened its excellent research facilities to me, the University of Minnesota Library loaned me important material, and Kent State University's Alumni Development Fund financed an excellent typist. Many thanks are due my wife, Estelle, who typed several drafts and graciously and sympathetically put up with the whole project. Janet McGarry carefully typed and retyped these pages. Also, I am indebted to the editor of *Mid-America* for allowing me to reuse material in Chapter 2 that originally appeared in his journal.

Stow, Ohio   R.H.J.
June 14, 1960.

The Civil War in the Northwest

1

The End of One War

TUESDAY, SEPTEMBER 2, 1862, DAWNED CLEAR AND COOL. The brilliant blue sky contrasted pleasantly with deep green foliage highlighted by glistening beads of moisture from Monday's hard rain. It was a beautiful late summer's morning in Virginia, even if it was also a day of retreat for the Union Army of Virginia. By mid-morning roads only yesterday cursed by soldiers as sinkholes of mud now powdered with fine dust those who used them. Over Fairfax Road, terribly exhausted troops trudged toward the fortifications near Alexandria. Among them rode Generals John Pope and Irvin McDowell, escorted by part of the First Ohio Cavalry. This was McDowell's second sad circuit from Bull Run to Washington, Pope's first. Pope, who bragged that he came from the West where he saw only the backs of his enemies, now let the enemy see his. Worse still, the eastern soldiers he commanded had resented this slur on their ability from the first, and now they openly jeered him. At that moment, since they had no confidence in McDowell either, it would have been difficult to discover two more unpopular men in Union blue.[1]

Meanwhile, news of the defeat had reached and alarmed the capital on Monday. With reluctance, President Lincoln had placed the very available General George C. McClellan back in command, this time of Union armies in the defenses of Washington. On this same bright Tuesday morning General-in-Chief Henry W. Halleck wired Pope of this news. As they trotted toward Munson's hill, Pope and McDowell noticed several horsemen riding toward them. One of the approaching officers, in a

[1] Bruce Catton, *Mr. Lincoln's Army*, 34, 50–53. Of the many descriptions of this day, Catton's is the most colorful.

clean uniform and vainly sporting a yellow sash, astride a splen-
did black horse, they recognized as McClellan. Handsomely at-
tired, he contrasted sharply with Pope and McDowell, who wore
the dust of retreat over rumpled uniforms. Salutes exchanged,
McClellan informed Pope of the change in command, and apparently granted his request to go on to Washington. With an
air of personal triumph, McClellan indicated he was going to
see what the firing on the horizon was all about. As the man with
the yellow sash rode off, the dusty ones doubtless felt a fresh
stab of humiliation, or perhaps contempt, as the cheers of the
former Army of the Potomac men saluted the return of their
hero.[2]

But Pope did not continue on to the city of confusion. He set
up his headquarters at Balls Cross Roads, within the fortifications
of Washington, in Virginia. He telegraphed his safe arrival to
Halleck and awaited orders. Pope believed himself still in command of his army, but was uncertain of just what McClellan
commanded. Next morning he asked for clarification of his status.
If a frightened Washington did not know, Pope at least knew
that one battle did not make a war. Washingtonians had pan-
icked, had conjured up a debacle worse than first Bull Run, and
feared Robert E. Lee's legions would be in their midst momen-
tarily. There was despair in the city, deepened by the stories of
the scared, the shirkers, the undisciplined refuse of the Union
armies who carried fantastic fairy tales of complete defeat. Defeat? Yes, and that was all it was. Pope knew it had been no rout.
Had not John F. Reynolds and George Sykes courageously held
Henry House Hill to cover the initial withdrawal? Had not
he anticipated Lee at Chantilly? Had not dashing one-armed
Philip Kearny and Isaac Stevens died in the rain while repuls-
ing (Thomas J.) Stonewall Jackson? Certainly the army had
been beaten, for a number of reasons, which Pope felt did not

[2] *The War of the Rebellion: A Compilation of the Official Records of the
Union and Confederate Armies* (Series I–IV, Index and Atlas, 74 vols. in 132,
Washington, 1885–1901), Series I, Vol. XII, Part III, 798, hereafter cited as
Official Records; T. Harry Williams, *Lincoln and His Generals,* 159–63; Catton,
Lincoln's Army, 50–53.

all directly arise from the battlefield. And this army, numbly fatigued and confused from days of marching and fighting, had been defiant enough to stop Stonewall. A less spirited group might not have had any fight left. Lesser men might just have run for the defenses of Washington. The ranks of the Army of Virginia were riddled, and, to be sure, some of the officers and many of the men hated him, but nonetheless this army was intact. Next time, Pope sighed, but even as he prepared for it, he did not know there would not be a next time.[3]

The General sent out cavalry reconnaissances to keep tabs on Lee's movements, and wanted to send sizable infantry forces after Lee too, but was unsure of his authority. He reminded Halleck that action should be taken promptly. "We ought not to lose a moment in pushing forward fresh men while the enemy is weakened. . . . I am ready to advance again to the front with fresh troops now here. . . . Let us not sit down quietly, but push forward again. . . . I would have attacked yesterday," but who is in command? The reply from across the River noted only that McClellan commanded the fortifications and a reorganization of the army would be made, and would Pope report in person to Halleck. "Old Brains" was being evasive. Reorganization was what they wanted? Pope, who could not conceive that McClellan would be permitted to command a field army again, the next day presented plans to Halleck for his army's reorganization. Strengthen the original three corps and add a new one, he asked. On Friday, Halleck told McClellan that Lincoln had removed Pope, but did not inform Pope until after that General heard it by rumor.[4]

Immediately, Pope again asked where he stood. He requested that his official report, sent off that morning, be published. In view of mounting criticism that clearly made him the goat of Manassas, he believed this only just. The public should hear his side. His removal would underline the unfavorable impression

[3] *Official Records*, Series I, Vol. XII, Part III, 808, 809; Margaret Leech, *Reveille in Washington* 1860–1865, 190, 196, 197; Francis F. Wilshin, *Manassas*, 35–37.
[4] *Official Records*, Series I, Vol. XII, Part III, 808, 809, 810, 811.

the country had of him. His reputation would be ruined. He asked, have I conducted my campaign badly or not? "If I have, I am prepared to shoulder the blame, but if, as both you and the President inform me, my course has met your entire approval, I am entitled to be shielded from unjust censure."[5] Though Lincoln and most of his cabinet sympathized with Pope, the President believed the bitter charges it contained would only increase demoralization in Washington. It was also clear to Lincoln the intense bad feelings between McClellan and Pope made it impossible for them to serve in the same army. And since McClellan had a knack for organization and also had the confidence of the troops, Pope would have to be sacrificed. But McClellan need not gloat over this personal victory: Lincoln told the cabinet the restored command was only temporary. In effect, this was the nature of Halleck's reply to Pope. Since the Army of Virginia was consolidated with the Army of the Potomac, Pope must await assignment from the Secretary of War.[6]

On Saturday, September 6, Pope was ordered to fight Indians in Minnesota. The resentment inside the man was nearly unbearable. It is significant that in his whirlpool of humiliation he did not resign: and here it is that the soldier in Pope asserted itself. He may not have liked his treatment, or his new station, but under the veneers of bombast and pride soldierly discipline ultimately compelled him to follow his superior's directions. The ten days that it took him to gather his effects together, leave the pulsating capital, and travel across the thousand miles to St. Paul, afforded him plenty of time for reflection. Was his career gone? Were his twenty years of service blighted beyond repair? Was this his fault or the fault of those who conspired against him? He had not been afraid to fight. Maybe he had not fought well in Virginia, but there had been so many obstacles. As has been so aptly observed, Pope "had many of McClellan's faults in reverse. He was aggressive where McClellan was timid, rash

---

[5] Ibid., 812.
[6] Williams, Lincoln and His Generals, 50–53; Official Records, Series I, Vol. XII, Part III, 813.

where McClellan was cautious. . . . McClellan magnified dangers, Pope minimized or did not see them."[7] But Pope would never have evaluated himself that way. If his career had flashed through his puzzled head, in search of his mistakes, perhaps the beginning would have been at the military academy.

His appointment to West Point came as a result of the family's political connections, but he had been proud of the opportunity nevertheless, and he had been a good cadet, too, even if his fast mouth had not made him too many friends. On that far distant day of the first of July, 1842, he had graduated seventeenth out of a class of fifty-six. James Longstreet, a key man in his recent defeat, had ranked fifty-fourth in that same class! As a topographical engineer his duty, by and large, had been interesting. The first two years he spent as a raw shavetail in Florida, and in the next two he surveyed the northeastern United States bounary. During the Mexican War, Pope could proudly recall, he had been twice brevetted for gallant and meritorious conduct, once at Monterrey and again at Buena Vista. Then it was off to Minnesota to conduct surveys and explorations. After that it had been back to the Southwest, where he served the Department of New Mexico as its Chief of Topographical Engineers. In 1853 he supervised the survey of the southwestern Pacific railroad route, and also experimented with artesian wells on the "Staked Plains" of New Mexico. The only really dull time had been the year of lighthouse duty! But—and here a smile might have crossed his face—if the duty was dull, the time had been livened up by other events. He had married, in 1859, Clara Pomeroy Horton, of Pomeroy, Ohio. And the next year, 1860, he blasted as vacillating the policy of President Buchanan in an address at Cincinnati. It had nearly cost him his commission (he was a captain by then), for court-martial proceedings had been started against him. But Postmaster General Joseph Holt intervened, and the proceedings were dropped. From then on, his military life had been full. There was the trip to Washington as a member

[7] *Official Records*, Series I, Vol. XIII, 618; Williams, *Lincoln and His Generals*, 158.

of President Lincoln's escort. There was the terribly dull duty in Chicago as mustering officer, but he marked time by pestering Washington for a general's commission, which finally came in May. True, it was a volunteer's commission. In July of 1861 he was transferred to Missouri, and from October through February he tangled with Confederate Major General Sterling Price, whom he chased into Arkansas. Then he successfully directed the Army of the Mississippi at New Madrid, and was rewarded with a second star. The capture of Island No. 10, another well-executed maneuver, followed. He became something of a celebrity for New Madrid and Island No. 10, and he developed a few military notions of his own, concerning movement and cavalry. Halleck didn't give Pope much opportunity to exercise his own ideas, though, in the snail-like advance upon and siege of Corinth. It was Pope's outfit that pursued the rebels to Baldwin in June.[8]

Then came the recognition he believed he deserved. President Lincoln called Pope east to command three scattered corps now called the Army of Virginia. Pope could not have been happier in his moment of triumph, but at the same time there were some misgivings. Yes, as he thought about it now, the misgivings seemed to outweigh the original pleasure. He was outranked by Irvin McDowell, John C. Frémont, and Samuel P. Heintzelman, who were to serve under him. In fact, Frémont was so upset (he had been Pope's superior in the West) he gave up his military career. Also, Pope recalled, with the military man's penchant for such things, that he had been promoted over Joseph Hooker, John F. Reynolds, James B. Ricketts, and Fitz-John Porter. But then, Porter had previously been promoted over him, so there was some satisfaction in that. Worst of all, McClellan, who was

---

[8] George W. Cullum, *Biographical Register of the Officers and Graduates of the U. S. Military Academy at West Point, N. Y., from . . . 1802 to . . . 1866–67,* Vol. II, 42, 49, 50, 70; *House Executive Document* No. 4, 29 Cong., 2 Sess., 90; *House Executive Document* No. 8, 30 Cong., I Sess., 141; James Grant Wilson and John Fiske, eds., *Appletons' Cyclopedia of American Biography,* Vol. V, 68–69; *Official Records,* Series I, Vol. III, 415, 527–72; Vol. VIII, 77–79, 81, 85, 566, 590; Vol. X, Part I, 653, 774, 801, 861.

Pope's junior in point of service, and who had even resigned his captain's commission in 1857, was promoted over him. For all concerned, the situation had been bothersome.[9]

Virginia! When he had come east in June, 1862, he certainly never believed he would be going west again in September! The whole trouble lay in the Old Dominion. He had got off on the wrong foot. In an attempt to instill confidence in his troops he had told them that in the West it was the backs of the enemy he had seen. Why should this have insulted them? He thought of it only as a pep talk, they thought he was an ill-bred braggart. Why did they not understand him?[10] General Order No. 5, the one in which he ordered the troops to subsist on the countryside, and General Order No. 6, in which he explicitly told his troops that "movements . . . must always be made with celerity, and no delay in such movements will be excused . . . on any pretext" had been designed to keep his troops mobile, unchained to long supply lines, and able to move fast. His officers could not understand this, even when he made an example of John P. Hatch. Also, Virginians did not receive the former order well. But then this was war.[11]

Criticism of those orders was not as severe as that directed at General Order No. 7, which held citizens responsible for any act detrimental to his troops or lines of communication. The civilians did not understand that disruption of railroad or telegraphic communications, the shooting of stragglers, or pillage of supplies, could be serious to an army in the field. Pope did not want to waste time or manpower in rear area repairs and guard duty. This was for the safety of his command! Also General Order No. 11, intended to stop leakage of military information to the enemy and to prevent sabotage or guerrilla activity behind his lines, was for the protection of his men. If these sounded

[9] *Official Records,* Series I, Vol. XII, Part III, 435; Cullum, *Biographical Register,* Vols. I and II, *passim.*

[10] Jacob D. Cox, *Military Reminiscenses of the Civil War,* Vol. I, 222–23, says Stanton suggested this order; *Official Records,* Series I, Vol. XII, Part III, 473–74.

[11] *Official Records,* Series I, Vol. XII, Part II, 24, 50.

harsh to civilians, it was because they were unused to the reality of war. Was it wrong to bring to the Virginians—they were rebels, weren't they—consequences of secession? Besides, he intended to be fair: he did not intend to allow looting by his soldiers. General Order No. 18 clearly stated that "neither officer nor soldier will be permitted to leave his command while on the march, or enter any house without a written permit from his brigade commander."[12] These were routine orders, even in their own time, for an army at war. Yet they rubbed people the wrong way.

Where had his campaign gone wrong? He used his cavalry hard, and before Jackson's flanking operation began, horses and men were worn out, and as a result his intelligence was faulty. That was part of it. But if McClellan had only stirred up some trouble on the Peninsula, just enough to keep Lee worried, Jackson and Richard S. Ewell couldn't have been spared to race to Cedar Mountain and bother him! Lee had the daring to divide his forces before McClellan evacuated Harrison's Landing; Pope smugly thought that the old fox had McClellan's number, all right, but look what it did to him! Why, Cedar Mountain was fought before the Army of the Potomac even began to leave. Even then, if McClellan had stirred, they would have had Lee in the bag. They could have come on Richmond from both sides! It was true that the order to evacuate had reached Harrison's Landing before Cedar Mountain, but it was five full days after that battle before McClellan began to move. All was not lost yet, for if the Army of the Potomac could have reinforced Pope before Lee concentrated on him, the jig would have been up for Lee anyway. Still, there had been hope, and almost victory, for Pope caught Lee in a serious military gamble that could have—should have—resulted in disaster for the gray armies. When he discovered Jackson behind him at Manassas the answer was clear. Concentrate on Jackson, destroy him, then turn his superior force (it would be superior if Jackson were destroyed) on Lee, and mop him up. But there were too many slip-ups between

[12] *Ibid.*, 51, 52, 52–53.

the knowledge of what to do and the execution of the plan. The army was tired from its marching and countermarching. Subordinates were not carrying out their assignments. Others were passing their own judgment on orders he issued in ignorance of the actual situation. Jackson proved slippery, and eluded him until Longstreet was in view. Pope did not realize Longstreet was so close, or he could have withdrawn farther and awaited the rest of the Army of the Potomac. Instead, he vented his anger at men like Fitz-John Porter, who clearly disobeyed an impossible order. Had Porter only acted more quickly to begin with: but then, he had not. Pope might have conceded this was a mess, might have realized he did not have his finger as squarely on the situation as he thought he had. His strategy was not faulty, it should have worked, but he could not bring himself to see it was he, as much as anyone, who had defeated himself.[13]

Pope may have recalled the original directive he received from Lincoln the previous June. In an ironical fashion, part of that directive had been carried out. He was supposed to protect "western Virginia and the national capital from danger or insult," and although the danger and insult had occurred, Lee, at least, was not in western Virginia or Washington. The rest of the order would have been a tremendous task for any officer, for Pope also was to have "in the speediest manner attack[ed] and overcome . . . Jackson and Ewell" and "reliev[ed] General McClellan and captur[ed] Richmond." There was scant comfort in such thoughts.[14] And now there might be no chance to vindicate himself. That was the bitterest pill of all! The war was over for him. Of what use was the President's sympathy now?

But he had another job to do. This was the cold comfort of a soldier: there always was another job to do. As the railroad car jolted westward, he could look at the new orders. They were dated September 6, 1862:

[13] There are a number of accounts of this campaign. For example, see John C. Ropes, *The Army Under Pope;* George H. Gordon, *History of the Campaign of the Army of Virginia;* Kenneth P. Williams, *Lincoln Finds a General;* Catton's *Mr. Lincoln's Army,* and others.
[14] *Official Records,* Series I, Vol. XII, Part III, 435.

General: You will receive herewith an order of this Department constituting you commander of the Department of the Northwest. The Indian hostilities that have recently broken forth and are now prevailing in that Department require the attention of some military officer of high rank, in whose ability and vigor the government has confidence, and you have therefore been selected for this important command. You will . . . take such prompt and vigorous measures as shall quell the hostilities and afford . . . protection to the people. . . .

This Department has received no detailed information respecting the extent of the outrages . . . or the force engaged in their perpetration, and therefore must leave to your judgment . . . the measures to be taken. You will employ whatever force may be necessary. . . .

In conclusion I will add that you cannot too highly estimate the importance of the duty now intrusted to you, and you have been assigned to it because of the high confidence of the Government that you have the personal and military qualities to meet the emergency.

Yours truly, Edwin M. Stanton, Secretary of War.[15]

This new command, the Department of the Northwest, was officially defined in General Order No. 128:

Ordered, That the Department of the Northwest, including the states of Wisconsin, Iowa, Minnesota, the Territories of Nebraska and Dakota, with the troops raised, and to be raised in that Department, be, and they are hereby, placed under the command of Major General Pope, who will proceed forthwith to his command. . . .[16]

And though Stanton's words of praise rang hollowly in his ears, that was just what Pope did: proceeded forthwith to his new command. There, too, frightened men had risen to arms to defend their homesteads, farms, and villages, others led a parade of refugees hastily away from the frontier, still others lay

[15] *Ibid.,* Vol. XIII, 617.
[16] *Ibid.,* 618.

dead upon battlefields no farther away from their homes than their own front rooms. There was turmoil in Minnesota's verdant valley, and panic touched every rude settlement from western Nebraska to eastern Wisconsin. In the West Johnny Reb had an unwitting ally in the awesome Sioux.

2

Let Some Sadder Strain Prevail

Minne-ha-ha, laughing water
 Cease thy laughing now for aye,
Savage hands are red with slaughter
 Of the innocent today.

Ill accords thy sportive humor
 With their last despairing wail;
While thou'rt dancing in the sunbeam
 Mangled corpses strew the vale.

Change thy note, gay Minne-ha-ha;
 Let some sadder strain prevail. . . .[1]

As swiftly as the sun-kissed falls of this poem, excited Sioux warriors were tumbling across the prairies and forests of Minnesota, Dakota, and Iowa. John G. Nicolay, one of Lincoln's secretaries, telegraphed an urgent on-the-spot report to Secretary of War Edwin M. Stanton:

> The Sioux, mustering perhaps 200 warriors, are striking along a line of scattered frontier settlements of 200 miles, having already massacred several hundred whites, and the settlers of the whole border are in a panic and in flight, leaving their harvest to waste in the fields as I myself have seen even in neighborhoods where there is no danger. The Chippewas . . . are turbulent . . .

[1] Attributed to Captain Richard H. Chittenden on leave from Company E, First Wisconsin Volunteer Cavalry, and composed while he rode with a group of Minnesota cavalry to the relief of Fort Ridgely. Quoted from Nathaniel West, *The Ancestry, Life, and Times of Hon. Henry Hastings Sibley, LL.D.,* 250.

and the Winnebagos are suspected of hostile intent. . . . As against the Sioux it must be a war of extermination.[2]

This full-scale war broke out in Minnesota on August 17, 1862, a time as unfortunate for the Union as it was opportune for the Indians. In spite of the savage hands red with slaughter and the mangled corpses in the vale of the Minnesota, the war-whoops, tom-toms, and shotguns on the northwestern frontier were scarcely heard above the rebel yells, drums, and din of cannon fire in the South.

None the less, the noise in the north was portentous. The fighting quality of the Sioux was familiar to frontiersmen, for they had been allies of the English in the War of 1812, had helped the United States destroy the remnants of Blackhawk's tribe, had terrorized the California trail in the 1850's, and as late as 1857 a renegade group had massacred thirty-two settlers at Spirit Lake, Iowa. The 1862 uprising was the largest yet, however, and inaugurated a series of violent wars against the white intruder, who was unable to subdue the Sioux until after the battle of Wounded Knee, two weeks after the death of Sitting Bull, in 1890. The names of General George Crook and Colonel George A. Custer have become almost legendary; but the names of John Pope, Henry H. Sibley, and Alfred Sully, the men who first handled the Sioux problem, have been all but forgotten.

Numerous irritants combined to precipitate the savage explosion along the northwestern frontier in August, 1862. Originally, several tribes of the Sioux Nation roamed the extensive, beautiful, and fertile regions of northwestern Iowa, western Wisconsin, southwestern Minnesota, and adjoining Dakota Territory. Herds of buffalo grazed over rolling plains green with prairie grass and wooded groves that were reflected, along with cotton clouds, in the countless lakes, streams, and rivers; the home of colorful quail, grouse, ducks and other wild fowl, which

---

[2] *Official Records*, Series I, Vol. XIII, 599. Nicolay was in the Northwest on an assignment to the Chippewa Indians.

shared this vast area with such fur-bearing animals as otter, mink, beaver, and deer.[3] The attraction of this country was as strong for the frontier farmer as it was for the native Sioux, and the advance of the white settlers was as inevitable as was the expulsion of the Indian. A series of treaties over a period of sixty years compressed the Sioux into an ever-dwindling reserve that by 1858[4] had been reduced to a narrow, ten-mile wide ribbon of land along the south bank of the Minnesota River, which spanned the 150 miles from Lake Traverse to a point just below Fort Ridgely.[5]

The Mdewakanton and Wahpekuta[6] occupied the lands below the Yellow Medicine River, or the Lower Reservation, while the Sisseton and Wahpeton inhabited the area above the Yellow Medicine, the Upper Reservation.[7] A resident Indian agent, whose job included administration of the treaties, established two places for the transaction of his business; the Redwood (Lower) Agency, fourteen miles above Fort Ridgely, and the Yellow Medicine (Upper) Agency, at the mouth of the Yellow Medicine River. Around these establishments clustered small villages of residences, stores, warehouses, schools, and churches.[8] The indefatigable missionaries Stephen Return Riggs and Thomas Smith Williamson had schools and churches a few miles above the Yellow Medicine; at Lac qui Parle were the house and school of another missionary, along with a government storehouse and blacksmith shop; and at the Lower Agency was yet a third mis-

[3] Isaac V. D. Heard, *History of the Sioux War and Massacres of 1862 and 1863*, [13], 14. Cited hereafter as Heard, *Sioux War*. The tribes were the Mdewakanton, Wahpeton, Sisseton, and Wahpekuta.

[4] Charles J. Kappler, *Indian Affairs, Laws and Treaties*, Senate Document No. 452, 57 Cong., 1 Sess. (Serial 4254), Vol. II, 177, 586, 590, 594. Other treaties were: 1830, p. 218; 1836, pp. 347, 355, 357; 1837, pp. 366, 439; 1851, pp. 437, 438, 440. Cited hereafter as Kappler, *Indian Affairs*.

[5] Heard, *Sioux War*, 18.

[6] The spelling of Indian names varies from writer to writer. Where questionable the spellings used are those in Appendix I, "Revised Spelling of Names of Indian Tribes and Bands," in Kappler, *Indian Affairs*, Vol. I, 1021.

[7] Heard, *Sioux War*, 18.

[8] *Ibid.*, 21, 22.

16

BRITISH AMERICA

Pembina

Chippewa
Red River Bands

Devil's Lake

Red Lake

MINNESOTA

Cass Lake Winnibigoshish Lake

Lake Superior

Leech Lake

Ft. Abercrombie

Chippewa
Mississippi Bands

Chippewa
Lake Superior Bands

DAKOTA
TERRITORY

Pomme de Terre

Mille Lac

Ft. Ripley

Lake Traverse

Alexandria

Sauk Center

Princeton

Sunrise

St. Cloud

Taylors Falls

Big Stone Lake

Paynesville

Forest City

WISCONSIN

Lac qui Parle

Acton

Ft. Snelling

Sioux

Camp Release

Hutchinson

St. Paul

UPPER AGENCY

Yellow Medicine

Ft. Ridgely

Glencoe

LOWER AGENCY

Sioux Reservation

New Ulm

Henderson

Le Sueur

Lake Benton

Redwood

Cottonwood R.

Mankato

St. Peter

Winona

Lake Shetek

Madelia

South Bend

Winnebago
Reservation

La Crosse

Jackson

Winnebago

Spirit Lake

Fairmont

Blue Earth

Sioux Falls

Ocheydan

Iowa Lake

Estherville

Spirit Lake

Ft. Randall

Peterson

Yankton

Cherokee

Vermillion

Elk Point

Correctionville

Webster City

Sioux City

Sac City

Ft. Dodge

Ida

IOWA

NEBRASKA
TERRITORY

Little Sioux

0   25   50   75   100

Scale in Miles

MINNESOTA AND VICINITY, 1862

sion. Trading posts had been established at Big Stone Lake and at other points on the reservation.[9]

Living in scattered groups mostly along the Minnesota River were about sixty-six hundred Minnesota Sioux, while another three thousand or four thousand Yanktonai Sioux roamed nearby in Dakota Territory.[10] By 1862 part of the story was already familiar, since the proud Sioux were bound by treaties similar to those the government made with other tribes. They did not wholly understand the pacts or trust those who administered them. Ostensibly the white man aimed to civilize and educate the Indians by converting them to a stationary, agricultural people, but instead irritated these nomadic hunters. Eighty acres were allocated to a family, and annuities from a trust fund were disbursed annually by the secretary of the interior for purposes of education and agriculture.[11] Sioux Agent Thomas J. Galbraith boldly stated the policy of refining the Indians:

> By my predecessor a new and radical system was inaugurated practically, and in its inauguration he was aided by the Christian missionaries and by the government. The treaties of 1858 were ostensibly made to carry this new system into effect.
>
> The theory, in substance, was to break up the community system among the Sioux; weaken and destroy their tribal relations; individualize them by giving each a separate home, and having them subsist by industry—the sweat of their brows; till the soil; make labor honorable and idleness dishonorable; or, as it was expressed in short, *"make white men of them"* . . . .[12]

[9] *Ibid.*, also, Stephen R. Riggs, *Tah-Koo Wah-Kan, or the Gospel Among the Dakotas*, 107, 312; cited hereafter as Riggs, *Gospel Among the Dakotas*. Henry Benjamin Whipple, *Lights and Shadows of a Long Episcopate*, 61–62; cited hereafter as Whipple, *Lights and Shadows*.

[10] *Report of the Secretary of the Interior*, 1863, *House Executive Document No. 1*, 38 Cong., 1 Sess. (Serial 1182), 410; report of Thomas J. Galbraith, Sioux Agent, dated St. Paul, January 27, 1863. See also *House Executive Document No. 68*, 37 Cong., 3 Sess. (Serial 1163), 38: included in this document is another copy of Galbraith's report plus other papers pertaining to the same subject.

[11] Kappler, *Indian Affairs*, Vol. II, 437, 438, 439, 440, 590–97.

[12] *House Executive Document* No. 68, 24–25; "Chief Big Eagle's Story of the Sioux Outbreak of 1862," *Collections of the Minnesota Historical Society*, Vol. 6, 884. Cited hereafter as "Chief Big Eagle's Story."

This program proved abortive. A few of the "annuity Sioux" became farmers, but most would not, and were hostile toward those who had. The farmers among them who dressed like the white men were known as either "Cut-hair and breeches" Indians or "Dutchmen," a name of opprobrium, while the others were called "Scalp-lock" or "Blanket" Indians. The few farmers made considerable progress in spite of harassment by their disdainful brethren. They had nearly three thousand acres under cultivation in the spring of 1862, and anticipated an abundant harvest, the estimated market value of which was about $119,400.[13] The white man conceded this to be a good beginning.

Christianizing the Sioux proved even less successful than making farmers of them. "Indeed, with quite a large majority of that people the settled purpose not to change their religion and the customs of their fathers was manifest."[14] The lure of getting a feather as the mark of a warrior and their reluctance to do such squaw's work as farming showed the vigorous influence of their customs, even occasionally upon Indians who were supposed to be civilized. Tribal ties were so strong that many participated in the outbreak of 1862 even though they realized the ultimate futility of their action.[15]

Sioux pride and egoism dwelt behind the mosaic of causes that induced warfare on the northwestern frontier. Chief Big Eagle, thirty-two years after the uprising, gave reasons for the war similar to those already noted, but substituted for Galbraith's dim view of the Indian an equally dim view of the white man. Big Eagle disparaged the presence of traders at the annuity payment (which they attended to collect their debts, just or unjust) and told how the Indians mistrusted them. The superior attitude of the white man also irritated the Sioux (because "the Dakotas did not believe there were better men in the world than they"),

[13] *House Executive Document* No. 68, 15–16, 26, 34.
[14] Riggs, *Gospel Among the Dakotas,* 391; Whipple, *Lights and Shadows,* 62. In the nine months after the opening of the first mission at the Lower Agency, Reverend Hinman was able to confirm only seven of the several thousand who lived near by.
[15] "Chief Big Eagle's Story," 387, 390.

as did the white man's abuse of Indian women. Big Eagle blamed the whites for the "Blanket" *versus* "Farmer" controversy. When Galbraith enlisted a volunteer company of half-bloods at the agencies, the Sioux were convinced the North was desperate in its struggle with the South. Big Eagle also criticized the change in administration in 1861, the appointment of new agents and a new Superintendent of the Northern District, Clark Thompson, and the innovations they brought to the management of Sioux affairs. Galbraith and Thompson had unjudiciously attempted to substitute goods for money in the annual payments, and Thompson foolishly encouraged the Sioux to expect "a further bounty" without telling them this would be a part of their 1862 allowance. In order to come in and get this "great gift" the Indians skipped their annual hunt, which would have brought them more benefits than the goods did. When the Sioux finally learned that this bonus was an advance on the next year's annuity, they became "greatly exasperated." Thompson spoke of the weakened condition of the frontier, which seemed to present the red men with a good opportunity to recover their lands. Many Sioux hoped a war might once again unify them. They believed their enemies, the Chippewas, and the Winnebagos as well, would assist them.[16] Accounts other than Chief Big Eagle's agree that the major causes of discontent were the treaty and the annuity delay, combined with the chance to retake the land they had bartered away.[17]

There was much discussion of these matters among the Sioux, who substituted temper and pride for reason and became belligerent that summer. On June 25, as the payment of annuities usually took place about then, they made a demonstration at the Upper Agency and inquired about their money. Galbraith told them he did not expect the payment to arrive before July 20, issued them some provisions, and sent them home.[18] On July

[16] *Ibid.*, 384–87; Stephen R. Riggs, *Mary and I, Forty Years with Sioux*, 147–48. Cited hereafter as Riggs, *Forty Years.*

[17] *House Executive Document* No. 68, 16–17, 28, 29.

[18] Heard, *Sioux War*, 44–46; *House Executive Document* No. 68, 16; *House Executive Document* No. 58, 38 Cong., 1 Sess. (Serial 1189), 11–12.

14, about four thousand annuity Sioux and one thousand Yank-tonai (who were not included in the payments, but who claimed a share) came down to the Yellow Medicine to collect their money. Galbraith was puzzled as to how to deal with them since the money still had not arrived, but he put them off and kept them fed until August 1, when his supplies were nearly used up. On August 4 the Sioux surprised the agency and the troops on guard and forcibly broke into the government warehouse. The troops succeeded in restoring order, and Galbraith, assisted by soldiers of the Fifth Minnesota Volunteer Infantry, and the missionary, Riggs, issued the "annuity goods and a fixed amount of provisions, provided the Indians would go home and watch their corn, and wait for payment until they were sent for."[19] The Indians withdrew and a serious incident was temporarily avoided.

Stories of the Civil War seemed to have a psychological effect on them also. One observer reflected that the effect of war stories "operates very powerfully upon the warlike Indians,"[20] while another remarked that "the war for the Union, has been a fruitful source for trouble among the Sioux, exciting inquiry, restlessness, and uneasiness. The effect . . . upon the savage and superstitious minds of the Indians can be easily imagined.[21] Perhaps "If there had been no Southern war, there would have been no Dakota uprising and no Minnesota Massacres!" There were rumors that Confederate agents fomented the trouble but, though this was given some credence, it was never proved. Also the English in Canada were thought to have implicated themselves to some extent in the outbreak.[22] This too was never satisfactorily demonstrated, although the Indians in the following years did

[19] *House Executive Document* No. 68, 17; *Executive Documents of the State of Minnesota for the Year 1862*, pp. [415]–416. Hereafter cited as *Minnesota, Executive Documents, 1862*.

[20] Riggs, *Gospel Among the Dakotas,* 330.

[21] *House Executive Document,* No. 68, 29.

[22] *House Executive Document* No. 68, 2, 8, 29; Board of Commissioners, *Minnesota in the Civil and Indian Wars, 1861–1864,* (2nd. edition), 729; *Report of the Secretary of the Interior, 1862 (House Executive Document* No. 1, Vol. 2, 37 Cong., 3 Sess., Serial 1157), 8, 9, 232; John G. Nicolay, "The Sioux War," *The Continental Monthly,* Vol. III (January, 1862), 197.

receive supplies from north of the border.[23] Certainly, the Sioux seem to have had sufficient provocation for war without urging from the Confederates or the English.

Rumors also rumbled along the frontier that the Sioux were not alone in their intent to evict or kill the white man. A simultaneous uprising of the Chippewas was narrowly averted, and some Winnebagos were virtually forced into the affair. The Winnebagos had been relatively quiet, since they were in no position to be otherwise. Their reservation was in the heart of very good land, and as a result they were hard pressed by settlers who coveted this land and who scarcely needed the excuse of a war to take it. The Winnebagos lived in double jeopardy after the outbreak, fearing the Sioux, who threatened to exterminate them unless they joined in, and apprehensive of the whites, who bore them more animosity than ever, just because they were Indians, and because some of them had joined the uprising. Their agent swore to their loyalty, and had two companies of troops stationed "in their midst, which . . . allayed their fears" apparently. He had to admit that Winnebagos were present at the massacre of the Lower Agency, however, and was not sure that a few did not take part.[24] The Winnebago chief, Little Priest, and a handful of his warriors probably participated in the outbreak, but in the main, the Winnebagos were at peace.

The secretary of the interior saw an even larger pattern, involving nearly all the Indians west of the Mississippi. An Indian agent in Utah had written on August 5 that the Shoshone were attempting to organize the "Cum-um-bahs, the Gros Utes, and the Shoegars, or Bannack Diggers" in a war against the whites and were in fact already committing depredations; an agent of the overland mail company informed the postmaster general that "a general war with nearly all the tribes east of the Missouri River is close at hand"; the acting commissioner of Indian affairs on September 19, in a public advertisement, warned of the dan-

[23] Joint Committee on the Conduct of the War, *Supplemental Report of the Joint Committee on the Conduct of the War,* "Report of Major General John Pope," Vol. II, 198.
[24] *Report of the Secretary of the Interior,* 1862, 174–76, 177, 227–31, 236–37.

ger of crossing the plains; and a missionary, Peter J. De Smet, warned of the excited attitude of the Gros Ventres, the Arikaras, the Mandans, the Assinaboines, and the Blackfeet, and strongly suspected that traders from north of the border were exciting them. He also had heard that the Missouri Sioux were agitated.[25] Captain James L. Fisk, who took an expedition to the mines in the northern Rockies, reported that the Assinaboines were saucy, and that "their conduct convinced me that they were knowing to the raid of the Sioux Indians." While this seemed to the secretary of the interior to indicate a general conspiracy in the West, its existence in more than coincidence is doubtful.

Tenuous evidence sustained a belief that a premeditated plan of attack was concocted by the Sioux, Chippewas, and Winnebagos of Wisconsin. As mentioned before, a few Winnebagos almost certainly took an active part, though most of them did not. Hole-in-the-day, an influential Chippewa chief, was accused of carrying on "a correspondence with Little Crow, leader of the Sioux raid." Evidence against this is strong. Both Big Eagle and Galbraith admit that the tribes were enemies, and, for this reason, the general belief seems to be with coincidence rather than collusion.[26]

Coincidence or collusion, general or local, the Indian situation in the whole West was incendiary. On the part of the Minnesota Sioux, the "spark of fire, upon a mass of discontent" was "one of those accidental outrages at any time to be anticipated on the remote frontier."[27] On August 17, 1862, a small hunting party

[25] *Report of the Secretary of the Interior*, 1862, 357, 358, 359; *Official Records*, Series I, Vol. XIII, 592, 645.

[26] *Report of the Secretary of the Interior*, 1862, 201; *Official Records*, Series I, Vol. XLI, Part III, 127; George W. Sweet, "Incidents of the Threatened Outbreak of Hole-in-the-Day and Other Ojibways at the Time of the Sioux Massacre of 1862," *Collections of the Minnesota Historical Society*, Vol. 6, 401 (hereafter cited as Sweet, "Incidents"); Samuel J. Brown, "In Captivity: the Experience, Privations, and Dangers of Samuel J. Brown and Others while Prisoners of the Sioux . . . ," *Senate Miscellaneous Document* No. 28, 56 Cong., 2 Sess. (Serial 4029), 2 (hereinafter cited as Brown, "In Captivity"). Ojibway and Chippewa were used synonymously.

[27] *Report of the Secretary of the Interior*, 1862, 204–205, report of Lieutenant Governor Donnelly of Minnesota.

murdered several settlers at Acton, Minnesota, after a quarrel among themselves over some hen's eggs. Accounts vary as to whether or not they were drunk, but it is almost certain that the slaying of the whites was not premeditated. Since the Indians expected trouble over the homicides anyway, they apparently decided to wage a preventive war.[28] This so-called "accidental outrage" began one of the worst massacres in the history of the United States.

In this same section of the frontier the United States Army maintained four garrisons: Fort Abercrombie, Dakota Territory, on the Red River of the North, roughly fifty miles above Lake Traverse; Fort Ridgely, Minnesota, about twelve miles northwest of New Ulm on the north bank of the Minnesota River; Fort Ripley, Minnesota, on the Mississippi River about forty miles above St. Cloud; and Fort Randall, Dakota Territory, on the southwest side of the Missouri River about forty-five miles west of Yankton. The military Department of the West (which then embraced this area) reported to the adjutant general's office, January 1, 1861, that fourteen companies of the regular army with a total of 879 men were on duty at those posts.

With the secession of the Southern states beginning in December, 1860, and continuing on through the winter and spring of 1861, along with the raising of an army in those states, it seems nearly inconceivable today that professional troops of the regular army were not replaced by local militia sooner than they were. Within a month of Lincoln's inauguration, the government began to concentrate these forces, however, and the regulars began to withdraw eastward on April 13. With the exception of one group, they had departed by the following August. The last unit went east in January, 1862.

The void created by the removal of regulars from the frontier posts was filled by the local volunteer troops. Those of the Minnesota volunteers who were assigned to the frontier, even though these assignments were at first brief, were disappointed

[28] *House Executive Document* No. 68, p. 31; Heard, *Sioux War*, pp. 54–61; Riggs, *Forty Years*, 153; "Chief Big Eagle's Story," 389–90.

to draw such unglamorous duty. Only nine companies were now deemed necessary. Forts Ripley and Ridgely were garrisoned by four companies of the First Minnesota Volunteer Infantry on May 28 and 29, and June 6, 1861. Two more companies of the same organization reached Fort Abercrombie June 10, 1861, but they were ordered south along with the rest of the regiment eleven days later. For a few days Abercrombie and Ripley apparently were unmanned until the arrival of companies from the Second Minnesota Volunteer Infantry in July. Fort Randall was garrisoned by three companies of the Fourteenth Iowa Volunteer Infantry, which was mustered into service in September and October of 1861. Fort Randall was occupied only by one company of the Fourth Artillery, from August, 1861, until the Iowa troops arrived in October that year.

Six companies of the Second Minnesota were stationed at Abercrombie, Ridgely, and Ripley until October 14. Garrison duty on these posts over the winter fell to detachments of the Fourth Minnesota Volunteer Infantry, who were relieved in the spring of 1862 by detachments of the Fifth Minnesota. That spring only seven companies were used to hold the frontier; of the Fifth Minnesota, Company B garrisoned Ridgely, C Ripley, and D Abercrombie; the same three companies of the Fourteenth Iowa remained at Randall; and Company A, Dakota Cavalry was mustered into United States service on April 29, 1862, and was stationed in detachments at various points along the Missouri River in Dakota Territory. Also at Ridgely in United States service was an ordinance sergeant to look after the six pieces of artillery left there by elements of the Second, Third, and Fourth Artillery Regiments that departed in the preceding spring, and also an Indian interpreter, a sutler, and a post surgeon.[29]

On June 18, 1862, the commanding officer at Fort Ripley sent

[29] *Minnesota in the Civil and Indian Wars,* 5, 79, 198, 243, 244; *Minnesota, Executive Documents, 1862,* 206; *Official Records,* Series I, Vol. XIII, 248; *Report of the Adjutant General and Acting Quartermaster General of Iowa 1862,* Vol. I, xiii, Vol. II, 323–24; *Senate Miscellaneous Document* No. 241, 58 Cong., 2 Sess. (Serial 4591), 10.

fifty men of Company C to Fort Ridgely. This detachment, with another fifty men of Company B, proceeded "forthwith . . . to the Sioux Agency on the Yellow Medicine River, and . . . [reported] to Major Thomas Galbraith, Sioux Agent at that place, for the purpose of preserving order and protecting United States property during the time of the annuity payment for the present year." Led by Captain John F. Marsh, the command included a twelve-pound mountain howitzer and rations for fifteen days. They arrived at the Upper Sioux Agency on the Yellow Medicine on July 2.[30] Since the annuity payment failed to arrive after the expiration of about two weeks, Marsh sent a detail to Fort Ridgely for another fifteen days' rations and a second mountain howitzer. The 779 lodges of Indians encamped about the Agency, including Yanktonai and Cut-Heads not entitled to annuities, worried Marsh.

Following the altercation at the warehouse and after the Indians were sent back to their homes to await the payment, the group from Ripley was ordered to return there, since Captain Marsh did not anticipate any further danger. They left on August 17. On the same day, one officer and six men of Company B were detached to St. Peter to provide transportation to Fort Snelling for the company of fifty recruits Galbraith enlisted at the agencies. Remaining at Ridgely was Captain Marsh and 76 men.[31]

On August 17, the day of the murders at Acton, the troops on frontier duty were disposed in the following manner: Company B, Fifth Minnesota, at Fort Ridgely (minus one officer and six men en route to St. Peter); Company C, Fifth Minnesota, garrisoned at Fort Ripley with about thirty soldiers, as the other fifty men were en route back from Fort Ridgely. At Fort Abercrombie was Company D of the same regiment, with nearly eighty men; at Fort Randall were Companies A, B, and C of the Fourteenth Iowa with 295 on the roll. Near by in Dakota Territory

---

[30] *Minnesota in the Civil and Indian Wars*, 245 (Special Order No. 57, Fort Ridgely, June 29, 1862).
[31] *Ibid.*, 245–48.

was Company A, Dakota Cavalry, that mustered 92 men. At Fort Snelling, the recruiting and muster of the Sixth, Seventh, Eighth, Ninth, Tenth, and Eleventh Minnesota Volunteer Infantry regiments was in progress, with about seven companies of the Sixth at full strength, or approximately 550 recruits, and other regiments at various stages of completion. But Fort Snelling was nearly ninety miles from the scene of the outbreak, and Fort Randall was even more distant, nearly two hundred miles from Ridgely.

In 1860–1861 the War Department required nearly nine hundred regular troops to secure the area. However, in the summer of 1862, there were on duty at the same frontier posts almost three hundred fewer troops in half the number of organizations previously thought necessary, and these were relatively green soldiers. Fort Randall, the most remote, was garrisoned by more than half the number of men on duty in this region. In the central Minnesota area, less than half the number of soldiers occupied the frontier posts than were present two years earlier. Here, from a military point of view, was a very weak link in the chain of frontier defense. The raw, unarmed troops mustering at Fort Snelling constituted a remote and shaky reserve corps with any utilization in the frontier district of questionable value, or, in view of the military situation in the South, of equally questionable assignment there.

News of the disturbance reached the governor of Minnesota on August 19, and almost immediately the whole northwestern frontier was aflame. The secretary of the interior, in his annual report dated November 20, almost matter-of-factly mentioned that

> In the month of August last the Sioux Indians in Minnesota most unexpectedly commenced hostilities . . . with a degree of cruelty and barbarity scarcely paralleled by any acts of Indian warfare since the first settlement of this country. . . . A large extent of country, in an advanced stage of improvement, was rendered utterly desolate. It is estimated that the number of lives destroyed by the savages is not less than 800. This outbreak

27

was so sudden and unexpected that the settlers were taken by surprise, and were found without the means of resistance or defence. . . . The Sioux Indians are connected with kindred tribes, extending . . . to the Rocky mountains. The various tribes, united, can bring into the field ten thousand warriors. They are supplied with arms and ammunition to a considerable extent. They have it in their power to inflict great injury . . . throughout the whole region.[32]

The commissioner of Indian affairs, in his report of November 26 to the secretary of the interior, reported

> It is estimated that from eight hundred to one thousand . . . unarmed settlers fell victim to the savage fury ere the bloody work of death was stayed. The thriving town of New Ulm, containing from 1,500 to 2,000 inhabitants was almost destroyed. . . . Meantime the utmost consternation and alarm prevailed throughout the entire community. Thousands of happy homes were abandoned, the whole frontier was given up to be plundered and burned . . . and every avenue . . . was crowded with the now homeless and impoverished fugitives.[33]

Superintendent Thompson placed the massacre figure at six hundred to eight hundred lives, "the destruction of an immense amount of property," and "barbarities . . . horrible beyond description."[34] Lieutenant Governor Ignatius Donnelly of Minnesota found the territory between Fort Ridgely and St. Peter "completely abandoned by the inhabitants; the houses, in many cases, left with the doors open, the furniture undisturbed," but went on to say, "I do not think that, when all the facts are ascertained, the number actually killed will much exceed *two hundred*."[35]

In Dakota Territory, frightened frontiersmen abandoned inland settlements such as Sioux Falls and retreated to stockades

[32] *Report of the Secretary of the Interior,* 1862, 7–8.
[33] *Ibid.,* 171.
[34] *Ibid.,* 199.
[35] *Ibid.,* 203, 210.

at Fort Randall and the Yankton Agency. The Indians burned Sioux Falls after it was abandoned. Governor William Jayne of Dakota Territory, formerly a physician in Springfield, Illinois (later mayor of that city) and a close friend of Lincoln's, pleaded with General James G. Blunt, commander of the military Department of Kansas, that as a result of the situation in Minnesota

and that attack upon our settlement at Sioux Falls and . . . each days' news of additional butcheries of families . . . a general alarm pervades all our settlements. Family after family are leaving our territory and whole settlements are about to be broken up. We must have immediate aid . . . or else our territory will be depopulated. I have ordered . . . all the militia [to active duty] . . . but we are to a great extent without arms and ammunition— a few thousand people at the mercy of 50,000 Indians should they . . . fall upon us.[36]

Schuyler R. Ingham, acting as agent for Governor Samuel J. Kirkwood of Iowa, visited the northern border of Iowa and reported he "found many of the inhabitants in a high state of excitement, and laboring under constant fear of an attack by Indians. . . . [Many] families were leaving their homes and moving to more thickly settled portions of the state."[37] Alarmed, Kirkwood apprised Secretary of War Edwin M. Stanton that the Yanktonai were joining the Minnesota Sioux "and threaten our whole northwestern frontier. The settlers are flying by hundreds. We lack arms. . . . Something must be done."[38] Algernon Sidney Paddock, secretary of Nebraska Territory and at that time acting governor (later—1868—governor of Wyoming), hastily telegraphed Stanton that there were "Powerful bands of Indians returning from Minnesota into northern settlements. Nebraska settlers by hundreds fleeing. Instant action demanded. . . . Territory without credit or cent of money."[39] Charles Robinson, gov-

[36] *Official Records,* Series I, Vol. XIII, 613.
[37] *Adjutant General's Report, Iowa, 1862,* Vol. II, 861; *Official Records, Series* I, Vol. XIII, 638.
[38] *Official Records,* Series I, Vol. XIII, 620.
[39] *Ibid.,* 621.

ernor of Kansas, requested arms for the state militia because Indians threatened the border, mobilized what organized militia remained after national calls, and also all able-bodied men. The whole northwestern frontier feared a general Sioux war.

While telegraph wires hummed the alarm and panic-stricken settlers fled, the Sioux ravaged the Minnesota Valley. Presumed to have 1,500 warriors, but never employing more than half that number at any one time, they were earnestly attempting to exterminate the white settlers from the Dakota border to the Mississippi River. The Indians were divided into two parties; one, the lower party, attacked major points such as Fort Ridgely and New Ulm, with other raids and engagements as those at Redwood Ferry and Birch Coulie. The upper party raided in the northern counties and attacked Fort Abercrombie. There were also many sorties by individual Indians all along the frontier.

The Sioux had no planned campaign in mind, only the general desire to reduce Fort Ridgely and New Ulm and to move swiftly toward the Mississippi, and in the process to bring the whole of the Winnebagos into the war. Stubborn resistance at Fort Ridgely, New Ulm (even though it was temporarily abandoned), and Birch Coulie ended any such hope. The organization of the Indians, although under the over-all command of Little Crow, was in no way perfected; each band was semi-independent and many braves preferred to plunder on their own. This imperfect deployment, coupled with brave defense by volunteer troops in the beleaguered area, insured their ultimate defeat. The hope that a war on the whites would close the breach among them was chimerical, since some of the farmer Indians helped warn the settlements and protected individuals from the scalping knives of their brethren. Also, many chiefs took part halfheartedly, realizing the ultimate futility of the campaign.[40]

The extent of the panic occasioned by the descent of the Sioux warriors down the Minnesota Valley was reflected by the authorities of Minnesota, Iowa, Dakota, Kansas, and Nebraska.

[40] "Chief Big Eagle's Story," 387.

Preparations went along at a furious pace in order to ward off any attack, but frontier settlers fled for safer ground anyway. The evacuation of the Minnesota Valley and abandonment of Sioux Falls has already been alluded to; Bon Homme, Dakota Territory, also was deserted, and Yankton, Vermillion, Elk Point, and Richland were partially depopulated. A large group of settlers fled from eastern and southern Dakota to Sioux City, Iowa, in such haste that they left their stock and crops in the fields. Also many Iowans from Woodbury, Ida, and Sac counties fled to Sioux City. In Nebraska Territory the Brulé and Yanktonai were reported grouping to assail the Pawnee Indians as well as white settlers of that region. Families moved out of danger areas to the village of Columbus, Nebraska, in anticipation of such an attack.[41] The conspiracy rumor and the terrible toll and stories of the Minnesota Valley massacre added to the panic.

Relatively fresh in the minds of Iowans was the Spirit Lake Massacre by Inkpaduta and his band of outlaw Sioux in 1857, who had killed about forty persons. The possibility of a recurrence of such depredation on a larger scale was indicated by the carnage in Minnesota, and particularly by the fifteen settlers (more or less) slaughtered near Jackson, Minnesota, about twenty miles north of the Iowa border, and the same number massacred at Lake Shetek only forty miles north of the line. In Iowa itself, within three miles of Sioux City, two frontier defenders were ambushed before the Northern Border Brigade was organized, and bands of redmen were reported in the Little Sioux Valley. Horses and cattle were also reported stolen.[42]

Iowa commissioned Lieutenant Colonel James A. Sawyer to command a Northern Border Brigade of five volunteer companies to defend the northwestern border. These units were mustered at Fort Dodge, Webster City, Denison, Sioux City, and Chain Lakes, and held a continuous line of blockhouses from Chain Lakes to Sioux City. While some of them had signed for

[41] *Official Records*, Series I, Vol. XIII, 638, 644–45. The Brulé, as the Yanktonai, were a Siouan tribe.

[42] Riggs, *Forty Years*, 139; Heard, *Sioux War*, 99; Benjamin F. Gue, *History of Iowa*, Vol. II, 68–69.

nine months' duty, most of them served until December, 1863. Divided between Spirit Lake and Sioux City were the Sioux City Cavalry in United States service. Also in Sioux City for a while were "a squad of artillery from Council Bluffs and three companies of infantry from Council Bluffs and Harrison County," which troops, as was the case in Minnesota, had volunteered for federal service but had not yet been sworn in. All told, there were apparently about 350 troops in Sioux City that September.[43]

In Dakota Territory, the governor ordered "every male citizen in the Territory between the ages of 18 and 50" to "enroll himself in a company to be formed for home defense in his respective county, with such arms as he may have in his possession." In response, five companies, totaling 266 men, were raised. The 92 troopers of Captain Nelson Minor's Company A, Dakota Cavalry, in federal service since April, were already on the job. They guarded Yankton, Vermillion, and Sioux Falls in Dakota Territory and, according to some accounts, the company, or part of it, was driven from Sioux Falls before the city was burned.[44] Other depredations in Dakota, combined with the Minnesota massacre, lent much justification to the arming there. Two farmers were murdered within a mile of Sioux Falls, a mail carrier was shot down between Yankton and Sioux Falls, a stage driver on the Fort Randall road was shot, and two unarmed citizens were killed at a ferry within three miles of Yankton. In addition Yankton County "farmers were driven from their fields and shot at in their doorways, until forced to retreat to the town [Yankton] for safety."[45]

In contrast to Minnesota, or Iowa and Wisconsin, Nebraska Territory's pressing problem was a nearly defenseless wide frontier. A string of settlements on the Dakota side and Fort Randall protected her northeastern frontier along the Missouri; but

---

[43] Dan Elbert Clark, "Frontier Defense in Iowa 1850–1865," *Iowa Journal of History and Politics*, Vol. XVI (July, 1918), 376.

[44] *Senate Miscellaneous Document* No. 241, 9–10, 12, 24, 81; Doane Robinson "A History of the Dakota or Sioux Indians," *South Dakota Historical Collections*, Vol. 2, 301. Cited hereafter as Robinson, "History of the Sioux."

[45] *Senate Miscellaneous Document* No. 241, 81, 82.

west of the Missouri there was little cover. A thin line of troops guarded the central mail route and the Oregon trail from Fort Kearny west. Brigadier General James Craig, whose duty it was to protect the routes, wrote Stanton on August 23 from Fort Laramie: "Indians from Minnesota to Pike's Peak, and from Salt Lake to near Fort Kearny, committing many depredations. I have only about 500 troops scattered on the telegraph and over-land mail routes. Horses worn by patrolling both roads."[46] Too many Indians and too few troops had been Craig's problem since April when he had taken charge of the mail route from its eastern terminus to the continental divide. But the Indian problem was important in another way also. Benjamin F. Lushbaugh, agent for the Pawnee, reported on September 13 that

> Before leaving Nebraska much apprehension prevailed among the settlers there that the existing Indian troubles in Minnesota might extend to the former Territory. . . . I have received information from my agency that an attack of a serious character had been made upon it by the Brulé and Yankton Sioux.[47]

The secretary of the interior then reported to Stanton:

> It will be seen that the Sioux Indians, now in open hostility to the United States have commenced hostilities upon the Pawnees of Nebraska as well as upon the white settlers in that Territory. . . . There is danger that great sacrifice of life, as well as of property, will be incurred . . . in Nebraska.[48]

Because the "frontier people" were "much alarmed," the governor asked for, and was denied, authority to raise a regiment for the defense of the Nebraska border. Since April, Nebraska had no active home guards and no volunteer troops in United States service except two regiments in the east. Apparently there was no change in this status until Nebraska Territory was transferred to another department in November.

[46] *Official Records,* Series I, Vol. XIII, 592.
[47] *Ibid.,* 645; *Report of the Secretary of the Interior,* 1862, 267.
[48] *Official Records,* Series I, Vol. XIII, 644.

Edward Salomon, governor of Wisconsin, wrote Stanton on September 2:

> There is very great apprehension in the northwestern and central portions of the state on account of the Indians. . . . Families are leaving their homes for fear of the wandering bands. . . . The people must be protected . . . more arms must be forwarded immediately. . . . Our Lake Superior settlements, surrounded by large numbers of Indians, are entirely defenseless.

Salomon received no arms, but after a sharp verbal duel with Stanton he did get some ammunition. As Wisconsin had no adequate law sanctioning militia or military organization, Salomon had to entrust the arms he sent to the frontier "to some reliable men in different localities." Apparently this was enough.[49]

The Sioux caught the frontier at a time when they knew it was weak, suddenly creating for the local agencies the problem of finding troops and arms to secure themselves. Minnesotans felt this problem most urgently, since they were virtually unprepared. Governor Alexander Ramsey acted quickly on August 19. He stopped at Fort Snelling to see what troops were available, then hastened to Mendota to put his old political foe, Colonel Henry Hastings Sibley, in command of the relief expedition, and gave him a free hand to campaign as he chose. Sibley had lived among and traded with the Sioux for twenty-eight years, so he knew them well. Sibley and four companies of the Sixth Minnesota, not yet mustered into United States service, began to move up the Minnesota and on August 22 reached St. Peter. He waited there for supplies and equipment to catch up with him. On August 24 some two hundred mounted militiamen arrived, led by William J. Cullen, a former superintendent of Indian affairs. Six more companies of the Sixth Minnesota also appeared along with several other squads of mounted men and volunteer militia. The force now numbered nearly 1,400.[50] Sizable as this was, it was

[49] Reuben Gold Thwaites, ed., *Civil War Messages and Proclamations of Wisconsin War Governors*, 138–39.
[50] *Minnesota in the Civil and Indian Wars*, 735; West, *Sibley*, 254.

utterly inexperienced, from the green infantrymen of the Sixth to the horses of the mounted men. However, there were men of experience among the leaders, such as Sibley the frontiersman, and Minnesota Militia Colonel William Crooks, who had spent two years at West Point.

Charles E. Flandrau (associate justice of the State Supreme Court and militia colonel), hero of the defense of New Ulm, was given command of the Blue Earth country of Minnesota, from the Iowa border north to New Ulm. He headed a force of volunteer citizens, militia, and elements of troops from Fort Snelling originally intended for federal service. Above the Minnesota River elements of the Ninth Minnesota and irregular militia held Forest City and Glencoe.

On August 21, the secretary of state in Minnesota wrote the assistant secretary of war that "a most frightful insurrection of Indians" had broken out and that the governor had ordered out infantry, which was of little use in chasing Indians. He wanted authority to raise one thousand mounted men. The same day Ramsey telegraphed Stanton that "the Sioux . . . have risen," and reported that he had ordered up the Sixth Minnesota and made Sibley a colonel. Henry W. Halleck, the general-in-chief, wrote Ramsey that as soon as the Third Minnesota Volunteer Infantry was paroled it would be sent to him. On August 25 Ramsey wired Stanton and tried to get the draft postponed, but Stanton did not accede. Ramsey then telegraphed President Lincoln:

> With the concurrence of Commissioner [William P.] Dole I have telegraphed the Secretary of War for an extension of one month of drafting, etc. The Indian outbreak has come upon us suddenly. Half the population of the state are fugitives. It is absolutely impossible that we should proceed. The Secretary of War denies our request. I appeal to you, and ask for an immediate answer. No one not here can conceive the panic in the state.[51]

Lincoln replied on the following day: "Yours received. Attend

[51] *Official Records,* Series I, Vol. XIII, 590, 595, 596, 597; *Minnesota Executive Documents,* 1862, 370–74.

to the Indians. If the draft cannot proceed of course it will not proceed. Necessity knows no law. The Government cannot extend the time."[52] There were no further references to the draft. Even though the government would not extend the time, the draft did not proceed. For one thing, Ramsey needed the Minnesota troops mustering at Snelling, and for another, with some fleeing and others fighting on the frontier, volunteers or draftees would be hard to find.

Ramsey continued to look for federal military assistance. The same day he wired Lincoln, he also asked Halleck: "Could not Minnesota and Dakota be organized into a military department and General W. S. Harney be sent to chastise the Sioux?" On August 29, three days later, Halleck replied: "The War Department is not prepared at present to create a new military department in the west."[53] Halleck doubtless was much more interested in the operations of the Army of Virginia at that date.

Despite the desperate struggle before Washington, the frantic appeals from the frontier, along with the news of the atrocities and the extent of the Sioux uprising, apparently caused Stanton to see differently from Halleck the necessity for federal military intervention. And then, after the first few days of September, Stanton had a general without a command who could most conveniently be used in the Northwest.

[52] *Ibid.*, 599.
[53] *Ibid.*, 597, 605.

3

Another War Begins for Pope

IF ONLY BY DEFINITION, a massacre must be considered an awful affair, but the superlatives various writers have attached to the Minnesota catastrophe are both excessive and inadequate. The event has been designated the "most serious Indian massacre in American history," "the most serious Indian massacre the frontier had yet seen," "the most remarkable and noteworthy incident of the kind in American history," and more recently, "the bloodiest Indian massacre the West ever knew."[1] Extravagant though these phrases are, the carnage compares (if one accepts a conservative estimate of four hundred dead, and if such things must be graded on a scale of morbidity) with the most serious manslaughter in North America, ranking just slightly above the Fort Mims affair that led to the Creek War forty-nine years before, although less awesome than Opechancanough's outrages in 1622 and 1644 in Virginia. Compared with the sacrifice in the South, however, the disaster in the Northwest was insignificant. It takes no imagination to see why the country's attention was focused on Virginia and Maryland, rather than Minnesota.

While there is some disagreement over the casualties suffered that same summer at Second Bull Run and Antietam, still there is substantial agreement that the armies of Lee, Pope, and McClellan lost in killed, wounded, and missing about 46,400 men. The frontier circumstances in Minnesota made it nearly impossible to fix a definite figure for either whites or Indians. Contemporary estimates ranged from over three hundred to eight

[1] In order, these quotations are from Wilson P. Shortridge, *The Transition of a Typical Frontier*, 146; Frederic Logan Paxson, *The Last American Frontier*, 235; Lucius F. Hubbard and Return I. Holcombe, *Minnesota in Three Centuries*, Vol. III, 269; C. M. Oehler, *The Great Sioux Uprising*, vii.

hundred whites dead; later figures ran from four hundred to eight hundred, while Sibley's biographer claimed one thousand frontiersmen perished, that two thousand more were maimed sufferers, that eight thousand were made paupers, and that thirty thousand were fugitives.[2]

There is no speculation, however, that when the Sioux war cry echoed through the Minnesota Valley, three companies of the Fifth Minnesota Volunteer Infantry found themselves desperately on the defensive, in the midst of a sudden savage war they had not enlisted to fight. They bravely struggled to hold their ground and prevent the Sioux from sweeping past Fort Ridgely and New Ulm and into the more populated areas downstream, such as Mankato and St. Peter. When Fort Ridgely was alerted shortly before noon on August 18, Captain Marsh acted quickly. He sent a courier to recall Lieutenant Timothy J. Sheehan and his fifty men from their return trip to Ripley. In haste, Marsh set out with forty-six men to the rescue of Redwood Agency. "Only six miles from Fort Ridgely houses in flames, mutilated but not yet cold corpses . . . revealed the appalling nature of the outbreak," as did the frightened settlers fleeing for the fort, yet incautiously, Marsh marched on. The Sioux knew that troops would come running toward the agency, and they were ready. As the soldiers prepared to take the boat across the river at Redwood Ferry, a signal from the other bank unleashed chilling howls from dozens of red warriors who materialized out of the brush, guns blazing. The surviving troops took shelter in a thicket by the water, cut off from escape. The river was their only out, and in their attempt to swim for freedom Captain Marsh drowned. After dark, nineteen survivors, some badly wounded, straggled into Ridgely.[3]

[2] *Report of the Secretary of the Interior,* 1862, 210; *Report of the Secretary of the Interior,* 1863, 408; *Minnesota, Executive Documents 1862,* 9–10; Heard, *Sioux War,* 243; Whipple, *Lights and Shadows,* 105; West, *Sibley,* 249; William Watts Folwell, *A History of Minnesota,* Vol. II, 391–93.

[3] *Minnesota in the Civil and Indian Wars,* 248–50, 731; also John Ames Humphrey, "Boyhood Remembrances of Life Among the Dakotas and the Massacre of 1862," *Collections of the Minnesota Historical Society,* Vol. 15, esp. p. 345.

The Sioux bypassed Fort Ridgely that same day, moving down toward New Ulm. This was fortunate for Lieutenant Thomas P. Gere and the small garrison of twenty-nine men, for if the Sioux had followed up the ambush on Captain Marsh's detail by attacking Ridgely, it is doubtful that the garrison could have held out. As soon as Gere learned of Marsh's fate, he promptly sent to Fort Snelling for reinforcements. His courier had instructions to stop at St. Peter to recall Lieutenant Norman K. Culver with Galbraith's half-bloods. Meanwhile, Sheehan's tired troops returned to Ridgely after an all-night forced march. News of the outbreak had reached St. Peter before Gere's emissary, who found Lieutenant Culver and Galbraith already securing arms for the reservation enlistees, who called themselves the Renville (County) Rangers. Upon being informed of the situation at Ridgely by the messenger, Culver and the rangers returned to Ridgely on the afternoon of August 19. Refugees, as well as the soldiers, flooded into the fort, but only 25 out of more than 250 were armed. With the 51 men of Company B, 50 men of Company C, 50 Renville Rangers, the armed citizens, and the officers, the defense force consisted of about 180 men.[4]

At 2 P.M. on Wednesday, August 20, a sentry gave the alarm, and the Sioux began firing at the garrison from the cover of the wooded ravines that nearly surrounded the post. Several attempts were made to storm the post, but fire from the artillery, directed by an old regular, Ordinance Sergeant John Jones, cut short any such hope. The Sioux retired at dusk. On Friday, August 22, at about 2:30 in the afternoon, an excited guard called the defenders to arms again, and, according to Lieutenant Sheehan, "a much larger force attacked us on all sides." This assault was very determined, and the objective seemed to be the field pieces that had caused the redmen so much difficulty on Wednesday. "The balls fell thick all over and through the wooden building erected for officers quarters," that sheltered some of the beleaguered. "Still the men maintained their ground. The Indians prepared to storm but the gallant conduct of the men at the guns

[4] *Minnesota in the Civil and Indian Wars*, 250–51.

39

paralyzed them, and compelled them to withdraw after one of the most determined attacks ever made by Indians on a military post." In this second encounter, all the small arms ammunition was used up, and the garrison had to use makeshift balls. Even bullets fired by the Indians were recast by "men and ladies organized for that purpose," and reused. The total loss to the soldiers of the garrison in both collisions was only three killed and thirteen wounded. The buildings of the fort proper were still up after the affair, but "very much wrecked." All the outbuildings, except the guardhouse and the magazine were entirely destroyed by the garrison itself to deprive the attackers of cover. Most of the mules and oxen had been taken by the Sioux. Ridgely was on a constant state of alert until the garrison was finally relieved on August 27.[5]

Company D, Fifth Minnesota, the garrison at Fort Abercrombie, Dakota Territory, was divided. One lieutenant and thirty soldiers were stationed at Georgetown, about fifty miles downstream on the Red River, while Captain John Vander Horck and about fifty men occupied the main post. On August 13, orders were received to guard a treaty train which was coming through with Dole, Thompson, and others, to treat with the Chippewas of the Red River Valley. The commission itself had only reached St. Cloud when the news of the outbreak came to them. The order to guard the train was countermanded with instructions to hold it at the Fort. With this last directive was a proof slip from a St. Cloud newspaper that contained news of the outbreak. This was August 20, the first notice Abercrombie had of the war. A messenger met the train (which was moving ahead of the commission) to order it and the Georgetown detachment back to Abercrombie. The treaty train made it back later in the day on August 20; the men from Georgetown returned on August 23.

Reconnoitering parties from Abercrombie found the usual evidence of Indians on the warpath, and sent for reinforcements and ammunition. On August 30, the Indians drove off a herd of

[5] *Ibid.*, 252–53, 254–55; *Official Records*, Series I, Vol. XIII, 248–50.

stock, which was partially recovered the next day. But the Sioux did not offer a direct attack until daybreak on September 3, when they commenced a futile but furious six-hour engagement. On September 6, the redmen, with an increased force, began another determined assault. In this fight Company D lost only one killed and two wounded. For the next couple of weeks the Indians made travel hazardous. They assailed a dispatch escort of twenty men on September 21, leaving eighteen to ride back alive. Abercrombie was not relieved, however, until September 23. Even after Abercrombie was reinforced, the Sioux still persisted with hostilities. On September 26, at 7:30 A.M., they made a brief attack, only to be quickly repulsed, and pursued. The troops moved with such haste that the redmen were forced to abandon their "camp equipage, blankets, &c.," which the soldiers burned. Again on September 29, in the late afternoon or evening, the Indians threw themselves at the post, but "a few shells thrown in the woods" discouraged them. Captain Emil A. Burger noted in his report that he expected more trouble, because "camp fires can be seen at a distance of 3 to 4 miles." No other assault came, but the Sioux remained troublesome and the garrison had to remain constantly ready for them.[6]

Only thirty troopers of Company C were at Ripley with Captain Francis Hall, since the rest of the company was at Ridgely with Lieutenant Sheehan. None anticipated trouble with the local Chippewas since they had been friendly for many years, but on August 19 Hall received a request from the Chippewa agent at Gull Lake for protection. The agent believed these Indians were going on the warpath too. The next day Lieutenant Frank B. Fobes led twenty men toward the agency and met the agent and all the whites in full retreat. The latter warned the soldiers the Chippewas were coming down in force. Hole-in-the-day, the Chippewa chief, was ordered arrested, but he subsequently escaped after an exchange of gunfire with the troops.

[6] *Minnesota in the Civil and Indian Wars,* 255–57 (this is the account of Captain John Vander Horck, commander at Abercrombie until relieved by Captain Emil A. Burger); *Official Records,* Series I, Vol. XIII, 282–83.

A dispatch to St. Paul advised the governor of the situation, and the small garrison prepared for action. As in the case at Ridgely, Hole-in-the-day did not attack while the beleagured force was inadequate (only twenty-nine), in spite of the fact that he had 275 warriors ready. Ramsey promptly ordered one company of the Sixth Minnesota and two companies of the Seventh Minnesota from Fort Snelling to Ripley. By the time of their arrival Hole-in-the-day had five hundred warriors in camp ten miles west of the fort. Dole's party appeared shortly after the arrival of the troops and successfully headed off any Chippewa disturbance.[7]

The forts in the area were forts in name only, containing in all cases no barricade, stockade, or breastwork of any sort, merely barracks and storehouse buildings built around three or four sides of a square.[8] Had these positions been attacked at the outset of the outbreak, before Ridgely and Ripley were reinforced and barricaded, and before Abercrombie was fortified, the garrisons might have been massacred as Captain Marsh's command had been. Fortunately also, many citizens rallied to the defense at the forts and other points along the frontier, at New Ulm particularly. On August 19 the first attack came at New Ulm, and despite the "state of utter frenzy" and the fact that there was no organization for defense, the Indians were driven off at dark. That night Colonel Flandrau, who brought 150 armed men from St. Peter, reinforced the town. Earlier that day a detachment of sixteen men under Sheriff L. M. Boardman had arrived in time to participate in the defense.[9] Accompanying Flandrau's St. Peter Frontier Guards was a large squad from Le Sueur under

[7] *Minnesota in the Civil and Indian Wars*, 257–60. Account by Lieutenant Frank B. Forbes, Company C, Fifth Minnesota Volunteer Infantry; *Minnesota, Executive Documents*, 1862, 384–92.

[8] *Minnesota in the Civil and Indian Wars*, 251, 255, 258.

[9] Heard, *Sioux War*, 78–81; *Minnesota in the Civil and Indian Wars*, 731–33; Alexander Berghold, *The Indians' Revenge; or, Days of Horror, Some Appalling Events in the History of the Sioux*, Chapter X. The German edition, *Indianer-Rache, oder die Schreckenstage von Neu Ulm* (Graz, 1892), is nearly word for word the same as the English. While most of the contemporary accounts differ in detail, Berghold is one of the least reliable.

Sheriff Tousley of Le Sueur County, while on the same day Lieutenant Samuel Coffin led some of Captain A. M. Bean's Nicollet County Guards from Swan Lake to New Ulm.[10] Subsequently, eight companies were formed for the defense of New Ulm, and by August 23, the date of the second battle, there was a total strength of over nine hundred men. On August 19, the date of the first battle, there had been about 360 defenders.[11] Flandrau became over-all commander, and William B. Dodd, his first lieutenant, was second. Salmon A. Buell, a former naval officer, was "provost marshal, chief of staff, and general manager." On August 29 Governor Ramsey made Flandrau's command in southern Minnesota official. Flandrau had charge of the Blue Earth country from New Ulm south to the Iowa border, and set up headquarters at South Bend. These citizen companies served anywhere from five or six days to several months, the greatest number disbanding with the temporary retreat from New Ulm on August 25.

In other areas of the frontier, similar citizen organizations sprang into existence. At Fort Abercrombie, Captain Vander Horck mustered in seventy-nine citizens, who participated in all of the battles, under the command of Captain T. D. Smith. There were about forty-six citizens attached to Captain Richard Strout's company of the Ninth Minnesota, around Glencoe, Forest City, and Hutchinson, the same vicinity in which some sixty-three Sibley Guards under Captain George C. Whitcomb served. That area also boasted the Hutchinson Guards, seventy-seven strong, led by Captain Lewis Harrington. Among others were the Goodhue County Rangers, the Frontier Avengers (St. Peter), the Renville Rangers, and 22 men not otherwise identified who assisted at Fort Ridgely. Elsewhere, farther north, west, and east, other independent bodies of citizen volunteers patrolled

---

[10] *Minnesota in the Civil and Indian Wars,* 732–33, [754]–756, 764, 767–68.

[11] According to the rosters, the strength was 916 on August 23, and 366 on August 19, allowing for 16 men of Flandrau's St. Peter Guards participating on August 19. Also, doubtless some who took part in the first battle unattached became parts of organizations by the time of the second battle. Allowance must be made for some such duplication.

the frontier. The heavy response in citizen-soldiers was due partly to Ramsey's proclamation calling on all men in the counties
next to the seat of war to take their own horses and report to the
general in charge.

On August 23, Sibley dispatched Captain E. St. Julian Cox to
the relief of New Ulm, but Cox's command arrived too late to
fight. Two days later Captain Joseph Anderson led sixty soldiers to New Ulm, only to find it evacuated.[12] On the twenty-
sixth Sibley moved toward Ridgely. Colonel Samuel McPhail's
mounted men arrived at Ridgely the next day, and the rest of
Sibley's army marched in on the twenty-eighth.

On August 31 Major Joseph R. Brown took about 150 soldiers
on a reconnaisance in force to the Lower Agency. Brown, the
Indian agent who had preceded Galbraith, had 70 mounted men
of Captain Anderson's Cullen Guard, Captain H. P. Grant's company of the Sixth Minnesota, and two volunteers of each of the
Sixth's other companies, seventeen teams and teamsters, and
some citizens. Aside from the reconnaisance they were to bury
the dead. They met no Indians, found the agency destroyed, dug
many graves, and encamped about two hundred yards from
where Birch Coulie emptied into the Minnesota. The Sioux si-
lently surrounded the encampment at night on September 1, and
opened fire shortly before dawn on September 2. This had not
been the plan, but a soldier on guard spoiled it for the redmen
by shooting at moving grass that he thought meant a moving
animal. The camp roused as other sentries also fired, and confusion reigned. Painted warriors rose from the tall grass and
rained a torrent of bullets on the camp. Tents were riddled, and
horses whinnied, bucked the picket ropes, and fell. In the first
minutes of the mix-up, the soldiers managed to turn the wagons
over, crawl behind them and the dead animals, and burrow into
the tough prairie sod. There they remained and returned the
fire, through the hot sun of the day, without water, without food
(they couldn't reach the provision wagon or the river). After a
day of sweat and horror, sunset came, and darkness, but not

12 Isaac V. D. Heard, author of *Sioux War*, was a member of this company.

relief. The ammunition was nearly gone. There was no rescue. The casualties were "87 dead horses, twenty-two dead soldiers. . . . [and] sixty wounded soldiers." The fight continued uninterruptedly all through September 2 and 3. Sibley heard the noise of battle, and dispatched McPhail with fifty mounted men and Major Robert N. McLauren with 105 infantry to Brown's relief. Three miles from Birch Coulie McPhail's force was attacked, and he sent back for reinforcements. Sibley then moved his whole army forward and met McPail after dark. At dawn the combined forces moved to lift the siege. When the Sioux saw Sibley's long columns approaching, they fired a parting volley or two into the camp by Birch Coulie and disappeared. Rescued and rescuers alike turned to Ridgely.[13] Sibley did not resume his operations up the Minnesota for another two weeks.

It was at this juncture that Pope took command. Sibley, on September 16, was camped four miles west of Fort Ridgely readying his forces for their plunge into hostile territory. The fact that Pope had to act nearly alone, since as yet there was no staff or organization to help him, did not dim the vigor with which he faced the many new problems. First, he assured Sibley that he would "push forward everything to your assistance as fast as possible." Then Pope ordered four regiments from Wisconsin. Cavalry was unobtainable but apparently he hoped to mount two of the Wisconsin regiments to provide 1,000 mounted men. He ordered 2,500 horses.

Pope's plan, he told Sibley, was to place 1,000 soldiers, half on horseback, at Abercrombie; 500 more mounted at Otter Tail; 1,000 troops at Ripley; and 500 cavalry and 500 infantry at Crystal Lake. He planned to send expeditions from Iowa into Dakota along the Big Sioux River to occupy the Yanktonai while Sibley struck the Sioux of Minnesota. Pope proposed to put forage for 1,000 horses and rations for 2,500 men at Ridgely as a depot for Sibley, supplies for 500 horses and 1,000 soldiers at

[13] *Minnesota in the Civil and Indian Wars,* 736–39. See especially note 2, p. 736, account by Lieutenant James J. Egan of Captain Anderson's company; also pp. 306–10, report of Captain Grant; Heard, *Sioux War,* 131–37.

Abercrombie, and to build the necessary stables and quarters at each place. This judicious disposition of forces and stores he had planned before he found he could not possibly carry out the project that season. He directed Sibley to seize for military use all lumber, all the blacksmith's and carpenter's tools, "and everything else that may be useful now" at the Sioux Agency "or elsewhere in your reach" and to send the items thus requisitioned to Ridgely. Pope sent Captain Anderson D. Nelson to muster in Sibley's regiments and pay them and ordered Sibley to "move forward as rapidly as possible" and "to make no arrangement of any kind with them [the Sioux] until they are badly punished."[14]

Fortunately, Pope approved of both the commander and the plan he found in operation when he arrived. "I am rejoiced to find you in command," he wrote Sibley, and gave tacit approval of Sibley's move up the Minnesota valley. Before Pope arrived, Sibley had strung guard posts along the perimeter of settlement. Iowa, acting independently, had continued this security network; and by location, if not by design, so had Dakota merely by having her main strongholds on the Missouri River. Hence there was little need for Pope to give much thought to the defensive aspect of the situation. The only expedient changes he could make would be offensive in character, and since troops were not available to send north from Dakota to cut off reinforcements or escape, he could only assist Sibley in every respect possible, try to bolster existing defenses, and plan for the future.

Sibley, with around 1,400 infantry, but only 27 horsemen, nonetheless prepared to move forward as fast as possible in spite of the absence of cavalry and the greenness of his new levies. He believed that the savages were assembled near Lac qui Parle about sixty miles above Ridgely, and his chief worry was that he might not be able to overtake them should they not offer battle. His half-bloods believed they would stand and fight no farther away than Lac qui Parle. Another worry of Sibley's was the safe recovery of the white captives. He had little doubt that even his inexperienced troops could whip the Indians, and as he told

[14] *Ibid.*, 648–49.

Flandrau, "they will be met with their own weapons and their own style of warfare.[15] Sibley advanced upstream watched all the time by small Indian parties, and on September 22 camped at Lone Tree Lake, about three miles east of Wood Lake.

Ironically enough, it was a few of the troops of the Third Minnesota, the only supposedly disciplined body Sibley had, who on the morning of September 23 on their own initiative decided to go over to the Yellow Medicine Agency (two miles distant) and replenish their stock of potatoes. Four of five teams crossed the bridge over the creek and spoiled the ambush the Sioux had ready for Sibley. These few men were fired upon, precipitating the battle. The redmen dashed toward the main camp about 7 A.M. "whooping and yelling . . . and firing with great rapidity." The Renville Rangers and the Third Minnesota formed a skirmish line and stopped the frontal charge while five companies of the Seventh Minnesota and two companies of the Sixth "at a double quick and amid a shower of balls" cleared a near-by ravine the Indians attempted to use to flank the troops. The battle raged for two hours, the "6-pounder and the mountain howitzer being used with great effect."[16]

They were "repulsed at all points with great loss" and "retired with precipitation." Only 500 braves attacked Sibley, although 800 more were assembled near by at Yellow Medicine but took no part in the fight. The official report listed four killed and thirty-five or forty wounded among the soldiers. The Sioux lost in the neighborhood of thirty killed and many more wounded, although the troops found only fourteen bodies.[17]

Aside from the defeat of the Indians, the battle at Wood Lake

[15] *Official Records,* Series I, Vol. XIII, 637, 650–52.

[16] *Ibid.,* 278–79; *Minnesota in the Civil and Indian Wars,* 159–60, 311–12, 351–52, 743–44.

[17] *Official Records,* Series I, Vol. XIII, 278–79, 679. This is Sibley's official report. However, as usual the number of casualties is a point of dispute. Heard agrees with Sibley's report (*Sioux War,* 174–75) as far as casualties, but believes there were nearer 800 Indians engaged. Folwell disagrees with Heard as to casualties, listing seven killed (*A History of Minnesota,* Vol. II, 181), but agrees substantially with Heard as to the number of Indians involved (II, 179); accounts in *Minnesota in the Civil and Indian Wars* vary. The monument on the site lists seven killed.

had three other important aspects: it made final the division among the Sioux into two groups, those who wished to fight and those who wished peace; most important of all, the victory insured the delivery to Sibley of the white captives; and for this victory at Wood Lake Sibley was soon made a brigadier general.

From time to time, various individuals among the Indians had communicated with Sibley, the first instance after Birch Coulie. Sibley left a note attached to a stake on the battleground. It read, "If Little Crow has any proposition to make, let him send a half-breed to me, and he shall be protected in and out of camp." On September 7 Little Crow sent two braves under a flag of truce to Sibley. The letter they carried blamed the outbreak on the mishandled annuity, and listed other insults to the Sioux. Little Crow admitted he had "a great many prisoners, women and children." As for the war, he said, "It ain't all our fault. The Winnebagoes were in the engagement [too]." Sibley replied, "You have murdered many of our people without sufficient cause. Return the prisoners under a flag of truce, and I will talk with you like a man." This brought the same messengers and the same truce flag on September 12, with Little Crow's answer.

We have in Mawakanton band One Hundred and fifty five prisoners—not includ the Sisiton & warpeton presoners, then we are waiting for the Sisiton what we are going to do with the presoners they are coming down. they are at Lake quiparle now. The words that il to the govrment il want to here from him also, and I want to know from you as a friend what way that il can make peace for my people—in regard to prisoners they fair with our children or our self jist as well as us.

[We have 155 prisoners with the Mdewakanton band, which does not include the prisoners held by the Sisseton and Wahpeton. We are waiting for the Sisseton to come down before we decide what to do with the prisoners. They (the Sisseton) are at Lac qui Parle now. The words that I want to say to the government I shall want to hear from the government also, and as a friend I want you to tell me how I can make peace for my people. In regard to the prisoners, they fare as well as we do.]

48

GENERAL JOHN POPE

GENERAL HENRY W. HALLECK

Sibley answered,

> You have not done as I wished in giving up to me the prisoners
> taken by your people. It would be better for you to do so. . . .
> You have allowed your young men to commit nine murders since
> you wrote your first letter. That is not the way for you to make
> peace.

Along with Little Crow's missive, one of the couriers managed
to smuggle out word from the dissenters, Wabashaw and Taopee, that revealed the division in the Indian ranks:

> Little Crow has been opposed to me in everything that our
> people have had to do with the whites. . . . I have been kept back
> by threats that I should be killed if I did anything to help the
> whites; but if you will now appoint some place for me to meet
> you, myself and the few friends that I have will get all the pris-
> oners that we can, and . . . go to whatever place you will appoint.

Sibley then told Wabashaw and Taopee that he would be glad
to receive all who were true friends to the whites, with as many
prisoners as they could bring, and all they had to do was to
gather on the prairie with a white flag in full sight of his troops.[18]
On the following day, September 13, Sibley addressed a notice "to those of the Half-Breeds and Sioux Indians who have not
been concerned in the murder and outrages upon the white settlers," obviously hoping to exploit the split among the Sioux, by
informing them that he would take the innocent under his protection but punish the murderers.

Since Sibley showed no inclination to offer any terms, Little
Crow and the Lower Indians chose to offer further resistance.
Because Wabashaw and Taopee were Lower Indians, they were
powerless to do anything. But the Upper Indians, or part of
them, led by Paul Maza-ku-ta-ma-ne, a farmer Indian, believed
that if his faction could get control of the captives and return

[18] *Minnesota in the Civil and Indian Wars,* 741, 742. Heard, *Sioux War,* 147–
50; *Official Records,* Series I, Vol. XIII, 631–32, 679–80, 688.

49

them, then most of the Upper Indians would escape the retribution they all feared. But Paul was unable to secure the prisoners. "Let us keep the prisoners with us, and let them share our fate," spoke one of the Lower group, and so the council decided. Two more councils were held. It became more and more apparent that the differences between the Upper and Lower Sioux, especially between the bands of Red Iron and Standing Buffalo, on the one hand, and Little Crow, on the other, were irreconcilable. A proposal that they try to make a treaty for British help against the Americans brought a cynical remark from Paul: "They are ruled by a petticoat, and she has the tender heart of a squaw. What will she do for men who have committed the murders you have?"[19] From September 14 to 24 Sibley received additional letters from among the peace faction, all of which expressed the desire that they not be mistaken for the guilty.

Sibley used the day after Wood Lake to bury the dead and to communicate with the half-bloods concerning the white hostages, before marching to their camp near Lac qui Parle. He reached that vicinity on the twenty-sixth, and bivouacked about a quarter of a mile away. This position became known as Camp Release. Meanwhile, Little Crow fled in haste with twelve or fifteen prisoners, and friendly Indians and half-bloods arranged to turn the remainder over to Sibley. Shortly after his arrival, Sibley with staff and bodyguard, rode over to take possession of the captives.[20] Sibley reported he recovered "107 white captives and 162 half-breeds."

Other hostages were two women and five or six children who had been seized by the bands of White Lodge and Lean Bear at Lake Shetek on August 20. Although Lean Bear was killed in the fray, the party headed west, throwing a scare into the Dakota settlements and murdering two settlers near Sioux Falls. From there they moved northwest, going into quarters at the mouth of Beaver Creek (now in North Dakota). They remained there

[19] Heard, Sioux War, 150–57; Minnesota in the Civil and Indian Wars, 742–43.

[20] Heard, Sioux War, 181–85; Minnesota in the Civil and Indian Wars, 312, 352; Official Records, Series I, Vol. XIII, 664, 666, 667, 679–80, 687, 695, 708.

for some weeks until a group of miners on their way down the Missouri from the Idaho country discovered them. By chance the prospectors found the Indians held white captives and near-ly became victims of the Sioux themselves. The miners arrived at Primeau's Trading Post, located just above old Fort Pierre, on November 15, and told their story. Several young Indians, called the "Fool Soldiers," set out to rescue the prisoners. These Indi-ans were youths, just in their late teens and early twenties, and had for one of their leaders one Waneta (the Charger) who was reputed to be a grandson of Captain Meriweather Lewis. They met White Lodge's band coming down the river in search of provisions, and after some dickering with the reluctant White Lodge, exchanged the hostages for some horses. This took place on November 19. After some hardship on the way back to the trading post and fear of being overtaken by White Lodge, the repatriates were eventually delivered to Fort Randall about the first of December.[21]

The rescue completed, Sibley determined to round up the re-mainder of the Sioux. On October 3, he sent four Indians to camps of Sioux that professed peace. Little Crow, unsuccessful in his war, now had only five who remained loyal to him. Sibley told the "Mdewakantonton, and Wahpeton . . . who have sepa-rated themselves from Little Crow," that they must surrender themselves immediately, or he would attack them. He promised only the guilty among them would be punished. In response to this threat, the redmen began to come in and surrender—an amazing deference to the power they believed Sibley held.

All the Sioux did not come in, of course. The group of about one hundred men under White Lodge and Sleepy Eyes (Lean

---

[21] Doane Robinson, "A History of the Dakota or Sioux Indians," *South Da-kota Historical Collections,* Vol. II, 301–13. This rescue, the full story of which did not come to light until 1898, was verified by Robinson, who "spent much time in ascertaining . . . the facts . . . and interviewing . . . each of the surviving Indi-ans. . . ." (note 508, p. 313). Robinson also states that Waneta's relationship to Captain Lewis "was a matter of common notoriety among the Indians" (note 504, p. 307). See also an account of this by John Pattee, "Dakota Campaigns," *South Dakota Historical Collections,* Vol. V, 285–88; and *Report of the Secretary of the Interior,* 1862, 519, 520, 523.

Bear's band) were encamped on the Missouri River. Standing Buffalo and others of the Upper Sioux were believed en route to the buffalo country to the west.[22] In order to insure the capture of all he could, Sibley wanted to flush the country between his camp and Big Stone Lake. Another expedition would be necessary to sweep westward from Lac qui Parle to the Coteau des Prairies.[23] An expedition to fulfill the first objective was abandoned; but on October 13 Lieutenant Colonel William R. Marshall of the Seventh Minnesota took one company of the Seventh, one of the Sixth, and forty-five recently mounted men of the Third, under Lieutenant Swan, on the second errand. They brought in about 139 warriors, squaws, and children, two weeks later. On October 15, twenty-five horsemen under a Sergeant Fox accompanied a scout and Captain Orlando C. Merriman beyond Lac qui Parle and captured a total of sixty-two Indians. Around October 24, the Third Regiment was all mounted and moved with Sibley to the Lower Agency, where Camp Sibley was established. From there Lieutenant Swan and the Third began a reconnaissance through the southwestern frontier, and returned to Fort Snelling about three weeks later.

Besides Sibley's column pushing up the Minnesota River, another smaller expedition was organized at Fort Snelling for the purpose of going to the relief of Fort Abercrombie. At Sauk Center, where they had been sent immediately after the news of the outbreak, were Captains George G. McCoy and Theodore H. Barrett of Company H, Eighth Minnesota, and Company G, Ninth Minnesota, respectively. Upon their arrival they found the company of mounted men under Captain Ambrose Freeman already there. Freeman had wanted to march to Abercrombie, but had felt too weak to set out alone. McCoy, under

---

[22] *Official Records,* Series I, Vol. XIII, 709, 711–12, 717–18, 724, 728, 734, 735.

[23] The Coteau des Prairies is a geological fault line running roughly in a horseshoe shape between the source of the Minnesota River and the Big Sioux River, with the bend of the shoe to the north. The Coteau des Missouri runs from near the Canadian border along a general line east of the river, between that and the James River, south to South Dakota's northern border.

orders to Sauk Center, did not feel authorized to move on. However, Captain Barrett, on his own responsibility, joined forces with Freeman and struck out for Abercrombie on September 14.[24] Meanwhile, at Fort Snelling, Captain Emil A. Burger took command of the main column, composed of Captain George Atkinson's Company of the Eighth Minnesota, Captain Rollo Banks's Company of the Seventh, about sixty men of the Third under Sergeant Abraham F. Dearborn, and one field piece. They departed for Abercrombie on September 10. Burger dispatched a messenger to Freeman and Barrett, asking them to await the arrival of his troops before continuing to Abercrombie. On September 19 the troops met at Wyman's Station, and arrived at their destination on September 23 without a serious incident.

On September 30, a detachment of the Third Minnesota and Freeman's company escorted about sixty citizens to safety at St. Cloud. The companies of the Seventh, Eighth, and Ninth regiments apparently remained in the vicinity of Abercrombie for the time, but the Third, after reaching Ft. Snelling on October 7 and being mounted, were sent to Camp Release and put under the command of Lieutenant Swan.

The strength of the expedition to Abercrombie was about 450 to 500 men, there being "approximately" sixty soldiers of the Third, "thirty to forty" men of Captain Freeman's company (although their roster shows 75), ninety of the Seventh Minnesota, 170 troopers of the Eighth Minnesota, seventy soldiers of the Ninth Regiment, and an undetermined number with the field piece, wagons, and other equipment.[25]

Farther south, in Dakota Territory, a portion of the Dakota Cavalry led by Sergeant Abner M. English fought an hour's battle with a small party of Sioux in late August or early September, and reported from time to time the presence of other war parties and Indian signals. This same detail fortified Yankton. Captain Minor brought his squad over from Vermillion, anticipating

[24] *Minnesota in the Civil and Indian Wars,* 161–62, esp. note on 161, and 744–45.

[25] *Minnesota in the Civil and Indian Wars,* 162, 375–76, 410–13, 448–49, 745, 762.

trouble, but finding none, left Lieutenant James M. Bacon in command of forty men at Yankton and returned to Vermillion. Shortly after the evacuation of Sioux Falls, Captain Minor and a detachment of cavalrymen put to flight another war party and recaptured some of the plunder taken in the Minnesota raids. Later, in November, Minor met and defeated a party of about forty Minnesota Sioux at Sioux Falls.[26]

On November 24, Pope ordered three companies of the Forty-First Iowa Volunteer Infantry to reconnoiter in force up the Missouri, to arrest any Minnesota Sioux they came across, and to discover the possibility of recovering the white captives discovered by the party of miners on their journey downstream the previous week. Company A of the Forty-First relieved the Dakota Cavalry, and the Dakota Cavalry went into winter quarters at Fort Randall. Captain Andrew J. Millard and the Sioux City Cavalry arrived at Randall to assist the operation by visiting the Indian camps in the vicinity. On November 26 Captain John Pattee with Company B, Forty-First Iowa, Captain Minor's Company A, Dakota Cavalry, and a detachment of seventeen men of Company A, Forty-First Iowa, organized as a battery with a twelve-pound mountain howitzer and a three-pound rifled gun, began the march toward Fort Pierre. There was some delay occasioned by the arrival of the paymaster, but on November 28 they resumed their journey in the snow. The following day the expedition met the party of whites previously rescued by friendly Indians. In camp that night, the newly-paid troops donated five hundred dollars to the rescued settlers in view of their impoverished condition. They were escorted back to Randall, and on November 30 Pattee again began to move toward Fort Pierre.[27]

The command arrived at the fur-trade post of Fort Pierre (160

---

[26] A[bner] M. English, "Dakota's First Soldiers," *South Dakota Historical Collections,* Vol. IX (1918), 245–48, 249, 251, 253–55. Hereafter cited as English, "Dakota Cavalry."

[27] Pattee, "Dakota Campaigns," 284–85, 287, 288; English, "Dakota Cavalry," 260–62. The Fourteenth Iowa's designation was changed to the Forty-First Iowa that fall.

miles up river from Randall) on December 5. Pattee, after learning that the Minnesota Sioux previously encamped near by had moved 200 miles north to avoid him, decided to return to Randall. The Dakota Cavalry returned immediately to avoid wasting forage rations, and Pattee, with the battery, followed shortly thereafter. Company B remained at Fort Pierre as a precautionary measure.

In January, Pattee received a report that a number of Sioux camped fifty miles upstream were wearing articles of white men's clothing, with the obvious connotation that they had been participants in the summer's slaughter. Pattee took eighteen men of the Dakota Cavalry on to the bitter cold prairie and returned with sixty-three prisoners. Seven of these were sentenced for participation in the raids in Minnesota, but managed to escape.[28] This was the last of active campaigning until the following spring.

From late September through November, 1862, the Department of the Northwest began to assume a more business-like form. Staff and organization began to emerge with the additions of Brigadier Generals John Cook and Washington L. Elliott, who, along with Sibley, were for a time Pope's principal assistants. Nearly as important as the generals, was the arrival of Colonel Robert E. Clary, the new chief quartermaster, an experienced career man of over thirty years' service. On November 23, General Order 19 divided the department into administrative districts. Sibley commanded the District of Minnesota, Cook the District of Iowa, and Elliott the District of Wisconsin. In October, Nebraska had been detached from Pope's department and attached to the Department of the Missouri.

This organization naturally superseded the volunteer militia arrangement in Minnesota. The first section of this to be replaced was Flandrau's Department of the Southern Frontier. Pope sent five companies of the Twenty-Fifth Wisconsin, under Colonel Milton Montgomery, to relieve Flandrau. Colonel Montgomery made his headquarters at New Ulm, and detachments

---

[28] Pattee, "Dakota Campaigns," 290–91; English, "Dakota Cavalry," 261–64.

occupied the Minnesota towns of Leavenworth, Fairmont, Winnebago City, and Madelia. Montgomery arrived at St. Paul on September 20, and at South Bend, Minnesota, Flandrau's headquarters, about October 1. Flandrau dissolved his company on October 5. The other five companies of the Twenty-Fifth Wisconsin, under Lieutenant Colonel Samuel J. Nasmith, moved into Minnesota's north central area, and occupied Sauk Center, Painesville, and Acton at about the same time as Montgomery took over in the south.[29] Since Sibley's command contained very little volunteer militia, it remained in service. In Iowa, the Northern Border Brigade was not replaced; and in Dakota the militia technically remained on duty, but its strength by the first of October was probably only one-third or less its authorized enrollment.[30]

[29] *Minnesota in the Civil and Indian Wars,* 741; E. B. Quiner, *The Military History of Wisconsin . . . A Record of the Civil and Military Patriotism of the State in the War for the Union . . .* 734–35; *Letter Books, Department of the Northwest,* Vol. I, 6, 18, 31, 44 (Mereness *Calendar* cards 6, 20, 35, 44).

[30] *Senate Miscellaneous Document No. 241,* 24–25.

4

The Sirocco Campaign

SIBLEY'S SUCCESSES IN Minnesota had not stilled the storm on the prairie. It was not that the battle of Wood Lake had not been decisive, for it did end major Sioux disturbances in Minnesota. But the power and will of the Sioux was not broken, and the ominous possibility of renewed attacks draped the northwestern frontier in the crepe of fear. Sibley's small mounted force was inadequate to scatter the redmen after the rescue at Birch Coulie, and was almost helpless to prevent the escape of Little Crow, White Lodge, and others after Wood Lake. Minnesota may have been mollified, but there was no prospect of peace.[1] Nearly every tribe west of the Mississippi was restless, and all reports indicated a spread of the hostilities. From Fort Pierre, a fur-trade post on the Missouri, notice had come as early as June, 1862, that

> The Uncpapas, Blackfeet, and Upper Yanktonais have this last spring acted with us more as a people at war with us than otherwise. Whenever they met a white man they ill-treated and abused him, and in many cases whipped him. . . . I say nothing of their yearly depredations at Fort Union and Berthold. . . . These Indians now have gone so far they cannot go back. . . . They not only insult and abuse us, but also the government. The greater portion refuse annuities, hold council, and advise with the English at Red River, and tell us every day they do not recognize the American government, as having any control of them.

Only the Minneconjou, Sans-Arc, and Two Kettles tribes were still on good terms with the government, the agent added, but

[1] West, *Sibley*, 260–61.

two-thirds of the remainder of the Upper Missouri Sioux were clearly hostile. They resented the white man using the Missouri as a highway and attempted to close it to white travel.

In fact, nine of their chieftains in July, 1862, delivered a message to the Indian agent at Fort Berthold that was at once an indictment and a challenge. They bravely announced:

> We do not want the whites to undertake to travel on our lands. . . . Boats carrying passengers we will not allow. . . .
>
> We beg of you for the last time not to bring us any more presents, as we will not receive them. . . .
>
> We notified Bear's Rib yearly not to receive your goods; he had no ears, and we gave him ears by killing him. . . . If you have no ears we will give you ears. . . .
>
> The whites in this country have been threatening us with soldiers. All we ask of you is to bring men, and not women dressed in soldier's clothes. . . .
>
> You may get this and tear it up, and tell your Father that we are all quiet and receive your presents, and by this means keep your place and fill your pockets with money. . . . Tell our Great Father what we say, and tell him the truth.[2]

Governor Jayne of Dakota Territory noted the Yanktonai were quiet, although the passage of Minnesota Sioux through their country alarmed the settlers. The Rees (Arikaras) and the Gros Ventres near Fort Berthold remained on good terms, but the friendly Piegans, Bloods, and Blackfeet, who totaled about nine thousand, were also upset over the number of whites in their country, and were determined to resist further encroachment. The Poncas were peaceful but the Brulé Sioux were not. In other words, except for the Yanktonai and scattered small groups, the Sioux were generally antagonistic not only to the whites, but to other Indians as well.[3]

The mixture of the belligerent Minnesota Sioux (or Santee, as they are sometimes known) among the Yanktonai and the prob-

---

[2] *Report of the Secretary of the Interior*, 1862, 216–19, 336–41.

[3] *Ibid.*, 319–33. The Piegan, Blood, and Blackfoot tribes were all Blackfeet, in fact.

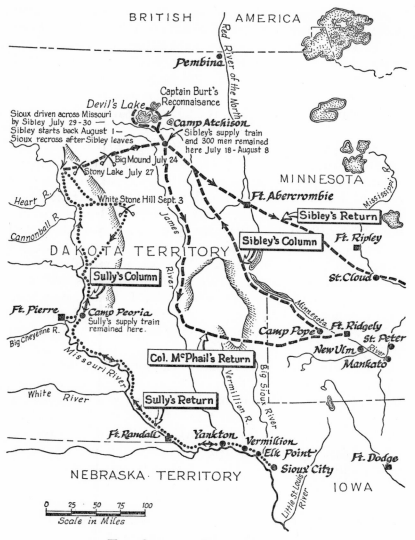

BRITISH AMERICA

Pembina

Devil's Lake   Captain Burt's Reconnaisance

Camp Atchison

Sioux driven across Missouri by Sibley July 29-30 — Sibley starts back August 1 — Sioux recross after Sibley leaves

Sibley's supply train and 300 men remained here July 18 - August 8

Big Mound July 24
Stony Lake July 27

Heart R.

White Stone Hill Sept. 3

MINNESOTA

Ft. Abercrombie

Mississippi

Sibley's Return

Sibley's Column

Ft. Ripley

Cannonball R.

DAKOTA TERRITORY

James River

St. Cloud

Sully's Column

Ft. Pierre

Camp Peoria
Sully's supply train remained here.

Big Cheyenne R.

Minnesota River

Camp Pope

Ft. Ridgely

St. Peter

New Ulm

Mankato

Missouri River

Col. McPhail's Return

White   River

Sully's Return

Vermillion R.

Big Sioux River

Ft. Randall   Yankton   Vermillion

Elk Point

Ft. Dodge

Sioux City

Little St. Louis River

NEBRASKA · TERRITORY

IOWA

0   25   50   75   100
Scale in Miles

THE SIROCCO CAMPAIGN, 1863

ability of alliance with hostile kinsmen of the Missouri frightened the Dakota settlers and officials. Jayne, Walter A. Burleigh, the Yankton agent, and James S. Williams, a Dakota judge, wrote Lincoln on Christmas Eve, 1862, that "Little Crow, White Lodge, Sleepy Eyes, Pawn, and Big Head, with from five hundred to one thousand Santee and Yankton warriors, are now on the Missouri River, above Fort Pierre, preparing for an early spring campaign against the whites."[4]

Lincoln passed this message to Halleck, who relayed it to Pope. On January 14, 1863, La Barge, Harkness, and Company (fur traders) petitioned the commissioner of Indian affairs for troops at Forts Pierre, Benton, and Berthold to protect the upper Missouri. "Perhaps you are hardly aware," they urged, "of the difficulties existing in that country. We have from Fort Randall to Fort Benton, a distance of some eighteen hundred miles, not a single military post, not a civil officer . . . not an officer or soldier of the army, indeed no . . . government of any kind." Samuel N. Latta, an Indian agent, wrote Dole, "I think we may have great reason to apprehend that they [the Sioux] will destroy any party . . . that may attempt to pass or be passed through their country."[5]

In February 1863, from his new headquarters at Milwaukee, Pope unveiled to Sibley the plans for a spring campaign. He would send three columns into Dakota, one west from central Minnesota, another north up the Big Sioux River from Iowa, and a third north along the Missouri River. To Army Headquarters in Washington, he added "all indications point to some serious and extensive operations against the white settlements, and it will be well to provide . . . against such an outbreak."[6]

Frontier security worried Sibley, since the extensive troop movement Pope proposed would leave few soldiers to protect the home front. So he asked to be reinforced. This brought a stinging reply from Pope, who told him,

[4] *Official Records*, Series I, Vol. XXII, Part I, 867.
[5] *Ibid.*, Part II, 104; *Report of the Secretary of the Interior*, 1863, 282–85.
[6] *Official Records*, Series I, Vol. XXII, Part II, 115, 116–17.

You have five and a half regiments of infantry, one nearly full of cavalry, and as much artillery as is needed for the force. You have plenty of horses to mount as much infantry as you desire. . . . So far as I know, there never yet has been assembled more than one-half of this force in this country for operations against Indian tribes. . . . Just consider, general, that you have under your command quite one-half of the force constituting the whole of the old army before the war, and which was scattered over our whole country. . . . I have little idea that the attack will be directed toward Minnesota. . . . On the contrary, all the information that reached us makes it certain to my mind that . . . it will be against the settlements in Dakota and along the Missouri River.[7]

Sibley was neither reassured nor convinced, argued that there would be a serious movement against Abercrombie, and obstinately repeated that he would need more men. Pope then answered that perhaps one brigade should go by way of Abercrombie and the Red River Valley rather than over the Big Sioux route, but at the same time asked Sibley to abandon scattered Minnesota picket posts and to use these soldiers in the field, with five or six hundred volunteers reserved at Ripley to watch the Chippewas. He promised to dispose of Sibley's Indian prisoners before the campaign began, to free their guards for action. By March 30 the captive Indians were not sent away yet, and their watchmen were not released, so the move up the Big Sioux River was abandoned. The column from Minnesota would detour northwest by Devil's Lake.[8]

Campaign plans were set June 1. The adjutant general was notified that Brigadier General Alfred Sully, who replaced Cook, would take his force up the Missouri River and meet Sibley's army turning westward from Devil's Lake in a gigantic pincer movement to trap the hostile Sioux, with three thousand men to hold the frontier against roving redmen. "These troops [the reserves] are established . . . along the whole line of outer settle-

[7] *Ibid.,* 119–20.
[8] *Ibid.,* 123, 186.

ments, and are certainly more than sufficient. . . . It is probable that you may be annoyed with complaints of insufficient forces . . . for the defense of frontier settlements. . . . I do not myself believe that one-half this force is needed." If the number that remained behind looked large, it was partly because the captive Indians had been relocated in April and May.[9] Pope also sought permission to cross the British boundary, should the Sioux flee rather than fight, so application to that effect was submitted to Richard Bickerton Pemmell, Earl Lyons, British minister to the United States. No such allowance was made.[10]

On March 30 Pope optimistically announced he intended to assemble two thousand cavalry, eight companies of infantry, and a battery of mountain howitzers at Sioux City and Fort Randall by April 15, so that the expedition could jump off by May 10, "the earliest moment at which the grass on the plains will subsist the animals." May 10 came and went, yet the expedition did not move. State officials held up the Second Nebraska Volunteer Cavalry for two months; Sully replaced Cook

[9] Ibid., 304–305. Sully was ordered to report to Pope in May, 1863. He brought a distinguished record into the department, although he was not in the best of health on arrival. Sully had been one year Pope's senior at West Point, had seen much western duty before Secession, and had served several years in Minnesota and Dakota while captain of the Second Infantry. He had been appointed colonel of volunteers in the First Minnesota Volunteer Infantry (February, 1862), but shortly after he was promoted to the permanent rank of regular army major of the Eighth Infantry (U.S.), and in this capacity he campaigned with the Army of the Potomac. Here he was twice brevetted, to Lieutenant Colonel for his work at Fair Oaks, and to Colonel for his action at Malvern Hill. Shortly after Antietam he was made Brigadier General of Volunteers. Another newcomer that same spring was Brigadier General Benjamin S. Roberts, also an old-timer, Military Academy, 1835, distinguished Mexican War record, ten years of illness, 1850–1860, but became Pope's inspector general for the Army of Virginia. Pope wanted to place Roberts in charge of the Missouri River expedition, but Stanton and Halleck demanded the selection of Sully. Either choice meant the removal of General Cook from the District of Iowa command. Cook joined Pope's staff at Milwaukee, Roberts commanded the District of Iowa for a time, Sully took the 1863 expedition into the field.

There were two other General officers who joined Pope that spring: Brigadier General Thomas C. H. Smith, a former member of Pope's staff of the Army of Virginia, who owed his general's commission to Pope, and Brigadier General Charles T. Campbell. At the same time Brigadier General Washington L. Elliott, who had joined Pope the previous fall, was relieved.

[10] Ibid., 198, 211, 289, 306.

in command; and steamboat transportation was delayed because the river was low. All in all, the Sully expedition did not
take the field until August, nearly a month after Sibley opened
the northern campaign.[11]

From mid-April through June 15, Sibley gathered his forces.
He did not depart on schedule either, but with less excuse. The
column left the rendezvous point, Camp Pope, on June 16, and,
averaging just under twelve miles a day, reached the foot of
Lake Traverse ten days later. Here he directed six hundred men
to Fort Abercrombie for supplies, while the main body continued on to the first crossing of the Cheyenne River. The campaigners waited here, at the spot they called Camp Hayes, for
the necessities from Fort Abercrombie. On July 11 the whole
group moved on through the intense summer heat, over the dry
and dusty prairie, with sunstroke a common hazard. "If the devil
were permitted to select a residence upon the earth, he would
probably choose this particular district for an abode. . . . Lakes
fair to the eye abound, but generally their waters are strongly
alkaline or intensely bitter and brackish. The valleys . . . frequently reek with sulphurous and other disagreeable vapors,"
commented Sibley, sounding as if he already longed for verdant
Minnesota. The alkaline quality of the lakes and streams tor-
mented the troopers, caused suffering and sickness and death
to the horses and mules as well as soldiers. In an attempt to
overcome the worst of the march across the prairie purgatory,
reveille sounded at two in the morning, and the weary soldiers
pitched camp at noon.[12] They could not escape the sun's heat
even then, for it enveloped and filled their dusty canvas tents
and wooden wagons. After six additional days of tedious tramp-
ing, the army halted ten or fifteen miles west of the second crossing of the Cheyenne, by a small lake. They entrenched there

[11] *Ibid.*, 186, 204, 211, 255, 260, 287, 288, 291, 306, 434; Part I, 361.

[12] *Minnesota in the Civil and Indian Wars*, 353, 354, 402–15, 439–54, 460,
749; *Official Records*, Series I, Vol. XXII, Part I, 355, 358–59, 361, 366–69, 381–
82, 907, 910; Part II, 349–50; Gabriel Renville, "A Sioux Narrative of the Outbreak in 1862, and of Sibley's Expedition in 1863," *Collections of the Minnesota
Historical Society*, Vol. X, Part II, 613.

and called the spot Camp Atchison. The object of the halt was to divest the column of the supply train and other impediments, to speed the march.[13]

In light marching order, Sibley's force resumed the trek on July 20, moving somewhat west of south. That same day a party of hunters from the Red River area crossed their path and reported a small band of Sioux encamped near Devil's Lake. Sibley sent three companies to "scour the country in that quarter"; the detachment hunted in vain for eight days and bagged only the son of Little Crow. This Indian, who had just fled from Minnesota, reported that his infamous father had been killed there in an attempt to steal horses.

In the next few days the soldiers, hustling along at sixteen miles a day, were so busy exercising their prerogative to damn the dust, the heat, and the march, that perhaps they did not feel the wary eyes of watching Sioux tracking them. On July 24, Sibley's scouts rode in hard and excitedly reported a large body of Indians on the prairie two or three miles ahead. Sibley quickly corralled his train alongside a small salt lake and began to dig in, when as if by magic redmen began to show themselves on the low hills and ridges that encircled the camp. One of Sibley's scouts cautioned the General that the Sioux would invite the white officers to parley, but not to accept, because it would actually be a trap. Some of the scouts struck up a conversation with a group of Indians close to the entrenching column, and the expedition's surgeon, resplendent in full uniform, rode up to join the group. An excited brave dazzled by the uniform apparently mistook him for a high-ranking officer and shot him, and the battle was on. The redmen, 1,000 to 1,500 in number, had been on a buffalo hunt, and apparently were so intent upon it and confident of their strength that they allowed Sibley to come upon them. The Sisseton and Wahpeton, led by Standing Buffalo and Scarlet Plume, had met Inkpaduta with his following of Yanktonai, and also the Sisseton bands of White Lodge and Lean Bear, the day before. They also knew a large body of Teton

[13] *Official Records*, Series I, Vol. XXII, Part I, 359–60.

GENERAL H. H. SIBLEY

GENERAL ALFRED SULLY

hunters was near by.[14] A six-pounder, quickly unlimbered, began to pour deadly spherical case shot at the hills, especially at "a hill toward the Big Mound." The Indians, under fire from the cannon and by troops who stormed the hills, fled. The cavalry kept up a running fight until darkness fell.[15] The Battle of Big Mound was over.

Two other engagements followed in short order, one on July 26 called the Battle of Dead Buffalo Lake, and the next on July 28 at Stony Lake. Hostilities might have been renewed the next day, but the campaigners were weary. They had fought Big Mound after a full day's march, and the cavalry pursuit had fatigued the horses. On July 26, the expedition removed to Dead Buffalo Lake, entrenched again, and fought a short skirmish with "increasing numbers of Indians . . . well mounted." The cannon, which kept the redmen generally at long range, caused them to withdraw without making a serious contest of it. On July 27, Sibley resumed the march, following the trail of the Indians as far as Stony Lake. On July 28, as the expedition was breaking camp to move on, the Sioux attacked. Indians appeared "in numbers that seemed almost incredible." They were foiled in an attempt to attack wagons that had begun to move out, because the cannon again kept them at a respectable distance until the train was closed up. Again, the Sioux were routed, and forced across the Missouri.[16] Retreating in haste, the Indians abandoned most of their transportation: the soldiers destroyed many carts and wagons and vast amounts of dried meat, tallow, buffalo robes and hides, cooking utensils, and "other indispensible articles," both after Big Mound and on the banks of the Missouri.[17]

Stony Lake was the most impressive of the three battles, because the Sioux were better organized and determined not to let Sibley fall upon their families. In that instance the redmen were successful, for their women and children escaped. At Stony Lake Sioux cavalry exhibited awesome strength massed for at-

[14] *Ibid.*, 353–54, 356; Robinson, "History of the Sioux," 318, 319, 323.
[15] *Official Records*, Series I, Vol. XXII, Part I, 352–72, 908–909.
[16] *Ibid.*, 354–55, 370.
[17] *Ibid.*, 356, 908–909.

tack on the prairie, showing Sibley's soldiers a spectacular mounted column, war paint and feathers glittering under the hot sun, five or six miles long from flank to flank, arranged in a semi-circle. If the troops were impressed, they weren't frightened off by the display. In his reports, Sibley judged about 2,300 Sioux, including Tetons, fought his soldiers in the final battle; although Turning Hawk, a participant, estimated only 1,600 warriors present. In any event, Sibley's force was not very badly hurt by the Sioux. Only three soldiers were killed, and four wounded, one fatally, while the soldiers claimed the Indians suffered 150 casualties. The colonel of the First Minnesota Mounted Rangers boasted his unit alone slew thirty-one, "all found with the peculiar mark of cavalry upon them." The Sioux modestly insisted that they lost only twenty-four braves in all three battles with Sibley.[18]

Even though the Sioux fled, Sibley could claim no victory. The Indians crossed the muddy Missouri at night, and in the morning clustered on the hills of the opposite shore, still defiant, determined to contest any crossing Sibley might attempt. The overall strategy had failed, for the redmen were not crushed in the vise prepared for them. Sully's column had not arrived. Sibley waited for two days, while daring braves continued to harass him, and were nearly successful in an attempt to stampede his livestock after dark on July 31. In hope of attracting Sully, Sibley advertised his presence with cannon signals and rockets, to no avail.[19] On August 1, the excitement over, the long return march began. The prairie was no more hospitable to the soldiers than before: "the earth was like a heated furnace, and the breezes that swept along its surface were . . . scorching and suffocating." Very likely the small war party that followed Sibley as far as the James River did not appreciate the heat any more than the soldiers. The tired troopers reached the James River Valley by August 7, and Camp Atchison soon after. Here Sibley divided his troops again, sent four mounted companies to pick

[18] *Ibid.*, 355–56, 370, 371; Robinson, "History of the Sioux," 319–23.
[19] *Official Records*, Series I, Vol. XXII, Part I, 356, 357, 368, 557.

up any Yanktonai stragglers near Snake River, a tributary of the James, to continue eastward to the Redwood River, then along the Minnesota to Ridgely. The main column headed directly for Abercrombie.[20] From Abercrombie, other scouting and reconnaisance parties were directed to follow other routes home. Three companies of cavalry cantered eastward through Chippewa country to Otter Tail Lake, then southeast to Ripley; one regiment followed the line of frontier posts as far as Ridgely "to reassure the settlers," the cavalry group that detoured along Snake, Redwood, and Minnesota Rivers next rode as far south as the Iowa line. The remainder of the force hiked directly to Fort Snelling, trudging in on September 12.[21]

On August 13, 1863, nearly two weeks after Sibley began his return from the Missouri, Sully began his march from Fort Pierre. This task force included the Sixth Iowa Volunteer Cavalry, eight companies of the Second Nebraska Cavalry, one company of the Seventh Iowa Cavalry, a battery of four guns, plus the usual supply train. Detailed figures on Sully's strength are not available, but he must have gone into the field with about 1,900 men.[22] The other three companies of the Seventh Iowa remained behind, along with two companies of the Thirtieth Wisconsin, two companies of Dakota Cavalry, and one company of the Second Nebraska. As near as ascertainable, two companies of the Thirtieth Wisconsin occupied Camp Peoria, ten miles north of Fort Pierre on the east bank of the Missouri River. The Dakota Cavalry rode monotonous frontier patrol duty, while Captain Minor and a detachment from Company A kept company with the relocated Minnesota Sioux at Fort Thompson, a recently erected stockade on the new Crow Creek Reservation. The remainder of the Seventh Iowa must have been divided

[20] *Ibid.*, 556, 907–908.

[21] *Ibid.*, 909–11.

[22] *Official Records*, Series I, Vol. XXII, Part II, 406. Pope gives the figure of not quite 1,200 as Sully's strength. An accurate account is difficult since there are no departmental returns between June 30, 1863, and December, 1863. Piecing together bits of information and doing a small amount of arithmetic produces an estimate of 1,831 without the battery or train.

between Fort Randall, Fort Pierre, and Sioux City. The Second Nebraska company was also at Randall. This left 550 troops stationed in a huge semicircle from Fort Pierre through Fort Randall to Sioux City, a very thin line compared to that in Minnesota.[23]

Sully depended largely on river streamers for supplies, but the low stage of the Missouri delayed his expedition until Pope prodded him enough to make him leave his baggage at Camp Peoria and ultimately march out on August 21.[24] The troopers carried rations for twenty-three days and forage for the transportation animals, and hoped prairie grass would suffice for the cavalry and artillery horses. The first two days, they went only eighteen miles, slow for an entirely mounted troop, but soon made better progress, as much as thirty-five miles in one day. Scouting parties brought in Indian stragglers who told of Sibley's battles; and the cautious campaigners saw "numerous signs of Indians in large numbers." Sully discovered a Mackinaw boat had been ambushed on its way downstream, its passengers massacred. It was apparent the Sioux recrossed the Missouri after Sibley retired eastward, probably to renew their buffalo hunt, since Sibley had destroyed their supplies. Sully's guides informed him that the Sioux always camped on the Coteau near tributaries of the James River, because there grass stayed green longer and buffalo were plentiful. Sully then headed east for the Coteau. Fortunately, he was a prudent man and conducted his march with great care. In front was an advance guard, off to the sides were flankers, provisions which were not unusual, but his train moved in parallel files, sixty paces apart, with troops on each side, and all loose stock in the center. An Indian war party cautiously followed Sully, but had no opportunity to make a nuisance raid. Company F of the Second Nebraska tracked down and destroyed an Indian camp of ten lodges, and further scoured the countryside in a reconnaissance of 187 miles, but

[23] Pattee, "Dakota Campaigns," 295, 298, 299; Quiner, *Military History of Wisconsin*, 790; English, "Dakota Cavalry," 264–70; *Senate Miscellaneous Document No. 241*, 10.
[24] *Official Records*, Series I, Vol. XXII, Part I, 555; Part II, 434, 496–97.

found no other Indians. Two companies of the Sixth Iowa scouted as far as the mouth of Apple Creek, located the cold ashes of Sibley's campfires, but no sign of the Mackinaw boat. On September 3, Major Albert E. House with three hundred men, riding well in advance of the column, suddenly discovered an encampment of over four hundred Sioux lodges. Just as quickly, House was surrounded but not attacked. These Indians boasted of their fight with Sibley, and tauntingly shouted they did not understand why the soldiers wanted to fight them, unless it was because they wanted to die. Notorious Inkpaduta, who was their leader, held up House's slaughter while he prepared for a ceremonious massacre. With some difficulty a hard-riding scout raced to inform Sully. About four in the afternoon Sully's eager army "at the sound of the bugle . . . with a cheer . . . in a very few minutes saddled up and were in line. . . . At full gallop . . . [they] made this distance of over ten miles in much less than an hour." Arriving at top speed with all but four companies of the brigade, Sully dashed into the Indian camp, and the boastful braves fled. Inkpaduta delayed too long. Darkness spoiled this Hollywood finish, but scattered skirmishing continued for two more days. The soldiers destroyed much Indian property, including "over 400,000 to 500,000 pounds of dried buffalo meat," and took 156 prisoners, 124 of them women and children. The amount of meat, even if exaggerated, is an illustration of the abundance of buffalo in the Dakotas and the red-man's ability to replace supplies Sibley destroyed. "The fight took place," Sully wrote, "near a hill called by the Indians White Stone Hill."[25]

Satisfied that the Indians were scattered in all directions, the troops turned back to Fort Pierre, reached Camp Peoria on September 11, and arrived at Sioux City by November 14. By his own estimate Sully had faced 1,500 Sioux, composed of "Santees, from Minnesota; Cut-Heads from the Coteau; Yanktonais and some Blackfeet . . . and . . . Uncpapas, the same party who fought General Sibley." A later guess cut the figure to only 950, because

[25] *Ibid.*, Part I, 555–61; Robinson, "History of the Sioux," 326–27.

among other things, the Uncpapas had returned to the Black Hills for their fall hunt and were not engaged.[26]

Sully suffered more severely than Sibley, his "killed number" fixed at twenty, with thirty-eight wounded. The official return listed seventeen dead, thirty-six wounded. Sully also reported 100 Sioux casualties, but his officers guessed 150. For once Indian estimates were higher, for they claimed 300 dead and 250 taken prisoner.[27] The real blow dealt the redmen obviously was not military defeat, but rather the serious loss of supplies. The United States Volunteers were not as formidable as a provisionless winter on the plains.

The demonstration in Dakota did not mean that the frontier behind the campaigners was quiet. There was enough real and imagined Indian activity to keep the settlers nervous, although the Sioux raids on the frontier in the spring and summer of 1863 were not nearly as vicious as the year before. Small foraging parties stole horses and killed several citizens in Dakota. A stage was ambushed on the Fort Randall–Sioux City road, and, although the fortunate driver escaped, a passenger, a sergeant of the Fourteenth Iowa Infantry, fell victim to the tomahawk, and the stage horses were taken. Seven children of a family near St. James, Nebraska, were massacred while their father was out with Sully. A detachment of the Dakota Cavalry hunted these Indians, members of White Lodge's band led by Inkpaduta's son. The pursuit was ordered even though Nebraska Territory no longer was within the department.[28]

So far as the Chippewas of Lake Superior were concerned, there was no trouble. Their agent wrote the Indian Bureau three times from May to August that "although there are a few Indians who would like to see another raid . . . they are so few . . . that I do not apprehend any difficulty." Hole-in-the-day, on behalf of the Mississippi Chippewas, sent a letter addressed "To my Great

[26] *Official Records*, Series I, Vol. XXII, Part I, 558; Robinson, "History of the Sioux," 324; Pattee, "Dakota Campaigns," 299.
[27] *Official Records*, Series I, Vol. XXII, Part I, 358, 360, 361–72; 559–60, 561, 563, 564, 567; Part II, 451; Robinson, "History of the Sioux," 324, 328.
[28] English, "Dakota Cavalry," 267–69; Pattee, "Dakota Campaigns," 296–98.

Father at Washington" protesting the treaty negotiated on March 11, 1863, which was in lieu of an unratified document made by Ramsey at the instigation of the Minnesota legislature in September, 1862. By the terms of this new agreement, much of their former reservation land was lost to them, and, according to Hole-in-the-day, the new lands were not "arable . . . enough to raise food for our families" and game was scarcer. The Chippewas of the Red River and Pembina came under a convention concluded by Ramsey in the fall, and Minnesotans hoped their hostile days were past.[29]

In Wisconsin the Winnebagos caused some consternation. Pope believed them to be Winnebagos who had escaped in anticipation of their removal from Minnesota. He reported to the adjutant general that there were about one thousand who "suddenly appeared in Juneau County. . . . They are very insolent, demanding everything they want from the whites, and taking when the articles are not given." They were reported destroying fields, and having in their possession plunder from Minnesota. Pope offered to send a force to collect them for shipment to the upper Missouri, but the Interior Department maintained he would have to take on the expense of moving and feeding them. Pope was "not willing to accept this arrangement." He added, "If these Indians are not proper subjects for the Indian Department, I have been mistaken as to the duties of that Department. I can easily protect the settlements by sending troops," but he thought the expense in men and money would not be worth it. Pope put the matter up to the War Department, who referred it to Halleck. In a letter to the secretary of the interior, Salomon, after having seen Commissioner Charles E. Mix's reply to Pope, in which Mix advised Pope that the Winnebagos in Wisconsin were old residents and not fugitives, admitted the accuracy of this assertion, but believed this no excuse for the government to "shift from the responsibility of controlling them." Since these Indians had no title to any land in Wisconsin and presumably

[29] *Report of the Secretary of the Interior,* 1863, 149, 150, 446, 448–51, 452, 453, 457–58.

also had no leave from the government to wander about, Salomon suggested they be sent to a reservation, and if they did not have one, one be provided for them.[30]

In mid-July the situation became serious enough for Pope to station a company of the Thirtieth Wisconsin at Lisbon to preserve order. One white woman and two Indians had been killed previous to the involvement of the soldiers. The Menominee Tribe, wishing to avoid trouble, wanted the wandering, uncivilized Winnebagos kept off their premises. Salomon distributed arms "at convenient points and to the proper parties, for border defense," and again asked the Department of the Interior for action. Petitions circulated in the affected section of Wisconsin, addressed to General Thomas C. H. Smith, Pope's district commander, demanded the removal of "these barbarians" and assured the government that if it did not take action "we shall be compelled, in self-defence, to exterminate them." Similar petitions were sent to the governor. This finally produced a mild stir among the bureaucrats at Washington, and the Indian commissioner sent a congressman, Walter D. McIndoe, to investigate. The Indian agent for the Menominees conducted an investigation on his own, and he warned the commissioner of danger to the Indians from the whites, noted some Potawatomis were involved as well as the Winnebagos, and that "these Indians are exceedingly filthy, uncouth, and . . . very impudent." He also reported that some of them, including their chief, Dandy, had been arrested by the military for their own protection. McIndoe later recommended they be removed in the spring, which would allow time for Congress to act. With this correspondence ceased for the time being, since the Indian Bureau did not apprehend any more trouble before spring.[31] This deferred the problem of wandering Winnebagos to a future time and left the matter up to Congress for a solution.

In other parts of the West, Indian conditions were no better.

[30] *Official Records,* Series I, Vol. XXII, Part II, 372–73; *Report of the Secretary of the Interior,* 1863, 476–80.
[31] *Report of the Secretary of the Interior,* 1863, 153, 481–93.

Most of the natives of eastern Oregon were hostile, and travel over the Oregon trail was very hazardous; savages in northeastern California were disturbed; in New Mexico the Navahos, Apaches, and to some extent the Utes were a "source of constant vexation and alarm"; the Cheyennes, Arapahoes, Kiowas, Comanches, and some of the Utes in Colorado committed depredations and caused "considerable excitement" there; and the Brulé Sioux attacked the Pawnees on their Nebraska reservation in May and June.[32] It is clear that Indian pacification and protection of the settlers were not problems peculiar to the Department of the Northwest.

While the Sibley and Sully columns were in the field or organizing for the expeditions, small parties of Indians kept up the pressure on the frontier. In Minnesota, the Eighth, and eight companies of the Ninth Minnesota Volunteer Infantry were broken into small detachments for daily patrol duty. In April a small party of Indians slew two citizens and an infantryman of the Seventh Minnesota twenty-five miles southwest of Madelia. On May 2 three men of the Eighth Regiment were killed near Pomme de Terre. A party of the Eighth had a skirmish in Wright County, and on September 1 a sergeant of that group was ambushed on the Paynesville–Manannah trail. On June 29 Amos Dustin and his mother were dispatched and his wife and one daughter fatally wounded while traveling near the Wright–Carver county line in Carver County. July 1 saw the murder of James McGannon in Wright County. And as before mentioned, a raiding party under Little Crow was broken up by his death. Oscar Malmros, Minnesota's adjutant general, wrote, "the Indians appeared suddenly . . . as if they had risen from the earth, a long distance interior of the frontier, and in the rear of the outposts." Every theft of cattle and other property was attributed to the Indians. Rumors of their presence multiplied.[33]

Since early spring frontier settlers had complained that fed-

[32] *Ibid.*, 131, 135, 136, 138–39, 147, 174–78.

[33] *Minnesota in the Civil and Indian Wars*, 353, 387; *Official Records*, Series I, Vol. XXII, Part II, 385, 403–406, 435, 449; *Executive Documents of the State of Minnesota for the Year 1863*, 341–45.

eral troops stationed in the state afforded "inadequate and insufficient protection." The volume of these complaints increased as the season advanced. Brigadier General Emil Munch of the Minnesota Militia, at the suggestion of Minnesota authorities, visited frontier counties to discover how well the settlers were armed, and urged them to form militia companies. On July 4, Malmros ordered the formation of a volunteer scout corps "for sixty days . . . to scour the Big Woods from Sauk Centre to the northern boundary line of Sibley County." James Sturgis became the captain of this body of sixty-eight men, who were divided into ten squads of varying size, and whose purpose, according to another order of July 20, was to exterminate "all hostile Sioux . . . to be found in the rear of our outposts." Members of the company were paid twenty-five dollars in addition to their regular pay of two dollars a day for "satisfactory proof" of any Indian slain by them. Private persons were allowed seventy-five dollars for the killing of any Sioux, a bounty that was raised to two hundred dollars on September 22. There was not much excitement for the volunteer scouts. One party tracked three Indians, bagged one, wounded another, and allowed the third to escape. The corps was kept in service for the full sixty days, and netted, according to the bounties paid, a total of two Sioux.[34]

[34] *Minnesota in the Civil and Indian Wars,* [594], 595; *Official Records,* Series I, Vol. XXII, Part II, 494; *Minnesota Executive Documents, 1863,* 192, 193, 195, 196, 198, 228–29, 339, 346, 348–49, 403, 470.

5

The Badlands Campaign

THE FOOTSORE SIROCCO CAMPAIGNERS had hardly returned from the parched prairies when Pope admitted the effort had failed. He wrote to Halleck, September 25, 1863, that additional action seemed advisable; that it would very likely be necessary for a strong cavalry force to make a demonstration against the Teton Sioux southwest of the Missouri River.[1] Reports trickled into department headquarters, as if to underscore Pope's point, that the Sioux were spending the winter in preparation for resistance to any further encroachment on their territory, were determined to block the navigation of the Missouri and close the northern emigrant route, and, as far as a few were concerned, to strike also at the white settlements.[2]

Agents for Chouteau and Company complained in March, 1864, that "the Sioux are now on Powder River and threaten to clear out all the whites, besides Fort Union and Berthold." Another said, "This whole section [of the upper Missouri] . . . is in a terrible foment. The Sioux are centering in large crowds in the angle formed by the Yellowstone and Missouri." In April, Sibley heard that the Tetons were assembling preparatory to joining the Yanktonais, although it was not certain that the first group had warlike intentions. Fort Union, with only a handful of men to guard it, feared attack by the Tetons. Rumors reached Sully that they had a piece of artillery "with which they intend to stop boats" on the Missouri, but, assuming the story was true, he supposed the gun was not large enough to be very formidable. By April 30, Sibley learned that 2,500 lodges of hostile Sioux had

1 *Official Records*, Series I, Vol. XXII, Part II, 570.
2 *Ibid.*, Vol. XXXIV, Part II, 152, 625, 677–78, 688, 712.

concentrated at the mouth of the Heart River. In mid-May, Gabriel Renville, Sibley's chief scout, reported that small parties of hostile Indians were on the way to the settlements, and that White Cloud's band threatened camps of the scouts near the head of the Coteau-des-Prairies. Renville informed Sibley that the hostiles prevented some of the former Minnesota Sioux, who desired peace, from going to Abercrombie to sign the conditions. Sibley advised Pope that some of the refugee Sioux in the Red River settlements north of the border had avowed to do what mischief they could along the Red River.[3]

By May 16, Sioux raiders struck south of the Minnesota River, first at Spirit Lake, then in the vicinity of the Cottonwood and Watonwan rivers, where one settler was killed and another wounded. After receiving Sibley's notice of this raid, Pope told him it was "not necessary to telegraph of these small raids, which are to be expected for a time. Neither is it judicious in other ways to make such things public, as they only tend to create unnecessary and injurious alarm and excitement on the frontier." A few days later he added that it was unlikely the Indian raids would continue for more than a few weeks, and would cease after the expedition took to the field. Sibley made no comment on this second point, but disagreed with Pope on the main matter. "It is quite impossible to keep secret any of these outrages on the border, and the course I have pursued is the only one which seems to promise success in quelling needless alarm connected with the hostile demonstration." The matter was left to rest and neither referred to it again.[4] The Sioux did not confine their nuisance raids to Minnesota. In Dakota Territory they constantly harassed details of soldiers outside the fortifications, particularly between Forts Randall and Sully. As late as June 12 they drove off forty cavalry horses from Randall, which later were recovered.[5]

Part of Pope's plan for frontier protection and the coming cam-

[3] *Ibid.*, Part II, 743; Part III, 33–34, 219–20, 330, 356, 368–69, 578–79.

[4] *Ibid.*, Part III, 694, 679–80, 712; Part IV, 57, 58.

[5] English, "Dakota Cavalry," 271; *Official Records*, Series I, Vol. XXXIV, Part IV, 331.

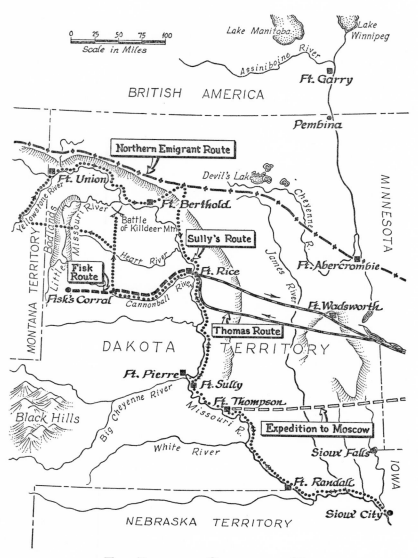

THE BADLANDS CAMPAIGN, 1864

paign included a network of new border forts. Pope wanted to establish a post on Devil's Lake in early spring and to move Fort Abercrombie due west to the James River or the upper Cheyenne. Along with Fort Sully on the Missouri, the proposed bases would cover the whole valley of the Red River and protect the settlements at the same time. Halleck inquired about building a fort on the Red River, for which Congress had made an appropriation, but Pope thought it unnecessary. Abercrombie and Pembina were both on this river and the contemplated setup would enclose the area in its defensive cover anyway.[6]

Pope directed Sibley to establish the James River and Devil's Lake forts, and in addition "the whole cavalry force in your district . . . [will] sweep the whole region now occupied by hostile Indians north of the line from Fort Pierre to Abercrombie." Sully's orders were to establish a post somewhere on the Yellowstone River southwest of Fort Clarke. No hint of the season's expedition was given Sibley other than telling him he would be informed of the campaign in due course.[7]

In a lengthy dispatch Sibley answered Pope with counter-recommendations. His suggestions began with the proposal to abandon the idea of a post at Devil's Lake, "which would be extremely difficult of access and of comparatively little importance." He suggested in its place that a fort be erected on the Re Ipahan, or the head of the Coteau-des-Prairies, an eminence six hundred feet above the surrounding plain, and midway between the valleys of the Red River, the Minnesota, and the James. The location was well supplied with water and timber and could protect the approaches to the Minnesota Valley. He thought a post on the James impractical, since above the mouth of the Snake River the valley "is singularly destitute of wood." Sibley suggested a post on the Cheyenne River on a line slightly northwest of Abercrombie where "timber is abundant." By occupying these points, he believed that "all the essential conditions of protection to trains bound for the goldbearing regions

[6] *Official Records*, Series I, Vol. XXII, Part II, 570, 729–30.
[7] *Ibid.*, Vol. XXXIV, Part II, 100, 109–11.

of Idaho would be fulfilled," and the advance of any savages from the upper plains toward Minnesota and Iowa would be blocked. Sibley also advocated a post on the Missouri near the place his expedition touched the summer before, since this was a favorite crossing place and commanded a choice hunting ground.[8]

It is questionable that Pope studied Sibley's recommendations carefully before sending Halleck his plans for the operations in the spring, which were merely an expansion of the brief orders he sent Sibley and Sully. Pope was convinced of his own position regarding the disposition of troops and the location of the proposed forts, in spite of Sibley's logical reply; and, after chiding Sibley for asking for more troops (Sibley wanted to keep in his district the veteran Brackett's Battalion, home on re-enlistment furlough), bundled the location question into a package labeled "I need not go further with this matter at present as I shall expect to see you and General Sully here together . . . [when] the whole subject can be gone over."[9]

In February Halleck telegraphed approval of Pope's project, "subject to such modifications as experience may suggest." On the following day Pope made arrangements to have Sibley come to Milwaukee for a conference, and requested Sully to be present also. What occurred at the conference is anybody's guess, but in a March 9 press release Sibley said that "the points where military posts are to be established are not yet determined upon with sufficient precision to enable me to mention their precise location," which seems a victory for his views over those of the department commander. But even though Sully also wished Pope would give up the idea of the post at Devil's Lake, Pope would not budge in that regard. On March 15 "for the information and guidance of Generals Sully and Sibley," Pope again restated his original directive for the construction and location of the new forts. The forthcoming campaign was to be conducted in connection with the establishment of these new posts. Sully was to march his cavalry up the Missouri River to Bordache Creek,

[8] *Ibid.*, 152–56.
[9] *Ibid.*, 155, 256–59, 303.

where Sibley's horsemen would join him, and the combined force would continue up river to bring the hostile Indians to battle. Sully also was supposed to send four companies of infantry up on steamboats to establish a fort on the Missouri due west of the Devil's Lake post. And if practicable, Sully was to establish the post on the Yellowstone. There was no change in Sibley's instructions: the construction of the forts on the James River and Devil's Lake remained his job. Sibley remarked to Sully that he could not see how the Devil's Lake postion could be established during the current season, but intended to do the best he could. In March Halleck suggested Pope build a post on the Powder River, but Pope answered that it would be difficult to supply.[10]

Toward the end of March Sibley asked Pope if he might use some discretion in locating the James River fort, alluding to Pope's oral remark that such could be located on the head of the Coteau if timber was not available on the James. Pope replied that he considered any point east of the James out of the question, and the problem was dropped until the end of May. In May the War Department prematurely named these new bases. Fort Wadsworth was the post on the James, Fort Hays at Devil's Lake, Fort Rice on the upper Missouri, and Fort Stevenson on the Yellowstone. On May 26, in consequence of an urgent order for troops to go south, Pope had to consider abandoning the erection of Fort Hays, for he would be too shorthanded to construct or garrison it. Nothing more came of these discussions before the expedition went into the field in June.[11]

Meanwhile, Charles Larpenteur, the veteran fur trader and traveler in the area, and now also Sully's commissary for the 1864 campaign, questioned the seriousness of the Indian situation. A businesslike man, he also had made arrangements with the Chouteau Company to take charge of Fort Union. When the steamer *Benton,* loaded with fifty tons of commissary freight, put into Fort Randall on the way upstream, the military told

[10] *Ibid.,* 330, 340, 350, 541, 594–95, 607–608, 622–25, 665, 677.
[11] *Ibid.,* 720–21, 793–94; Part III, 565; Part IV, 56, 57.

him the Sioux were camped near Fort Berthold determined to stop navigation. Larpenteur was not worried. "Those who knew neither the country nor the Indians believed all this rubbish," but he did not, and the *Benton* steamed on. At Fort Sully the commander informed him headquarters had decided steamers could not proceed without escorts. Larpenteur replied that the reports of Indian concentration on the Missouri were exaggerated because there was little game on the river, which would make it impossible for 1,500 lodges to remain in camp together. Larpenteur continued that he "should not be at all surprised if we did not see a single Indian on our journey," although he admitted there would be some danger. The military was convinced, and the *Benton* left Fort Sully on May 9, saw no Indians until they came to the mouth of the Heart River, and only a few peaceable ones after that. They arrived at Fort Union on May 31.[12] Once there they found the Sioux such a nuisance that the garrison kept behind closed gates all the time.[13]

Back in Milwaukee, the department headquarters was concerned with getting the columns into the field as early as possible. On March 18 Pope directed Major Edwin A. C. Hatch to abandon Pembina and "relieve the garrison at Fort Abercrombie as soon as practical," which Sibley believed would be about April 20. On April 15 Hatch was told to keep three of his four companies at Abercrombie, one to patrol the route to Pembina. The fourth company, divided into halves, was to relieve the garrisons at Pomme de Terre and Alexandria, and remain there until further notice. The Eighth Minnesota, at Abercrombie, was marched to Sauk Center. On March 3 and April 18 six companies of the Thirtieth Wisconsin left to join Sully. Brackett's Battalion followed from St. Paul on May 2. By the end of April, Sibley proposed to rendezvous his brigade at Camp Pope. The Minnesota contingent was to depart for Dakota May 28.[14]

[12] Charles Larpenteur, *Forty Years a Fur Trader on the Upper Missouri: The Personal Narrative of Charles Larpenteur, 1833–1872* (Elliott Coues, ed.), Volume II, 355–60.
[13] *Ibid.*, 360.
[14] *Official Records*, Series I, Vol. XXXIV, Part III, 541–42. Brackett's Bat-

Forty-nine "deserters from the rebel armies," were assigned to Captain McCoy's company of the Eighth Minnesota, sixteen of whom were to be assigned to garrison duty. Presumably, these deserters came from Camp Chase, Ohio, under a War Department ruling of the previous September that ordered "rebel deserters who have been drafted into the U. S. service will be sent to Camp Chase . . . [and] distributed among the regiments in the Department of the Northwest."[15] If the department expected more such troops in time for the campaign, none arrived; nor were any others mentioned at this time as replacements for or additions to any troops scheduled to go in the field.

On May 13, and again on May 20, Pope cautioned Sully to be prepared to move in order to establish Fort Rice and meet the brigade from Minnesota as scheduled, whether or not the Missouri would permit navigation from Fort Pierre. Pope was concerned that Sully might fail to meet the Minnesota contingent and would repeat the unhappy occurrence of the previous year. Sully was slightly worried about the same thing, only this season the worry was augmented by the fact that the Minnesota troops would have to rely on him for supplies after reaching the Missouri. On May 25, Sibley sent a lengthy and detailed order to Colonel Minor T. Thomas, Eighth Minnesota Volunteers, delineating his duties as commander of the troops leaving Camp Pope, and giving in full his route, along with numerous other suggestions. Then on May 26, the Sixth Minnesota was ordered south, causing some last minute shuffling of soldiers and delaying the departure for the Missouri ten days. The temporary void created by the removal of the Sixth threatened to mean the with-

---

talion, commanded by Major Alfred B. Brackett, originally was designated the First, Second, and Third Minnesota Light Cavalry, and had enlisted in October, 1861, at Fort Snelling. After being sent to Missouri, they were brigaded with companies from Iowa, Nebraska, and Missouri, the combination being first called the Curtis Horse, then the Fifth Iowa Cavalry. They were veterans of Fort Donelson, Shiloh, Lockridge Mills, and other engagements. They were sent back home for reenlistment in March, 1864, and reassigned to the Department of the Northwest. An additional company was recruited to make a full brigade, as well as other replacements for those who did not re-enlist.

15 *Ibid.*, Series III, Vol. III, 791; Series I, Vol. XXXIV, Part III, 504-505.

holding of four hundred men from the Thomas column, but the prompt accession of companies of the Veterans Reserve Corps for guard and garrison duty allowed the full complement to join Sully.[16]

The Minnesota, or Second, Brigade included the Eighth Minnesota Volunteer Infantry, mounted on Canadian ponies, under the command of Lieutenant Colonel Henry C. Rogers; six companies of the Second Minnesota Volunteer Cavalry, commanded by Colonel Robert N. McLaren; two sections of the Third Minnesota Battery, one of six-pounder smooth bore guns, and one of twelve-pounder mountain howitzers, directed by Captain John Jones; and about forty-five scouts, with Colonel Thomas leading the whole. There were over ninety six-mule teams carrying supplies and twelve ambulances for those who would need them. The aggregate number of mounted and armed men in this group, including the group of scouts, was nearly 1,600. Sibley gave the total figure as 1,550.[17]

On June 6, to the tune of "The Girl I Left Behind Me," the expedition marched. The men of the Eighth Regiment were astounded to see so large a body of troops assembled together, after having spent their entire organized existence in scattered units on the frontier; for many the novelty of marching through a new country held some interest, but at best the journey to the Missouri was uneventful. Accompanying the Second Brigade were between 120 and 160 emigrant wagons, not of Captain Fisk's party.[18]

Meanwhile, the First Brigade of the Northwest Indian Expe-

[16] *Ibid.*, Series I, Vol. XXXIV, Part III, 579–80, 662–63, 694; Part IV, 14–15, 40–42, 57, 58, 103, 135, 136, 152–53, 170–73, 184–85, 274.

[17] *Ibid.*, Part IV, 288; *Minnesota in the Civil and Indian Wars*, 388; Lieutenant David L. Kingsbury, "Sully's Expedition Against the Sioux in 1864," *Collections of the Minnesota Historical Society*, Vol. 8, 449. Colonel Thomas estimates there were 2,100 men, and so does Kingsbury, then a sergeant. But assuming the organizations were at nearly full strength, that is, 1,000 in the Eighth Minnesota, 600 in the units of the Second Minnesota Cavalry, 100 men in the Third Minnesota Artillery, and the 45 scouts, the number would be only 1,745.

[18] *Minnesota in the Civil and Indian Wars*, 388, 451, 752; Kingsbury, "Sully's Expedition . . . in 1864," 451–52.

dition was organizing in Iowa and Dakota. Brackett's Battalion of Minnesota Cavalry reached Fort Sully, the rendezvous for Sully's troops, on June 15. Others in this contingent were eleven companies of the Sixth Iowa Cavalry, commanded by Lieutenant Colonel Samuel M. Pollock, three companies of the Seventh Iowa cavalry, led by Pattee, two companies of Dakota Cavalry under Captain Nelson Minor, a company called "The Nebraska Scouts," headed by Captain Christian Stuffts, and "The Prairie Battery," of four mountain howitzers and the usual complement of men directed by Captain Nathaniel Pope; numbering in all about 1,800 troops.[19]

Governor Newton Edwards of Dakota Territory reflected his people's fears when he complained to Pope in June that his frontier would be left virtually undefended after Sully went up the river. Pope was at first somewhat terse in his reply, remarking that "General Sully was assigned to command of the forces in Dakota Territory and charged with the protection of its frontier. . . . The sole object of his expedition is to accomplish this" by breaking the power of the Sioux. Pope went on, "General Sully is not a man to neglect so obvious a duty," and concluded with a discussion of his plans for the erection of the new forts which should not only protect the Dakota settlements but "secure peaceful relations [with the Sioux] thereafter."[20] This tranquilizer seemed to be all that was necessary for the governor, who sent no more protests to the department.

On June 26, the First Brigade marched out of Fort Sully to meet the Second Brigade up the Missouri. On June 28, the topographical engineer and naturalist assigned to the expedition, Captain John Feilner from the First U. S. Cavalry, was killed a short distance from the main column. Captain Minor and Com-

---

[19] Ingersoll, *Iowa and the Rebellion,* 686; English, "Dakota Cavalry," 273–74; Pattee, "Dakota Campaigns," 301–302. Ingersoll alone guesses at the strength of the Sully brigade. Taking minimum figures, there should have been at least 360 men with Brackett, 880 in the Sixth Iowa, 240 in the units of the Seventh Iowa, 160 in the Dakota Cavalry, 60 in the battery, and 80 with the Nebraska Scouts, or 1,780.

[20] *Official Records,* Series I, Vol. XXXIV, Part IV, 604–605.

pany A, Dakota Cavalry, were sent in pursuit of the Indians, three in number, whose bloody heads Sully mounted on poles as a warning to others. According to a Sioux historian, news of this action "flew as upon the wings of the wind to every Dakota camp from the Oglalas on the Platte to those in farthest Canada" precipitating the retreat of the Indians into the Bad Lands, "where the white men . . . could not come." On June 30, the First Brigade reached Swan Lake Creek, where they met the Second Brigade the next day.[21]

The boats with supplies arrived at nearly the same time enabling the united command to march off again July 2; on July 9 the steamers ferried the army across the Missouri at the proposed location of Fort Rice. The vessels previously brought up four companies of Colonel Daniel J. Dill's Thirtieth Wisconsin, who were engaged in erecting the new post.[22] After a ten-days' rest, the expedition, leaving behind all surplus baggage and equipped with rations for sixty days, hiked up the Cannon Ball River Valley expecting to find a large camp (1,500 to 1,800 lodges) of Sioux, according to a scout's report. But the Indians had moved on before the expedition arrived, leaving behind only warm ashes of recent camp fires. Sully now crossed northward to the Heart River, and followed this westward to its source. "Trails and other signs, and frequently signals, smoke by day and fires by night" let the men know they were not alone in this previously unexplored country. The march was a rugged one, for the area was nearly barren of vegetation, and water was very scarce and of poor quality. The animals "suffered intensely . . . and many were shot" when they became unable to support their riders. Scouts reported a large village at Ta-ha-kouty (Killdeer) Mountain on July 24. Sully corralled the teams and the emigrant

[21] Pattee, "Dakota Campaigns," 302–305; English, "Dakota Cavalry," 275–78; Robinson, "History of the Sioux," 330; *Official Records,* Series I, Vol. XXXIV, Part III, 168–69.

[22] *Minnesota in the Civil and Indian Wars,* 389; Kingsbury, "Sully's Expedition . . . in 1864," 452–53; *Official Records,* Series I, Vol. XLI, Part I, 135; Vol. XXXIV, Part IV, 628–29. The steamers used were the *Marcella, Sam Gaty, Chippewa Falls, General Grant, Isabella, Tempest, Island City,* and the *Alone,* according to Joseph Mills Hanson, *The Conquest of the Missouri,* 53.

train, left with them tents and every disposable article possible, and sufficient dismounted men for protection. Taking only
enough wagons to carry ammunition and rations for eight days,
the lightened expedition began a rapid march northward. At
10 A.M. on the morning of July 28, Sully came upon the Indian
camp. Killdeer Mountain was a small chain of very high hills,
criss-crossed with thickly timbered ravines, and well watered,
situated on a branch of the Little Missouri. This was on Sully's
right. There was a steeply rolling prairie on the left and in front.
On the top and the sides of the hills, at the base of the mountain
to the right, and on prairie hillocks in front, the Sioux waited.
Because of the timber-filled ravines it was impossible to charge
them, so the cavalry were dismounted and deployed, the few
light wagons were quickly closed up, and the army advanced
driving the redmen before them until they reached the plain
between the mountain and the hills.

Large groups of Sioux remained on the flanks. The Second
Minnesota Cavalry drove the Indians on the left off, while Brackett's group struck at those on the right. The redmen turned on
Brackett, but with the help of skillful artillery fire the Indians
were driven off. Another feathered war party rode up on the
rear, but the artillery was hastily turned in their direction, and,
aided by a few companies of rear guard, they were beaten off.
Discouraged, the Sioux began to dismantle their camp and hurry
the squaws and children off as Sully began to close in. His left and
right flanks moved forward as the artillery cleared the wooded
ravines. "By sunset no Indians were on the ground," but were
scattered over the mountain. They maintained a rear guard on
top of Killdeer, but four companies of the Eighth drove them off.

There was no pursuit because of the rough terrain, and the
troops spent the night on the battlefield. The redmen were not
finished, though, for the following evening at dusk the soldiers
were attacked in camp about six miles from the previous day's
field, and two guards were killed. The Sioux were repulsed in
short order, and did not make any further demonstrations. Sully

returned to the corral on July 30, having marched 172 miles in six days.[23]

At the battle of Killdeer Mountain, Sully claimed to have faced "at least 5,000 to 6,000 warriors, composed of Unkpapas, Sans Arcs, Blackfeet, Minneconjous, Yanktonais and Santee Sioux" with 2,200 of his troops (the remainder being at the corral). None of the other officers estimated the number of Indians the troops confronted. Indian sources place the figure at 1,600. Sully estimated the total number killed about 100 to 150; the Indians claimed to have lost thirty-one. Sully listed five dead and ten wounded soldiers from this fray.[24]

The whole command took up the westward journey again with only six days' rations remaining. Scouts doubted that Sully's wagons could make it through the rough terrain of Dakota's Bad Lands, but in order to meet the supply steamers on the Yellowstone he would have to try.

It would take over a month to circle south. Besides, a Yanktonai scout believed he could get the wagons across "with some digging." When they came upon the Bad Lands August 6, even Sully agreed crossing would be nearly impossible, and were it not for his short rations he would not have tried. Sully waxed eloquent as he attempted to describe the view nature presented him. "It [the country before them] was grand, dismal, and majestic." The badlands were a huge colorful basin, which Sully estimated to be six hundred feet deep and twenty-five miles in diameter, "filled with a number of cones and oven-shaped knolls of all sizes, from twenty feet to several hundred feet high, sometimes by themselves, sometimes piled up into large heaps on top of one another, in all conceivable shapes and confusion." Sully hardly attempted to describe the color, which seemed to change as the sun moved, a rainbow of grays and gray-purples shading into brick reds and relieved by greens from "the few scrub cedars" that clung to the sides of some of the hills. Once

[23] Kingsbury, "Sully's Expedition . . . in 1864," 453–57; *Official Records*, Series I, Vol. XLI, Part I, 141–44.

[24] *Official Records*, Series I, Vol. XLI, Part I, 142–44; Robinson, "History of the Sioux," 334.

in this awesome area they found it to be covered with pieces of petrified wood, and even some stone stumps sixteen to eighteen feet in diameter, "the remains of a great forest." Sully lamented the absence of any naturalists, because in iron-ore and lava rock they found fossil impressions of "leaves of a size not known to any of us." From a "distance at sunset it looked exactly like the ruins of an ancient city." With much hard work and much digging, the expedition made twelve miles the next day, camping on the bank of the Little Missouri. That night Indians stampeded horses from a cottonwood grove, but the troopers recovered them. During the next day, part of a working party, commanded by Pattee, was driven back to camp. The Indians, shooting from the bluffs, fired into the camp itself until the battery drove them off. The column engaged in a skirmish the next day, shortly after crossing the river. Again, the battery dislodged the Indians. Desultory attacks were made on the troops and the emigrant train during the whole day, but no attack was made in very great force. Coming to a small lake and spring at the day's end, there was another sharp skirmish, but the Indians again retreated. The next morning, a group of Sioux made a show in force, but were beaten and fled. Sully's "road lay through a succession of mountain gorges, down deep ravines, with perpendicular bluffs so narrow only one wagon could pass at a time, intersected with valleys down which the Indians could dash onto any point" of his train. The wagons stretched out three or four miles, and moved very slowly, since in front the road had to be cut or dug, and because the heavily-loaded ox wagons of the emigrants could only move at a snail's pace. Sully was troubled for the safety of the emigrants, because there was a large number of women and children among them. But they crawled on, hunting a road before them and fighting off Indian forays. Toward the end, the Sioux killed their guide, who carelessly moved too far from the party. Sully estimated that in crossing the Bad Lands his soldiers killed at least one hundred redmen. After leaving the Little Missouri, the group found the vegetation destroyed by myriads of grasshoppers, so that the animals were "almost starved." A number had to be abandoned and shot. Once on the plains again they found the grass burned out by the sun or eaten by the grasshoppers, and the water quite alkaline. They met with no more Indians, then, and reached the Yellowstone August 12.[25]

Waiting for the troops were two light-draft steamers, the *Chippewa Falls* and the *Alone*, each carrying about fifty tons of freight. The *Island City*, with a cargo of corn for the animals, had struck a snag near Fort Union and sank. This loss of forage caused another change in plans for Sully. Without corn he could not strike out to the northeast toward Berthold. Therefore, it was necessary to follow the course of the Yellowstone and the Missouri on the return, for there was some grass in the river valleys. This detour meant nearly one hundred miles of extra travel. The expedition crossed the Yellowstone on August 13, and, helping the boats across the rapids, and in turn being assisted by them in crossing the Missouri, managed to get to Fort Union by August 20. Here the emigrants who still followed the column left Sully's charge, heading west and taking with them "quite a number of [government] horses, mules, and oxen . . . a large number of pistols and other arms and property . . . and several deserters." They had traded whisky to soldiers for some of the arms. Sully sent a force after them, but they had made good time and were too far out to be caught. Sending the sick and wounded downstream by boat and leaving one company of the Thirtieth Wisconsin to winter at Fort Union, Sully headed downstream for Berthold and arrived there after a week's march. Around Berthold the Rees, Gros Ventres, and Mandans were busy collecting their corn, and asked once more for protection against the Sioux. For this reason, as well as to keep open communication with Fort Union, Sully garrisoned the place with a company of the Sixth Iowa Cavalry. He left Berthold on August 30 and in nine days was at Rice.[26]

On the way down to Fort Rice, the expedition conducted a reconnaissance in force to the eastward, for it was rumored that

[25] *Official Records,* Series I, Vol. XLI, Part I, 144–47.
[26] *Ibid.*, 147–51.

a large body of Sioux were headed for Devil's Lake, but although old Indian signs were plentiful the detachment encountered nothing more hostile than buffalo. Sully was convinced the Sioux had gone north of the border and complained to Pope of this refuge where they were "supplied with ammunition by people living under the British flag." At Fort Rice Sully met the lodges of different bands of Indians who had taken no part in the war and allowed them to go on a hunt supervised by fifty of their number whom he uniformed as police.[27]

Sully also found, much to his displeasure, that Colonel Dill, contrary to his orders, had furnished Captain James L. Fisk's emigrant train a convoy of fifty cavalrymen, poorly mounted, under the command of Lieutenant DeWitt C. Smith of the Dakota Cavalry, who had remained behind at Rice pending acceptance of his resignation. Actually, Pope notified Sully of the arrival of the Fisk train, but had left the escort problem to Sully's judgment. Fisk had followed a supply train from Ridgely to Fort Wadsworth. From there a detachment of the Second Minnesota Cavalry accompanied Fisk's party to Rice. At Wadsworth, it may be noted, was yet another emigrant train of 150 wagons.[28]

Sully, his displeasure heightened by the fact Fisk was corralled, surrounded by Indians, and crying for help, asked Pope "Why will our Government continue to act so foolishly, sending out emigrant trains at a great expense? Do they know that most of the men who go are persons running away from the draft?" Sully protested that "they curse and ridicule the expedition and officers in command. Fisk . . . was the loudest talker in this respect." The government would have done better to have bought out the emigrant train that had gone with him, as well as Fisk's, for three times their worth and saved money. Fisk was advised of the scarcity of grass and water, as well as the Indian hazard, Sully continued, but believed it was a trick of the traders to get him to go by way of Fort Berthold. Doubtless thinking Fisk

[27] *Ibid.*, 152–53.
[28] *Ibid.*, 151, 153; Vol. XXXIV, Part IV, 479; English, "Dakota Cavalry," 297; *North Dakota Historical Collections*, Vol. II, 424; *Minnesota in the Civil and Indian Wars*, 565.

deserved his fate, Sully sent a detail of 900 men (600 infantry and dismounted cavalry, and 300 cavalry) to bring the Fisk party back to Rice. The safety of Fisk was of no moment, but "the women and children, and my soldiers, *if no one else*, who were innocent of the folly of so small a party going into an enemy's country," troubled him as did his concern for his prospects of making peace with the Indians. "They [the Indians] would . . . take this emigrant train for a part of my command, and if they capture it the evil disposed in the nation would boast of it and urge the rest to continue the war." The controversial Fisk and his party were returned to Fort Rice on September 30, contrary to Fisk's wishes, but in harmony with the wishes of the emigrants. Details of the Fisk train's battle are not important to this narrative, so suffice it to say they were attacked 160 miles west of Fort Rice by around 300 Sioux, and called their skirmishes the "Battles of Red Buttes." During the time they were corralled they learned of the captivity of Mrs. Fanny Kelly, who was taken by the Sioux from a large emigrant train near Fort Laramie on July 12. Fisk bargained for her release, with no success.[29]

Pope, who in June had extended the courtesies of his department to Fisk, took a different attitude in a formal report to Halleck on October 6, 1864. He said,

> The complaints against this officer by General Sully are simply a repetition of the same statements made by General Sibley as to his conduct last year. . . . He [Fisk] manifested the same disrespect and used the same disrespectful language in regard to General Sibley that General Sully now reports. . . . [As he is beyond my control] I trust that the War Department will take such action in his case as the gross military offenses . . . warrant.

This did not stop Fisk from organizing two more expeditions.[30] In his report from Fort Rice, Sully told Pope that

[29] *Official Records,* Series I, Vol. XLI, Part I, 151–54; *North Dakota Historical Collections,* Vol. II, 427, 428, 434–35, 438, 440.
[30] *Official Records,* Series I, Vol. XXXIV, Part IV, 478–79; Vol. XLI, Part I, 132.

The Indian expedition . . . has been a success in every respect as far as it was in the power for anyone or any body of troops to make it so. Circumstances . . . prevented it from being a perfect success. Had the Missouri River . . . [risen] in April instead of June, the boats . . . would have got up to Sioux City and other points of starting sooner; the command would have been in the field sooner. . . . But in spite of all this, the expedition has met the combined forces of the Sioux . . . completely routed them, destroyed a large portion of their camps . . . and scattered them in all directions. . . . I think they will never again organize for resistance. . . . Yet, owing to the vast extent of country [and] the safe refuge the Indians have in the British possessions . . . it will be exceedingly difficult to bring all the bands of the Sioux to a complete subjection. . . .

The expedition was considered a success, but not a complete one; Sully thought the Sioux were through as a unit but still dangerous in parties. Slowly making his way downstream, he reached Fort Sully early in October and the Crow Creek Agency on October 10. Shortly thereafter the command returned to Yankton and Sioux City. Brackett's Battalion continued on to Minnesota from Sioux City, arriving at Fort Ridgely on November 9.[31]

The Minnesota Brigade, with the exception of one hundred men of the Second Cavalry and two hundred men of the Eighth Infantry who went to Fisk's relief, left Fort Rice September 15, striking eastward across Dakota for Wadsworth and arriving there on September 26 after an uneventful trip. Four companies of the Second Minnesota Cavalry remained there in garrison, while the detachment of the Thirtieth Wisconsin that built the post returned with the balance of the brigade by way of Fort Ridgely to Snelling, where they arrived in mid-October.[32]

After the departure of the Minnesota Brigade for the Missouri, the construction of Fort Wadsworth, ordered to be located either

[31] *Ibid.*, Vol. XLI, Part I, 154–56; Part IV, 528; English, "Dakota Cavalry," 300–301.

[32] Kingsbury, "Sully's Expedition . . . in 1864," 461; *Official Records,* Series I, Vol. XLI, Part I, 169–70; Part II, 814.

on the James River or as near as possible to that place, was the next project. The valley was examined by Major John Clowney and Captain Lewis S. Burton of the Thirtieth Wisconsin Volunteer Infantry, who confirmed Sully's previous intelligence that there was not sufficient timber near the James to build a fort. A commanding position on the head of the Coteau between the James and the Minnesota border was chosen and work began. A company of the Second Minnesota Cavalry and three companies of the Thirtieth Wisconsin with a section of the Third Minnesota Battery, formed the garrison until the Thirtieth was relieved late in September.[33] Thus the post on the James, which was actually supposed to be a relocation of Fort Abercrombie, was not built on the James. The fort at Devil's Lake was never built by Sibley, due to the shortage of man power. The position on the Yellowstone also was not constructed for many reasons. The season was too far advanced, supplies had deteriorated and been lost, Sully was unwilling to spare men, and he was convinced that a central route such as Fisk attempted, or such as the expedition took, was not practical, and therefore a fort on the Yellowstone would serve no real purpose.[34]

Remaining on the frontier in Dakota Territory were two companies of the Thirtieth Wisconsin, at Fort Sully, along with three companies of the Seventh Iowa Cavalry. At Fort Randall was one company of the Sixth Iowa Cavalry; stationed at Sioux City was one company of the Seventh Iowa Cavalry. Two companies of the Veterans Reserve Corps were at Davenport, Iowa, and another company was at Keokuk. This meant that Sully left on guard and garrison duty about 1,750 troops. In Minnesota at Fort Ridgely were four companies of the Second Minnesota Cavalry, one of the Thirtieth Wisconsin, and a detachment of rebel deserters. At Fort Snelling was one company of the Second Minnesota Cavalry, one section of the Third Minnesota Battery, and two companies of the Veterans Reserve Corps. At Fort Aber-

---

[33] *Official Records*, Series I, Vol. XXXIV, Part IV, pp. 288, 381–83, 629; Vol. XLI, Part I, 39; Part II, 548.
[34] *Ibid.*, Vol. XLI, Part II, 81, 228, 628, 768.

crombie was Hatch's Battalion and at Fort Ripley was a detachment of the Eighth Minnesota. On June 30 these aggregated 1,859 men. In addition, one company of the Veterans Reserve Corps was stationed at Madison, Wisconsin, and two more companies were at Milwaukee.[35]

While the army was in the field the Indian problem on the frontier did not appear to be serious, or cause much alarm among the settlers until August. An unescorted ox train on its way across Dakota Territory from Mankato to Fort Thompson discovered no hostile Indians or any recent signs of any. Scouts reported that most of the Sioux northeast of the Missouri were encamped on the Coteau in the approximate vicinity that had been reported to Sully at Fort Berthold; although a large party fired on a group of Sibley's scouts, they later professed their friendship and showed credentials given them by Sully. Sibley, always apprehensive, on August 6 sent the commanding officer at Fort Abercrombie a dispatch stating that the use of the Minnesota Brigade on the southwest side of the Missouri was unexpected, and its effect was "to uncover the Minnesota frontier to the raids of all the bands of Sioux on this side of the Missouri," and hence Fort Abercrombie must exercise "double vigilance" and "constant and unwearied watch and guard."[36]

The first alarm of trouble since spring came on August 12 when a small party of six or eight Sioux killed one man, wounded another, and stole some horses about ten miles south of Garden City, escaping both Sibley's troops and some militia companies. The governor of Minnesota, Stephen Miller, ordered militia Colonel B. F. Smith, of Mankato, to form a company of mounted minutemen to co-operate with Sibley's troops in protecting the frontier. The main raiding party supposedly was a part of White Lodge's and Sleepy Eyes' bands, totaling about fifty men.[37] Sib-

35 Ibid., Vol. XXXIV, Part IV, 628–29. The aggregate present for duty in Sully's district was 3,871. Subtracting 320 (average) for the four companies at Fort Rice and 1,800 on expedition, leaves 1,851. This figure, as the 1,800, can only be tentative. The figures for Sibley's district are those given in the return, and did not include those in the expedition.

36 Ibid., 194, 348, 485, 493, 516–17, 591.

ley, upon receiving this last information from his scouts, complained to Pope that he had only three hundred men to guard the frontier from Sauk Center to the Iowa line, and deplored the fact that the War Department had taken the Sixth Minnesota away.

On August 17 a trooper on patrol duty informed the commandant of Fort Ripley that "A messenger came into Paynesville . . . with a report that hostile Indians had been depredating in the neighborhood of Norway Lake." A detachment of the Second Cavalry, sent north to investigate, found one dead cow and the tracks of three Indians. Some other cattle had been rustled but no trace of the thieves was found. More such reports came in. The case was well put by Smith, the Minnesota militia leader, who remarked to Malmros, Minnesota's adjutant general: "There are straggling Indians, but they are not easily caught. There is no chance to get at them or trail them through the dense thicket in these woods." He did not believe the damage was great enough to keep eight men busy on scout duty, so he sent two of them home. Two teamsters were killed between Abercrombie and Georgetown. Several Winnebagos were killed by a party of Sioux south of Sioux City. The shadowy children of the plains and, in many cases, just their spirits, kept the frontier in a state of agitation.

In what seemed the nick of time, more troops arrived in the department. On September 6, Pope advised Sibley that two full companies of the First United States Volunteers were being sent to reinforce them, adding that they were excellent troops. Two more companies of the same organization followed on September 30. Also on the way to Sibley was a company of Connecticut Cavalry, dismounted, which Pope urged be joined with the First U. S. Volunteers. In early September, 350 lodges of Sioux had arrived at the British settlements, making 1,000 to 1,200 warriors. Major Clowney reported from Fort Wadsworth on September 9, as he had before, no trace of any hostiles in his area. On October 3, Colonel Pfaender reported from Fort Ridgely that "There are

[37] *Ibid.*, 679, 697, 701, 709–10, 723, 724, 725, 738.

no more Indian rumors lately, and the scouts . . . report no signs whatever." And on October 8, the Minnesota Brigade of Sully's expedition returned to Ridgely, thus bringing the frontier garrisons to full strength.[38]

The nervous settlers in Minnesota communicated some of their feelings to Colonel Smith, who alleged "gross negligence" on the part of the U. S. troops on frontier duty, but did not accuse their commander of being remiss. Sibley blamed the removal of the Sixth Regiment, "relied on for that purpose," for the shortage of frontier guards, adding that it was because of

> pressing and reiterated representations from citizens of this state that there was no danger to be feared from hostile Indians and that it was . . . wrong to retain so noble a regiment . . . to guard against mere idle and baseless impressions of peril . . . when they should be battling . . . the rebels. . . . This fact should be known to the settlers who are so ready to . . . blame . . . any catastrophe upon the military officers of the district.

Apparently Minnesotans in more thickly populated areas did not fear another massacre, as did those who lived on the frontier.[39]

Actually the campaigns against the Sioux were only a small part of the department's activity. The disposition of the captured Indians, the draft, copperhead activity, and other matters provided excitement when the troops were not in the field. Some of these occurrences served to remind both the department and the people it ministered to that there was another war going on.

[38] *Ibid.*, 755, 792–93, 845–47, 928–30, 950, 966; Part III, 73, 87, 129, 336, 464, 598.
[39] *Ibid.*, Part III, 400–402, 432–33, 597–98, 628–29.

6

Civil Affairs, a Model Department

DARK CLOUDS OF MILITARY ACTION shrouded the sunshine of democracy in parts of the Union during the Civil War. Citizens found that the United States did not always apply the accepted axioms of Anglo-Saxon jurisprudence to their property, their rights, or their persons, even though by 1860 there was a strong American tendency against military interference in civil affairs. Over a century of precedent bound the government itself by law, forbade arbitrary action, and held its agents liable to damages for wrongful invasions of private rights. But so titanic a struggle had not previously been experienced by Americans, and bewildered by it, some accepted questionable doctrines of military necessity or "necessity knows no law."

Accusers fumed at Lincoln, called him a despot for suspending habeas corpus and ruling without Congress. Secretary of State William Seward used a network of secret agents to screen immigrants and émigrés, and spirited persons suspected of disloyalty off to prison without the formalities of legal procedure. The military arbitrarily arrested others and tried them before military commissions (*ex parte* Merryman, Milligan, Vallandigham, the execution of Mumford), even in areas where civil courts were open. An occasional newspaper was ordered from the streets.[1] This dismal shadow did not cloak the whole Union, however, and the spell it cast is not wholly representative of the time. No one will argue that the subject "cannot be passed over lightly: to do so would allow too small a value to civil guarantees,"[2] but not

[1] A fine, brief discussion of this topic can be found in James G. Randall, *The Civil War and Reconstruction*, 387–404.

[2] *Ibid.*, 404.

all military commanders acted as Benjamin Butler did in the Mumford case or as Ambrose E. Burnside did in the Vallandigham episode. John Pope is one example of a department commander who acted more circumspectly.

During the Minnesota uprising, the Sioux committed outrages against civilians and soldiers. On September 28, 1862, Sibley convened a military commission in the field to examine all the half-bloods and Indians camped near by, so that he could arrest and deal with the guilty parties. "I have no doubt we shall find some such in the number," he wrote.[3] Sibley indicated in this and other dispatches, that he did not expect to find many of the wrongdoers, doubtless assuming the worst offenders had fled. Meanwhile Pope ordered Sibley to make no treaty with the Sioux and to capture their chief, Little Crow, "and all others engaged in the late outrages and hold them prisoner until further orders." As Pope wrote this, Sibley informed him that sixteen Indian suspects were captured and "if found guilty they will be immediately executed"; although he was unsure of his legal power to do this. He remarked to Flandrau "perhaps it will be a stretch of my authority [to hang the guilty Indians]. If so, necessity must be my justification."[4] But more Sioux surrendered voluntarily than Sibley expected. By the end of the first week in October there were twenty under sentence of death, with others still to go before the commission.[5]

Although military commissions had met in the Western Department, the Department of Northeast Virginia, and in the Army of the Potomac earlier, Sibley's court was apparently the

[3] *Official Records*, Series I, Vol. XIII, 680; West, *Sibley*, 279; Heard, *Sioux War*, 188. Heard, recorder of the commission states that this was a military commission of inquiry. This description is inaccurate according to Articles of War 115–121, since no criminal charges are formed before a commission of inquiry, since it arraigns no prisoner, receives no plea, makes no finding of guilt or innocence, and awards no punishment. Thus Sibley called a military commission, and not in any sense a court of inquiry.

[4] *Official Records*, Series I, Vol. XIII, 686, 687, 688; Riggs, *Forty Years*, 179–80. Little Crow was a war leader of the Sioux. Flandrau was also a militia colonel and a noted Minnesota jurist.

[5] *Official Records*, Series I, Vol. XIII, 710, 712, 717, 720, 724, 738, 739, 740–41, 745.

first convened to try Indians. Halleck, as commander of the Department of the Missouri, in General Order No. 1, January 1, 1862, was the first Civil War officer to define in detail the nature and scope of military commissions. Later in 1862 similar action was taken by the department commanders of the Gulf, of Kansas, and of New Mexico. No such order existed for the Department of the Northwest, so if Sibley at times was at loss for proper procedure, it should have surprised no one.

On October 25 the commission adjourned to Mankato to inquire into Winnebago participation. It convicted none of that tribe. The court ended its sessions at Fort Snelling on November 5, having tried 425 Indians, half-bloods, and one mulatto; 321 of this number were sentenced, and of those, 303 condemned to hang.[6] The charges were largely compiled from information furnished by the missionary, Stephen R. Riggs, whose knowledge of the Sioux and their language enabled him to interrogate them, but the indictments were signed by either Sibley or his adjutant general. The settlers, some of whom had been captives of the Sioux, bore witness for the prosecution when necessary. Also, the mulatto, Godfrey, implicated many of his fellow warriors while he was under sentence of death.[7]

Sibley orally instructed the commission to insure each Indian a fair trial, to allow the accused the best possible defense, and

[6] *Minnesota in the Civil and Indian Wars,* 747; Heard, *Sioux War,* 231.
[7] Riggs, *Gospel Among the Dakotas,* 333–34; Heard, *Sioux War,* 251–52, 255. The form of charge and specification given below agrees substantially with that given in Folwell, *A History of Minnesota,* Vol. II, 196, note 12. In general the charge and specifications were:
"Charge. Murder.
Specification 1st. In this, that the said [name] did, at or near New Ulm, Minnesota, on or about the 19th day of August, 1862, join a war party of the Sioux tribe of Indians against the citizens of the United States, and did with his own hand murder . . . peaceable citizens of the United States.
Specification 2nd. In this, that the said [name] did, at various times and places between the 19th of August, 1862, and the 28th day of September, 1862, join and participate in the murders and massacre committed by the Sioux Indians on the Minnesota frontier.
By order of
      Col. H. H. Sibley, Com. Mil. Expedition
      S. H. Fowler, Lt. Col. State Militia, A.A.A.G.
Witnesses:"

to give the benefit of every reasonable doubt to the prisoner. In the nearly six weeks of trials the tribunal had to try at least twelve cases a day. As many as forty came before the commission one day, and thirty on some of the other days. Since a case was occasionally settled in five minutes, it is doubtful that any could have received more than cursory consideration. Mere admission of the second charge decided many cases. The court, in trying the Sioux, kept three major points in mind: first, the attack on New Ulm was on civilians, as were the assaults on many of the other towns, such as Acton and Hutchinson; second, there were many instances of murder and rape against civilians; third, there was much plundering. The fact that much of this was done by organized bands of Sioux and not just by individuals among them did not mitigate the offense, and therefore mere presence in a certain area at a certain time was thought sufficient to establish guilt. As far as this unfortunate concept is concerned, it is not without precedent in military law.[8] However, the commission tried them not only on these common premises, but also for the massacre at Birch Coulie, Minnesota, because those attacked were a burial party (it was also a reconnaissance), because it was composed of civilians as well as soldiers (the civilians were along voluntarily and must have been aware of the risk), and because the war party that assailed them were bound for New Ulm and points farther eastward. The culprits were also arraigned for the action against Captain Richard Strout's company in the Acton-Hutchinson (Minnesota) area, because civilian volunteers were with Strout and because there was no way for the whites to surrender (when outnumbered) since they could expect no quarter.[9] The legal basis for many of these points is a tenuous one at best, and a non-existent one in some cases. One factor, not in mitigation of the court's hasty and quasi-legal actions, may serve as a point of perspective: the people of Minnesota and many of the soldiers wanted to exterminate the Sioux,

[8] Heard, *Sioux War*, 252–58; William Winthrop, *Military Law and Precedents*, Vol. II, 1298, 1307.
[9] Heard, *Sioux War*, 255–56; Riggs, *Gospel Among the Dakotas*, 333–35.

and were it not for the trials, attempts to massacre the prisoners might have proved violent enough to be successful.

Although he was uncertain of his legal right to order the executions, Sibley was determined to proceed with only necessity for justification, but Pope was cautious enough to ask Halleck if he had the authority.[10] Article of War 89 enabled Pope to shift the burden to Lincoln since he did not want the blood of 303 hastily convicted Sioux on his conscience. The Article read:

> Every officer authorized to order a general-court martial shall have the power to pardon or mitigate any punishment . . . except the sentence of death . . . which . . . he may suspend, until the pleasure of the President of the United States can be known.

Lincoln acknowledged receipt of the list of the condemned, and asked to have the full record sent. During the time he had the

[10] *Official Records,* Series I, Vol. XIII, 688, 733, 755. Actually this is a complicated point in military law. However, Article of War 65 stated that: "neither shall any sentence of a general court-martial, *in time of peace,* extending to the loss of life . . . be carried into execution, until after the whole proceedings shall have been transmitted to the Secretary of War, to be laid before the President of the United States for his confirmation or disapproval, and orders in the case." [*Revised Regulations for the Army of the United States,* 1861, 509. Italics mine.] Since a military commission was similar to a general court-martial in constitution and procedure, and its actions subject to the same review, in the same manner and by the same authority [*Official Records,* Series I, Vol. VIII, 476–78; William Winthrop, ed., *Digest of Opinions of the Judge Advocate of the Army . . . Between September, 1862, and July, 1868,* 222], then the paramount question becomes whether or not this was wartime. By implication, interpretation, and statute, the commanding general in the field could enforce a death sentence in wartime [Winthrop, *Digest of Opinions of the Judge Advocate,* 23, 40; *United States Statutes at Large,* Vol. 12, 330–31].

The puzzle of whether an Indian uprising was a war is not found in the Articles of War except by interpretation, and the Indians could not be said to be a part of the Southern army of rebellion. It was accepted that a state of war could exist without a declaration, and that should a hostile force "either from without or within our territory . . . assail and capture our forts . . . our government and invade its soil" the President was bound to carry on a war [Robert N. Scott, *An Analytical Digest of Military Law of the United States,* 13–14, note 3]. The attorney general interpreted military law and regulations to apply the same during periods of Indian hostility as during war with a foreign power [Winthrop, *Military Law,* 136]. Certainly the lethal aspects of Indian uprisings were the same as the lethal qualities of war with anyone else, therefore from implication, interpretation, and fact, the Sioux uprising was a war. In the strict sense of military law, then, Pope could have carried out the death sentence.

matter under consideration, he was besieged with appeals. Ramsey, Pope, various state politicians, the Minnesota press, and apparently many of the people of Minnesota petitioned for the execution of all the Indians. One western protestant bishop, Henry B. Whipple, urged that an inquiry be made into the causes of the outbreak and that the Indian system be overhauled. Eastern voices rose in protest against the contemplated massacre. It was nearly a month before Lincoln announced his decision: thirty-nine Sioux were to be executed, and the rest held until further notice. Minnesotans anticipated such a decision, and despite the strengthened guards there were ineffective attempts by citizens to storm the prison and take the law into their own hands. After thirty-eight of the condemned were hanged (one got a reprieve) on December 26, the furor partially subsided.

All the excitement that fall was not confined to Minnesota. In November, Wisconsin experienced trouble with the militia draft. The draft machinery was the province of the state authorities, but when riots broke out in Ozaukee County and threatened in Milwaukee, United States troops were called to quell the disturbance and allow the draft to proceed. On November 11, the day after the rioting began, Governor Edward Salomon reported resistance and rioting at Port Washington as well to the Colonel of the Twenty-Eighth Wisconsin Volunteer Infantry, who sent eight companies to restore order, and the United States provost marshal arrested those involved.[11] Lincoln's proclamation of September 24, 1862, declared that all persons resisting militia drafts were subject to martial law, liable to trial and punishment by courts-martial and military commission, and were denied the benefit of habeas corpus. Of those arrested, the provost court found sufficient cause to imprison about 130.

Four companies of the Thirtieth Wisconsin Volunteer Infantry marched to West Bend, Washington County, to disperse a mob

[11] Quiner, *Military History of Wisconsin*, 146. The population of Ozaukee County, Milwaukee County, and Washington County was predominantly German, and the Germans in turn were staunch Democrats who still rankled over the election of a sectional president; they also had pressing economic reasons for wanting to avoid service.

hostile to the draft, and another company went to Green Bay. The draft in Milwaukee had been postponed to November 19, and to remove the possibility of a repetition of the scenes in Ozaukee and Washington Counties, seven companies of the Thirtieth and detachments of the Twenty-Eighth stood guard, while Governor Salomon proclaimed it was his duty to see the law enforced. The draft then proceeded with reasonable order under military observation.

Had matters ended there, those arrested would have been released within a few weeks. However, Salomon, to whom they were an acute source of discomfort, successfully urged that they be turned over to the Department of the Northwest. No federal hearing was given the men, and the War Department referred the matter to the cabinet. No decision was forthcoming before the following January, after the Wisconsin Supreme Court voided Lincoln's proclamation. At the same time a motion was pending to the United States Supreme Court for a writ of error.[12] Apparently Brigadier General Washington L. Elliott, who was temporarily in command during Pope's absence, paroled the prisoners. Later the Wisconsin Supreme Court denied the petition of the same agitators for a writ of habeas corpus. The justices avoided reversing themselves by pointing out that there was no evidence in the petition that any consideration of the court was due the draft rioters.[13]

The draft problem flared up again in 1863. On May 27 Pope told Halleck that "difficulties on account of enrollment for conscription take me back immediately to Iowa and Wisconsin. By prudence I hope they may be avoided." Some of the Wisconsin counties remained hostile to the draft, and an irate citizen from Dodge County shot an enrolling officer. In Iowa, a Davis County copperhead convention proclaimed its members would *"resist*

[12] *Official Records,* Series III, Vol. II, 765, 786, 843, 861, 867, 868, 882, 935, 943; Series II, Vol. V, 24, 164–65, 174, 179, 190.

[13] *Ibid.,* Series III, Vol. III, 103; a nearly complete account of this matter in its nation-wide aspects is presented in Fred A. Shannon, *The Organization and Administration of the Union Army, 1861–1865,* Vol. I, 259–92, Vol. II, 200–203.

to the death attempts to draft any of our citizens . . . and that we will permit no arbitrary arrests."

Immediately after his return, Pope reported to the Adjutant General that he did not anticipate further trouble over the enrollment in Wisconsin. He mentioned that Madison and Milwaukee had requested troops, and explained he "was very unwilling that the military should be brought into collision with either the civil authorities or the people," and concluded that the matter could be settled without military force. Pope characterized some of the assistant provost marshals as "rash, imprudent men, whose zeal outruns discretion. . . . Who rather desire to stir up a riot . . . to rid themselves of offensive opponents. . . . I shall endeavor to prevent this, and so far I have been successful." On June 20 he repeated these sentiments in more forceful language for the benefit of Colonel James B. Fry, the provost marshal general in Washington. Pope corrected Fry's impression that enrollment in Milwaukee had to be abandoned, stating that this did not "accord with my knowledge of the facts. The enrollment in Milwaukee was completed . . . strictly according to law, and by the aid of the municipal police force alone." Pope believed such protection sufficient, and declined to supply troops in the future unless necessity demanded it. The general then lectured the Colonel:

> The habit of resorting to military force in every trifling case of resistance or opposition to the laws is becoming sufficiently common to be alarming. Such a practice entirely supplants the civil authorities, sets aside time-honored means for the enforcement of the laws of this country, destroys in the citizen that feeling of personal interest in their execution . . . and prepares the public mind for the complete abdication of civil rule.

Pope urged the same policy upon the governor of Wisconsin.[14]

Nevertheless, Pope did make an attempt to reserve troops against a draft emergency. He told Halleck in July that the fears

[14] *Official Records*, Series I, Vol. XXII, Part II, 303–304; Series III, Vol. III, 395–96, 544–45, 579–80.

of Wisconsin authorities were well founded, and proposed that two veteran regiments from Wisconsin and Iowa be sent home to their respective states for recruiting and rest, and thus be on hand to prevent any trouble. He did not have sufficient troops for other than frontier guard duty because of the Indian expedition. Halleck could not spare old regiments for this either, and reminded Pope (in nearly the same words Pope had once used to Sibley), "the number of troops operating against the Indians . . . is double that of our entire army before the present war . . . if [it becomes] . . . necessary to employ force in Iowa and Wisconsin, such . . . must come from your own command."[15] So Pope made other arrangements, calling again on the Thirtieth Wisconsin and also upon other recently enlisted men.

The serpent of conscription raised its scaly head again in 1864. On August 1, Pope asked the provost marshals in his department if they would need military aid in enforcing the draft, ordered for September 5. Since most of Pope's troops were in the field, he had to plan the disposition of the few in garrison should they be needed. At Madison, the acting assistant provost marshal general for Wisconsin, Lieutenant Colonel Charles S. Lovell, asked to have four companies stationed at Milwaukee, with smaller detachments at Janesville, Prairie du Chien, Fond du Lac, Green Bay, and La Crosse. Lieutenant Colonel John T. Averill, the provost at St. Paul, anticipated no difficulty, but felt that fifty men at the headquarters of each subdistrict "for the purpose of guarding the conscripts there and in transit" would be adequate. Major Thomas Duncan, provost marshal at Davenport, Iowa, after consulting with state officers and his own assistants, reported there would be no serious draft opposition there, adding that all Pope need do was to lend him one Veterans Reserve Corps company already in Davenport if he needed it, but he thought the state militia could handle anything that would transpire. Pope told Lovell to confer with state authorities about enforcement, and also have new recruits, then assembling, quickly mustered into service and moved to Camp Washburn, Milwaukee. He also

[15] *Ibid.*, Series I, Vol. XXII, Part II, 384.

ordered the two companies of the Veterans Reserve Corps from Davenport to Milwaukee as a precaution against imminent trouble. The use of the Veterans Reserve Corps (unarmed veterans mustered for housekeeping services) for guard duty was protested at Davenport as contrary to their conditions of enlistment. On August 22, two companies of the First U. S. Volunteers (troops recruited into federal service from among prisoners of war) arrived at the draft rendezvous at Camp Randall, Wisconsin, although on the day the draft began they received orders to join Sibley at St. Paul, along with another company that had gone to Camp Washburn. So Pope repeated that Lovell arm the recruits at Milwaukee, which he considered adequate to preserve the peace.[16] In general, the draft in the Department of the Northwest proceeded quietly enough, in spite of the murder of an assistant provost marshal and a special agent sent to arrest draft dodgers in Iowa. Another assistant provost marshal in Iowa complained to Washington that mobs of men of draft age went "visiting" during the enrolling season, and similar groups from Minnesota passed through his state. This was bad enough, he lamented, but worse still was the fact that they would be back to vote! While trouble seethed in Wisconsin, there were no riots as in 1862, and Minnesota reported nothing worse than anxious moments.

Brigadier General Alfred Sully feared worse trouble than before if Lincoln's December, 1864, call for 300,000 volunteers fell short of its goal and a draft had to be held in February. On January 10, 1865, Sully suggested to Pope that cavalry be transferred from Sioux City to points of possible difficulty. Pope reminded Sully that the draft arrangements were the exclusive jurisdiction of the provost marshal, "the military only being auxiliary, and to be used when the necessity arises, on requisition of the . . . provost-marshal general or the governor." Sully's course, Pope continued, was to confer with the provost marshal and the governor; find if the grounds for alarm were reasonable and if they

16 *Official Records,* Series I, Vol. XLI, Part II, 512, 529, 565, 581, 590, 618–19, 813; Part III, 73.

were, to exhaust the means at the governor's and provost marshal's disposal to enforce the draft. He said, "If these means be not sufficient . . . it will then be time enough to act, bearing in mind that you are only furnishing military aid on requisition . . . and by no means originating measures of security yourself for the protection of these officers." Pope thought the governor of Iowa would be prepared for any emergency, however, "at all events . . . I desire written statements of the necessity for calling troops from the frontier at this time for such a purpose, and a requisition therefore from Major Duncan . . . provost-marshal general for Iowa.[17]

Copperhead activity was not as troublesome to the Department of the Northwest as it was to other areas, partly because state authorities acted with dispatch in such matters. From the neighboring Department of the Missouri, Major General Samuel P. Curtis forwarded communications to Pope concerning copperhead sentiment along the Iowa-Missouri border. One of these was a letter by J. M. Hiatt, provost-marshal general of the area, informing W. D. Gallagher, special agent of the Treasury Department, that "there is a disloyal element on the Iowa side, dangerous from its magnitude and its virulence" that supposedly was collaborating with similar elements in Missouri. The danger was that the Iowans could supply Missouri rebels with items which Curtis had restricted from trade. Curtis's concern seemed casual enough, his comment confined to the laconic endorsement:

> for the information of the commanding general, to show how restrictions on trade are urged by the agent of the Treasury. I would take off restriction on everything but arms and ammunition . . . if the loyal sentiment were not so earnestly opposed to it.

The provost marshal urged Iowa's governor, Samuel J. Kirkwood, to allow him "to vitalize and mobilize" the Southern Border Brigade. The provost, in turn, had been informed by a

[17] Richardson, *Messages and Papers*, Vol. VI, 271–72; *Official Records*, Series I, Vol. XLVIII, Part I, 506.

captain of the Clark County (Iowa) volunteer guard, that "northern rebels have become bold and insolent," and that the "meetings of the K.G.C. [Knights of the Golden Circle], as we believe, [are] nearly public." They displayed arms, the captain went on, and spoke of cleaning out the abolitionists. Particularly affected was a tier of counties: Madison, Decatur, and Clarke, located in South Central Iowa.[18]

Pope believed this information valid since it also came to him "through other reliable sources." This condition, he reported to Halleck, "is to be found in less, but increasing degree both in Wisconsin and Minnesota. The same reports are also sent to me from Dakota." Pope believed it was "impolitic to take any present action on the subject, but matters should be so arranged that the necessary steps can be taken" should there be any trouble. "I am not prepared to say how much or how extensive the danger is from these sources, but that organizations are being made in . . . Wisconsin, Iowa, and Minnesota to resist, by force . . . the conscription law, I do not doubt."

Brigadier General Benjamin S. Roberts had become so alarmed by copperhead activity in Iowa that he acted rashly, and Pope reprimanded him. Pope wrote,

> I regretted . . . your . . . stating that you had seized arms, &c., the personal property of the citizens of Iowa. I don't desire you to have anything to do with such matters. I have carefully refrained from allowing such things to be done here . . . I confine myself strictly to my military duty. I hope you will do the same. All such business has been turned over to the provost marshals or comes properly under civil jurisdiction.

Pope felt an army commander in a loyal state had no right to seize personal property on the chance it might be used in the future to resist the law. Pope believed the military commander could only act when federal law had been flouted and when the civil authorities were unable or unwilling to enforce it, and even

18 *Official Records*, Series I, Vol. XXII, Part II, 104–107, 160.

then only after proper application for his aid.[19] Fortunately, difficulties were averted in Wisconsin in 1863, and there was no draft in Iowa that year. There was some local trouble in Davis, Fremont (where the county court house was blown up), and Keokuk (Tally's War) counties, but these disturbances were quelled by the state without the assistance of the department.

Late in 1864, Wisconsin and Iowa experienced more copperhead trouble. On October 29, the governor of Wisconsin wrote that he had received information "from responsible and credible parties, that a secret organization against the Government exists at Shullsburg, La Fayette County . . . numbering eighty-five members" who sent for arms "within the past fortnight." The governor hoped Pope would permit no disturbance of the peace. Pope replied that he had forwarded the governor's note through proper channels to the acting assistant provost-marshal general for Wisconsin, and suggested that in the future such information be sent directly there. To allay the governor's fears, Pope added that he stood ready to help the state put down any breech of the peace.[20]

The governor of Iowa was next on the lecture list. The state militia turned over to the department a few captured guerrillas and bushwhackers who operated in conjunction with Confederate Major General Sterling Price's foray into Missouri, and who were alleged to have committed depredations in southern Iowa. Pope, however, had other ideas about their disposition, and on December 19 told the Iowa chief executive:

> Of course, I am quite willing to take charge of these prisoners and make the necessary disposition of them . . . but I would suggest . . . that the effect would be infinitely better if these men were tried and punished by the authorities of the State of Iowa. Having been captured by the State Militia . . . under your orders, they are . . . amenable to punishment by the authorities of the State. So long as these . . . bushwackers . . . understand that they are finally responsible only to the Federal authorities they will

[19] *Ibid.*, 397; Series III, Vol. III, 579.
[20] *Ibid.*, Vol. XLI, Part IV, 324, 433–34.

avail themselves of every opportunity in the absence of U. S. troops . . . to commit robbery and murder. Once let them understand that they will be promptly and summarily dealt with by the State authorities . . . without delay for reference to the U. S. authorities, and I feel sure your southern border will not long be invested.

Pope directed Sully to confer with Governor William M. Stone, adding that if Iowa was unwilling or unable to dispose of the prisoners, Sully should take them. The matter rested here, and Iowa handled her own troublemakers.[21]

Sully frequently received tongue-lashings from Pope too. One of the most important came for his seizure of public property. Sully faced a difficult situation: the government purchased large amounts of oats in Iowa and the West, which were shipped by rail from Sioux City to Dubuque, ferried across the river, and transshipped at Dunleigh (East Dubuque) for Cairo. Colonel Frederick Myers, the quartermaster at St. Louis, complained to Lieutenant Abram Williams, quartermaster at Dubuque, that the grain moved too slowly. Williams thereupon hurried the oats across the river and urged the railroad agent at Dunleigh to speed them down. But the agent delayed, and the grain at both Dubuque and Dunleigh overflowed the warehouses and was piled in the open. The agent complained that he had not enough cars or locomotives. Sully learned that large trains loaded with hogs and private freight were running (in Illinois) daily, so he ordered the railroad to stop shipments of private freight until the government grain was cleared out. "I knew," Sully reported, "that the road, being in a state not in my district, did not properly come under my care; but being on the spot and knowing the facts, I thought I would be justified in giving the order I did."[22]

Pope was horrified that Sully had acted outside his district (even outside the department), and had seized private property. "No railroads," he admonished, "even within the limits of your own command and for troops within your jurisdiction,

[21] *Ibid.*, 895.
[22] *Ibid.*, Series I, Vol. XLVIII, Part I, 529.

should ever be seized except under the gravest necessity." Still less justifiable, according to the commander, was the seizure of cars and railroads in another department. "If the necessity really exists, proper representations to that effect should be made . . . to these headquarters for any railroad property within the departmental area." Illinois railroads were in neither's jurisdiction, and Pope would never have thought of seizing them without orders from a superior authority. And if anyone outside the department requested such action, or if Sully was ordered by some authority over the department to perform any similar act, such orders were to be sent to Milwaukee for approval. Sully retorted, "You were mistaken in the idea that I seized the road . . . I merely gave them an order to ship Government freight first," and succeeded in getting nearly all of it moved out. However, in view of Pope's disapproval, Sully revoked the order stopping the shipment of private freight.[23]

The department also had to tolerate a certain amount of civilian interference. Pope discovered as early as 1862 that someone was scheming for his job when, after the Sioux problem had passed, he asked Halleck if he was to remain in the Northwest for the winter. Halleck did not know positively, but he remarked to Pope that "there has been urged upon the President a proposition to remove you and appoint a civilian (a member of Congress) in your place. I need not add that I have and will oppose it."[24] Senator Henry M. Rice (Democrat, Minnesota) was the individual under consideration. Rice was a former Indian trader, prominent in Chippewa affairs, and a member of several Senate committees, including the Committee on Military Affairs, which was a convenient lever for him to use to supplant Pope. The move would have had some popular appeal in Minnesota, and would have appealed to Rice too, since as a Democrat his re-election seemed doubtful during the war.

Pope was disturbed because this information seemed to indicate a Democratic plot: McClellan, his replacement in Virginia,

23 *Ibid.*, 506–507, 529.
24 *Ibid.*, Series I, Vol. XIII, 766–67.

was also a Democrat. But more important, he felt that if anyone should succeed him, it ought to be Sibley. He relieved his feelings with a caustic attack on Rice in a private letter to Halleck:

> His appointment [Rice's] will be based upon a knowledge of Indians and Indian character, acquired during many years of unlimited concubinage with Indian women. . . . Politically he is ruined, and he looks to this position to restore his broken political and material fortunes. Sibley has lived here longer than Rice . . . and is . . . a high-toned, honorable man, who has the respect of everybody, as he has conducted a successful campaign against the Indians, and has endured all the hardships and exposures of such service. The appointment of Rice, who has done nothing, will be a great and unmerited humiliation to him.[25]

Although the Rice appointment never materialized, the two Minnesota senators, Rice, and the renegade Republican, Morton S. Wilkinson, openly critical of the conduct of military affairs in the department, sought to create an independent body of troops that they might control. They prevailed upon Stanton to authorize Major Edwin A. C. Hatch to recruit a battalion of cavalry. This was an affront to Pope, who demanded a copy of "the order under which Mr. Hatch is acting" and proclaimed "he has no authority for announcing that he is to command troops in the service of the United States within this department." Pope told the War Department that such an organization was "a great and unnecessary expense" and recommended Hatch's authority be revoked. Even Halleck was in the dark about Hatch. Hatch's commission was not revoked, but he came under Pope's command and took orders from Sibley, to whose district he was assigned.[26]

Although Pope's personal conduct of some of the political affairs of the department, especially the Rice episode, were not always entirely satisfactory, civil affairs were generally well con-

---

[25] *Official Records*, Series I, Vol. XII, Part III, 826.
[26] *Official Records*, Series I, Vol. XXII, Part II, 371–72, 384, 569. Hatch's orders to form a battalion do not appear in the *Official Records*.

ducted. The brushes with Rice concerned the department only by implication, while the department's relationship with the states and territories was direct. Pope made no effort to interfere in their political affairs, and left civil matters in their hands as much as possible. The frequent lectures to his subordinates, especially to Roberts and Sully, illustrate Pope's views on most of these matters. When Lieutenant General Ulysses S. Grant, supreme commander of the armies, shook up the command positions in November, 1864, he proposed to make Pope commander of a new administrative area, the military Division of the Missouri, which included the former departments of the Northwest, Missouri and Kansas. "With Pope in command we may secure at least two advantages . . . namely, subordination and intelligence of administration."[27]

Forgetting his admonitions to various governors, and with characteristic boastfulness, but with essential accuracy, Pope reported to the Committee on the Conduct of the War:

> The usual questions, concerning the relations between the civil and the military authorities . . . arose in the department of the northwest. . . . I am gratified to say that . . . the laws of the United States, however disagreeable to the people, were fairly . . . executed, and at no time was there any conflict of jurisdiction or . . . opinion between the civil and the military authorities.

This, he added, was owing "to the good sense and patriotism of the people." One might have expected Pope to have added, "although I had to prod them along some," but he did not. Pope may not have been the best remembered field general, Lee and Jackson perhaps made him look very foolish at second Bull Run, but Pope had at least one quality that set him above some of his fellow officers: respect for civil law. He quite sincerely believed that civil law, authorities, and procedures should be either exhausted or incapable of action before the military could justly act, and to this principle he rigidly adhered.

[27] *Ibid.,* Vol. XLI, Part IV, 661, 672, 702, 709, 716, 717.

7

The Indian Problem in Fact and Fancy

THE REDMAN, WHO HAD TURNED THE NORTHERN LANDS of the sky-blue waters red with the blood of slain settlers, posed some unique military problems for Pope. One of them was the boundary, the imaginary line that divided British America from the United States. The Indian could step across this and laugh at piqued pursuers. One might compare this to the Yalu River problem that confronted the United Nations in Korea some eighty-eight years later. Under the circumstances, Pope realized the Indians could not be defeated until he either cut off their source of supply or obtained permission to pursue them into British America.

There was no question of the efficacy of this strategy, but perhaps its importance was magnified at first: "The complete results of our campaign against them [the Sioux] will be overthrown" if they could retreat to the shelter of British America. This problem never became really acute between 1862 and 1865, but in the military sense the redmen could use the boundary to prevent their destruction or subjugation. Sibley believed traders from the British Red River settlements were influential enough with the Indians to have "succeeded in deterring them from submitting to the government," which, while it was good business for the merchants, prolonged hostilities. Besides another argument for securing the border, it was a case for limiting trade.[1] This was the next logical step.

Sibley's concern exceeded even Pope's, and it was Sibley who drafted and put into effect an order which regulated commerce with British America, but Pope sanctioned and applauded Sib-

[1] *Official Records*, Series I, Vol. XXXIV, Part II, 69, 152.

ley's course. Sibley withheld all munitions bound through Pembina, Dakota Territory, for the English settlers to the north. Pope modified this directive and provided for transmission of freight bonded against the passage of goods into savage hands. The effectiveness of the change was questionable, and Sibley remarked to Pope in June, 1864, that he believed "much of the powder and lead thus transported was sold to the hostile Indians"; and the following January reports filtered back to the department that English traders visited the Indians and presented them with kegs of powder and sacks of bullets.[2]

Pope also considered it necessary to control Indian trade from his own side of the border. Before he had been in command a month he had asked Halleck to procure an order from the Interior Department revoking trade permits. Pope felt only Indian agents should be permitted among the tribes. The matter was referred to the President and his Secretary of War, who later intimated that instructions would be forthcoming. They never were. Pope next tried to deprive the Indians of annuity money due them under various treaties and he urged that under any circumstances the redmen should not be paid in cash because this would "stimulate the cupidity of unscrupulous men, both traders and others.[3] In February, 1864, Pope appealed to Stanton to adopt trade regulations. He attacked the annuity system as serving to attract only the undesirable element of the frontier, and blamed the Indian wars on "the conduct of the white men who have swindled them [the Indians] out of their money and goods." He insisted that eliminating the annual payment would also remove the avaricious whites.[4]

The following April, Halleck, who was in sympathy with efforts to limit trade and to bring the Indians under more realistic military control, acquainted Pope with the obstacles that the War Department faced in any attempt to accomplish such ends, when he wrote: "You probably are not fully aware of the diffi-

[2] *Ibid.*, Part IV, 450; Vol. XLVIII, Part I, 637.
[3] *Ibid.*, Vol. XIII, 706, 707, 737; Vol. XXII, Part II, 569–70.
[4] *Ibid.*, Vol. XXXIV, Part II, 260, 263.

culty of ascertaining and counteracting the baneful influence upon military operations exercised by speculators, through members of Congress and the civil departments of the Government. More especially is this the case in regard to Indian affairs." There clearly were heavy civilian pressures against regulation. Pope tentatively took matters into his own hands, no doubt hoping to present the government with an accomplished fact and thereby secure the desired result without constant bickering with the War Department.

In May, 1864, Pope told Halleck he had instructed Sibley merely to assure relocated Sioux in the vicinity of Devil's Lake protection from hostile Indians. To encourage farming they would be issued seed corn. "No treaty had been made with them," Pope continued, "nor shall I permit the treaty they have violated [by the outbreak of 1862] to be renewed without orders from the War Department. The Indians . . . will keep . . . [the peace], under the surveillance of the military authorities, without any money or other considerations and without expense to the United States."

A week later, Pope submitted a draft order establishing trade regulations with the Indian tribes within the department. This lengthy order contained sixteen paragraphs, in summary, as follows:

I. All trade permits were revoked; future traders had to have written permission from the War Department.

II. This permission along with a bond that pledged observance of these regulations had to be deposited with the commanding officer of the military district in which the trader would trade.

III. The district commander would designate trading posts near a military post. No trade was to be carried on.

IV. Certified price lists and invoices were to be filed at the nearby post.

V. A military council was to fix prices in the same manner as they did for Sutler's goods, and to publicly post the price-list, copies of which were to be forwarded to both district and departmental inspectors general.

VI. The military council also was to fix prices on furs or other articles the Indians offered for barter, by which the trader would be bound.

VII. Upon oath the members of the military council were to have no interest or connection with the Indian trade.

VIII. Trade was to be in goods, not money. Spirituous liquors were prohibited.

IX. No white man other than approved traders and immigrants passing through were to be allowed in the Indian country, and the latter were prohibited from trading.

X. Price-lists and regulations were to be explained to the Indians by interpreters whether requested by them or not.

XI. Traders violating regulations, and white men or half-breeds trading in violation of them, were to be arrested and their stock confiscated.

XII. Settlers at military posts were allowed to trade with the Indians in accordance with these regulations.

XIII. During periods of hostilities all trade was to be suspended.

XIV. The object of the regulations was to secure peace with the Indians "by making it clear to them they will be dealt with fairly and kindly . . . and in restraining all irresponsible persons who might wrong or plunder them."

XV. Commanders of military districts and posts were directed to encourage missionaries.

XVI. The commander of each military post was charged with the enforcement of these regulations and was held accountable for their strict enforcement.

At best this was an honest attempt to deal with the Indians as fairly as the military commander could conceive while still accomplishing the primary objective. But Lincoln did not approve these restrictions because, as Pope wrote to Assistant Secretary of War Charles A. Dana the following September, "It was not at the time thought judicious to authorize the issue and enforcement of these rules."[5] The occasion for correspondence with Dana was a complaint, forwarded to Pope by Governor Newton

[5] *Ibid.*, Part III, 33, 448, 565–67, 600; Vol. XLI, Part III, 125–26.

Edwards of Dakota Territory, about American traders who abused their licenses. Pope unsuccessfully used this opportunity to urge again adoption of his trade regulations.[6] However, in November, 1864, the Missouri Sioux were made party to the same sort of policy established for the Devil's Lake (Dakota Territory) Sioux the previous spring. Sully proposed to make peace with the redmen in that area, and if he succeeded, Pope told Halleck, the Indians would be allowed a treaty containing only a provision protecting them from the whites, provided the Indians committed no hostile acts, in which case the treaty would automatically end. Again, there was to be no monetary consideration, and until the War Department or Congress told him otherwise, he would not permit "intercourse between Indian agents and these Indians."[7]

Sully believed that peace could be made and maintained "provided the proper course is adopted, and that is to treat the Indians in the future with justice. Let them understand that the Government intends to see that they will no longer be the prey of dishonest agents and traders." Sibley was in substantial agreement. He thought that the payment of "large annuities to the Indians is a direct incentive to fraud on the part of unprincipled men, whether Government agents or traders. . . . I am satisfied that all intercourse between the Government and the . . . tribes, including the regulations for trade, would be more simple and satisfactory if confined strictly to the military channels."[8]

Several points of view were expressed by these men in a few words, but they both agreed with Pope on the need for trade regulations, even if their motives were not wholly military. By dealing fairly with the redman, yet not paying annuities to tempt the unscrupulous frontier trader, peace might be gained and kept. One says, and the other implies, that relations with the aborigines would be better handled by the military.

The problem of the trader continued after 1865. The com-

[6] *Ibid.,* Vol. XLI, Part III, 122–24.
[7] *Ibid.,* Part IV, 599–600.
[8] *Ibid.,* 651, 710.

mandant of Fort Rice, Dakota Territory, complained to Sully's adjutant general about British traders on the Missouri.

> [I] urgently request of the commanding general permission to break up these trading parties . . . and execute summary justice on the principals engaged. . . . I fear the consequence[s] in the spring. . . . I would respectfully urge upon the general commanding the evident necessity of more stringent rules . . . governing traders at different posts on this river. There are . . . at Fort Sully . . . some ten unauthorized petty traders who are governed by no law whatever; also at Fort Berthold there are four.

On February 1, 1865, in his last dispatch as commander of the Department of the Northwest, Pope wrote Sibley and Sully authorizing them to confer with Indians at their posts and to offer the Sioux peace during their good behavior in return for protection from hostiles. "No other treaty stipulations will be made," Pope ordered. "Payment of annuities or distribution of goods under former treaties will not be permitted," but the Indians should be encouraged by kind treatment to camp near the outer posts "and to trade with persons duly authorized to trade with them. . . . No Indian trader will be permitted to locate himself in the camps of these Indians, but will be assigned a place for his store . . . in the immediate vicinity of the military post." Pope's order also prohibited officers and soldiers from trading with the Indians on penalty of court-martial.[9] Thus it was that Pope, impatient with the War Department after a three-year struggle over his trade regulations, put the heart of them into effect by direct order.

From his viewpoint as a department commander, Pope honestly believed that he could see the way for creating a more realistic general Indian policy than that pursued by the government. As the chief military officer in the area, he could appreciate the army's responsibility for obtaining and maintaining order. But he lacked the power to secure a lasting peace, which led him to approach the War Department, and anyone else who

[9] *Ibid.*, Vol. XLVIII, Part I, 637, 719–20.

would listen, with his plan. Since his ideas never were taken seriously, Pope attacked the Indian Bureau and its superior, the Interior Department. Pope was well acquainted with the frontier, as were most regular army officers who had been in service before the war. The Indian was no stranger to him; he thought he understood the redman, and perhaps he did. Pope had no idea of territorial aggrandizement in mind, only a solution to the Indian difficulties from the military viewpoint. Since the army had to put down uprisings, quell disturbances, protect Indian agents, convoy supply trains, settlers, and emigrants, he felt it should deal with the Indians in all their relations.

On February 6, 1864, Pope outlined his plan to Stanton. It was so important to Pope that he later included it in his report to the Committee on the Conduct of the War. The letter began with an attack on the Interior Department's Indian policy, which Pope saw as "the result of temporary expedients, and not of well-considered examination of the subject." The system of treaties, reservations and annuities in both goods and money, created two classes of Indians: those whose lands were surrounded by white settlement, and those "who still maintained their roving life and their relation with the wild tribes," while at the same time depending on the whites for annuity payments. Those of the first type could not maintain themselves by hunting on their own small plots and others, like the Sioux, that took unkindly to farming became vagabonds dependent upon governmental support. Their money attracted a most unsavory element, the worst possible influence on the Indian, and made him a gambler, drunkard, and plunderer besides a vagabond. When the growth of settlement increased his land value, speculators influenced Congress to make a new treaty that involved more money and goods and removal of the Indians, thus opening their lands to the real estate agents and the treasury to the trader. "This process was repeated at no long intervals, the Indian tribe diminishing rapidly . . . and becoming thoroughly debased, until . . . they . . . fell . . . prey to hostile Indians or perished with disease and want." In other words it was futile to try to make white men of them, as the Indian agent, Galbraith, had put it two years earlier.[10]

Hope for the roving Indians was only slightly better, said Pope. They still had to come in periodically for their annual or semi-annual payments, only to be swindled there by the "Indian traders, whiskey sellers, and gamblers," which forced them back to the prairies to support themselves. The speculators robbed him of his land as the settlements encroached more and more, making him dispose of more and more of his land, until, "by contact with the depraved whites, he gradually parts with his whole country . . . and becomes one of the 'Reserve Indians'," and then follows the path of those in the first group. The recent Indian wars were brought about, Pope charged, by Indians who were "goaded by swindling and wrong and maddened by drink."[11]

The system of reservations and westward removals, Pope felt, had erected "a constantly increasing barrier to travel and emigration" which led to friction and violence between the Indians and travelers. When the whites were beaten, they called for troops, and an Indian war began. The contractors and other interested parties used every means to prolong these difficulties, which meant more bloodshed and expense. The Indian policy had been a woeful failure from either the humane or economic point of view, said Pope. He concluded, "I have passed ten years of my life in service on the frontier, and the facts herein stated are the result of observation and experience, and are familiar to every officer in the army who has served in the West."[12]

Pope called attention to his previous memorandums and suggestions to Halleck and Stanton in October of 1862. He reminded them of his proposals to collect, disarm, and secure the Sioux and Winnebagos at "some point far in the rear of the settlements," and his recommendation to use appropriations to build villages and to feed and clothe the Indians rather than for annuities. The Indians would therefore be unable to wander,

[10] *Ibid.*, Vol. XXXIV, Part III, 448; Vol. XLI, Part III, 123, Part IV, 600; Pope, "Report . . . to the Committee on the Conduct of the War," 192–93.
[11] Pope, "Report . . . to the Committee on the Conduct of the War," 193.
[12] *Ibid.*, 193–94.

white traders would be the less tempted since there would be no money payments, and the Indian would be "shielded from all the corrupt and debasing influences which have surrounded him in times past." The native would be, the General thought, in circumstances much more congenial to education, civilization, and Christianity. Also the Indian barrier would be removed, thereby eliminating one cause of hostility, and the government would be relieved of considerable expense.

Pope admitted he had not discussed or taken into account Indian claims to land ownership, and mistakenly added that "no government but our own has ever recognized Indian titles to lands on this continent." He shrugged off such questions as subjects fit only for abstract discussion, because "all history shows that the result will certainly be . . . the dispossession of the savage and the occupation of his lands . . . the only practical question . . . to consider, is the means . . . by which this result may be attained with the greatest humanity, the least injustice, and the largest benefit to the Indian, morally and physically."[13]

Pope proposed that annuity Indians who still observed their treaties should be removed to points far in the rear of frontier settlement, as he previously explained, "and . . . all other Indians be left to the exclusive management of the War Department and the military commanders in the Indian country." Pope showed a rare spark of modesty as well as determination when he remarked "although I hardly feel justified in recommending so extensive a reorganization . . . I consider it not improper to present these views" to those who have jurisdiction of the subject.[14]

Pope's criticisms of existing Indian policy were valid enough, even if one allows some exaggeration to a man trying very hard to make a point. Certainly in agreement with him were the local clerics, particularly the clear-thinking Henry B. Whipple, Episcopal bishop of Minnesota, a man of some influence in Indian affairs; the indefatigable missionary, Stephen R. Riggs; and

[13] *Ibid.*, 194–95.
[14] *Ibid.*, 195.

also Alexander Berghold, the New Ulm priest. Pope's subordinates made similar criticisms, as has been pointed out.[15]

The soundness of the plan to relocate annuity Indians east of the frontier was questionable in all but a military sense, and also difficult to accomplish. Military control of the Indians from any but the military viewpoint could be seriously debated. Some white officers, among them the infamous Colonel John M. Chivington and his henchman, Major Jacob Downing (both of the First Colorado Volunteer Cavalry), were not at all innocent of barbarities toward the Indians themselves. The massacre of five hundred Cheyennes and Arapahoes at Sand Creek, Colorado, on November 29, 1864, and the killing of forty Cheyennes at Cedar Bluffs, Colorado, on May 3, 1864, for which Chivington and Downing were responsible, along with the hanging of the thirty-eight Sioux by Pope's department two years earlier, does not exactly speak well for the idea that the military should handle the redmen.

It was true, and Pope might have argued that Chivington and Downing were volunteers, and not regulars, and therefore not schooled in a military sense of fair play, but Pope had strongly recommended the hanging of all 303 Sioux convicted by his military commission, although he shifted the final responsibility to Lincoln. Sully, who was also a regular, could not escape the charge of barbarism himself, for it was he who caused the heads of three Sioux to be cut off and mounted on poles as a warning to their tribesmen during the 1864 campaign. Pope's own thoughts had undergone some modification in the course of time, too. In late September, 1862, he wrote Sibley:

It is idle and wicked, in view of the atrocious murders these Indians have committed, in face of the treaties and without provocation, to make treaties or talk about keeping faith with them. The horrible massacres of women and children . . . call for punishment beyond human power to inflict. There will be no

[15] Whipple, *Lights and Shadows*, 5–6; Riggs, *Gospel Among the Dakotas*, xxii–xxvi, 327–28; Berghold, *The Indians' Revenge*, 62–66; *Official Records*, Vol. XXXIV, Part I, 907–908; Part III, 159; Vol. XLI, Part I, 949.

peace in this region by virtue of treaties and Indian faith. It is my purpose to utterly exterminate the Sioux. . . . They are to be treated as maniacs or wild beasts.

With his contemporaries in Minnesota, Pope had paled before the evidences of Sioux brutality. If the regular general officers behaved in this manner, then who was to be an example to the minor officers who poisoned provisions and let them fall into Sioux hands, and to the enlisted men who took scalps and sent home Indian skulls as souvenirs? It is true these were acts committed in war time, but who could say the integrity of the average officer or enlisted man had been better than that of the frontier farmer or hunter? The military mind might be more amenable to discipline, and perhaps a few officers might have had the high moral convictions that Pope seemed to think were inherent in all. So, while the military aspects of Pope's proposed Indian policy were expedient, and his criticisms of Indian policy accurate, the removal seemed impossible, and the military control of the Indians held no greater attraction for the non-military than did Indian-agent control for the military.

Pope believed, with some justification, that it was foolish to make treaties with the Indians, considering that in this manner "the Indians are bribed not to molest the whites. . . . It is a common saying with the Sioux that whenever they are poor and need powder and lead they have only to go down to the overland routes and murder a few white men, and they will have a treaty to supply their wants." Here, then, was another reason for not paying the Indians in goods or money. For if a treaty meant so little, why negotiate one? Why not just an agreement for protection, which they could understand. Pope tried to inaugurate this system, as noted, at Devil's Lake and on the Missouri.[16]

Secretary of the Interior John P. Usher, partially concurred with Pope's views. On December 5, 1864, using almost as urgent

[16] *Collections of the State Historical Society of North Dakota*, Vol. 2, Part I, 427, Part II, 106, 107, 109; English, "Dakota Cavalry," 278; *Official Records*, Series I, Vol. XIII, 686.

a tone as Pope, Usher reported that in all cases where Indians were hostile to the United States "trade and intercourse should be interdicted, until they [the redmen] yield. . . . I recommend that a law be passed, making it a penal offense for any person to carry goods, or supplies . . . into their country, for traffic; and that all persons, of whatever pursuit, shall be prohibited from trading . . . with them while they are in a state of hostility." However, concerning a change in the treaty system, Usher was adamant. "Much has been said . . . against the policy of the government in making treaties with the Indian tribes . . . but . . . while this nation is governed by the rules of civilization, such a proposition as not making treaties will not be entertained." Usher did, however, accept another vital point of Pope's thesis. "In negotiating new treaties," he remarked, "where good policy or existing engagements will admit of that course of action, stipulations for the payment of money annuities should be avoided."[17]

At least, the whole of Pope's argument was not lost. The General's views were more summarily discussed by William P. Dole, the commissioner of Indian affairs. He noted that first, before the 1864 campaign, Pope protested against the delivery of annuity goods to the Sioux of the upper Missouri, and declared that he would tolerate no interference by Indian agents until the campaign was over. Dole said, superciliously, "I had already instructed all of the agents not to distribute guns or ammunition," and added that the agents were told to co-operate with the military commanders in their operations. Commenting directly upon Pope's remarks, Dole soberly added, "While I am far from insisting that the policy thus far pursued has been in all cases best for the Indians . . . I still think it the best which the conditions of things and the times present to us." Dole admitted "that grave and serious mistakes may have occurred in the management of our Indian affairs . . . and that . . . many of the wars . . . have resulted from the wrongful acts of our own people," but, he continued, "I have yet to learn that the greed of military contractors is any less than is that of civilians as contractors; or

[17] *Report of the Secretary of the Interior,* 1864, 10.

that camp-followers and the 'hangers-on' around military posts are more virtuous than are those . . . who assemble around our Indian reserves."[18]

This final statement of Dole's is the most telling criticism of Pope's proposed policy. Certainly, Pope could not have expected the mantle of a military uniform or the words of an official order or the ink on a government contract automatically to endow a person with integrity. But many of his more practical suggestions concerning trade regulations, treaties, and annuities, may have had some influence on the enactment of restrictive legislation in those areas from 1866 through the 1870's. Actually, much more influence on Indian policy could have been exercised by the President, had he either the time or the inclination to do so, since a law of June 30, 1834, gave him the blanket power to "prescribe such regulations as he may think fit for carrying into effect the various provisions of any act relating to Indian affairs," and also through his power to create by executive order Indian reservations out of lands in the public domain. It may have been in knowledge of this that Pope addressed his thoughts to the Secretary of War.[19]

It also seemed to be the Indian Bureau's object to make white men of the Indians by converting them from nomadic to more settled ways. Even though he did not choose to express it this way, it was Pope's view that it would be better to make children of them. Take their allowance away so the bully would not be tempted to seduce them; shield them from harm but do not let them fight if provoked; and move them into a better environment so they might grow up peacefully. From the military viewpoint this treatment was not illogical. Since the military had the dirty task of cleaning up the mess every time the Indian saw fit to resist the treatment accorded him, it seemed as if the military ought to have the power to do their job efficiently. If general policy control was denied them, then certainly limited trade

---

[18] *Ibid.*, 171–72, 573–75.
[19] Kappler, *Indian Affairs*, 1–19, 23–29; Thomas Donaldson, *The Public Domain*, 243–44.

and treaty control ought to be theirs in times of stress. William Tecumseh Sherman, later commanding general of the army, reflected this same attitude in 1866 when he remarked that:

> We, the military, charged with a general protection of the infant settlements and long routes of travel, have to dispose our troops and act as though they [the Indians] were hostile; while by Act of Congress, and the acts of our executive authorities, these Indians are construed as under the guardianship and protection of the general government, through civilian agencies. . . . [While] Indians . . . always look to the man who commands our troops as the representative of our government.[20]

It has been fashionable to score the military for their brutal, fumbling, or selfish methods of dealing with the Indians. It cannot be denied that on occasion they acted as uncivilized as the savages with whom they dealt, and the wanton outrages such as Sand Creek must rest on their heads. But however sincere, and from whatever humanitarian viewpoint this type of judgment springs, it must be remembered that in matters of *policy* the issues must be determined by the soldier through the criteria of military expediency. This in itself cannot cloak the soldier's inhumanity, but it can explain why the military so often clashed with civilian bureaus. And, unlike the politically oriented Bureau of Indian Affairs, the altruism of theocratic reformers, the public press of compassionate areas behind the frontier, or even the more immoderate press of the border, Pope saw the department's problems through a soldier's eyes.

[20] R. Ernest Dupuy and Trevor N. Dupuy, *Military Heritage of America*, 311, quoting from Sherman's report to the secretary of war, 1866.

8

The Indian Problem in Fact

BEFORE THE TERRIBLE TROUBLE OF 1862 began, the Sioux shared
the beautiful northwestern frontier with their traditional enemies the Chippewas, with Winnebagos transplanted from Wisconsin, and with a growing number of white settlers. About
4,000 Chippewas hunted in the forests and fished the streams
and lakes set aside for them in northern Minnesota. In the
verdant Blue Earth country of south central Minnesota, about
2,000 Winnebagos huddled on a reservation, and about 400
more disturbed newer Wisconsinites by remaining in their old
homeland. With nearly 9,600 Dakota and Minnesota Sioux
added to the mixture, the Indian population of the northwestern
frontier totaled about 16,000. Not all of the problems concerned
the saucy Sioux.[1]

In 1862 the Chippewas were restless too. The Mississippi
bands located on Mille Lacs, Gull Lake, Sandy Lake, Pokegama,
Rabbit Lake, and Rice Lake, had stolen cattle, taken hostages,
and threatened the life of their agent, Lucius C. Walker, whom
they charged with fraud. Walker subsequently committed sui-
cide, and in fear of a Chippewa outbreak Captain Francis Hall
of Fort Ripley asked for reinforcements. Fortunately, Dole and
Thompson were on their way to negotiate a treaty with these
tribes for the safe navigation of the Red River of the North, and
had arrived at St. Cloud on August 19. When troops were sent
to protect the agency at Gull Lake, the Chippewa chieftain,
Hole-in-the-day, fired upon them and attempted to stir Chippewas to war.[2] Hole-in-the-day had mustered three hundred

---

[1] *Report of the Secretary of the Interior, 1862, 215–16, 240; Report of the Secretary of the Interior, 1863, 426–27.*

warriors, and some of the bands, notably the Pillager and the Otter-tail,[3] had joined him. However the Mille Lacs and Poke-gama bands had not done so, and the Commissioner was success-ful in alienating them from Hole-in-the-day.[4] This may have been a serious deterrent to the Chief, since he doubtless relied on the help of warriors from these bands. At any rate, he sent word to Dole that he wanted an interview. Hole-in-the-day was at first "insolent, defiant, and disrespectful," but Dole handled the affair well, and was able to secure peacefully "entire and unconditional submission" of the Chippewas. In the meantime, the legislature of Minnesota, desiring to avoid a Chippewa war, had delegated Governor Alexander Ramsey as head of a com-mission to negotiate a settlement with the tribe. The legislators had acted before Commissioner Dole was able to report his suc-cess. Such a treaty was negotiated over the Commissioner's dis-approval, although it was never ratified.

In 1863 there was no trouble with the Lake Superior Chip-pewas, but as noted previously, the Winnebagos caused some distress. Meanwhile there were additional Sioux problems after the 1862 campaign. Confined in federal custody in a stockade near Fort Snelling were the uncondemned among the redmen tried by Sibley's military commission. Their number, originally 1,658, dwindled to 1,601 by December. The 321 condemned, with 25 more to see to their personal needs, were at Mankato. After the mass hanging of the unpardoned thirty-eight (one of the original thirty-nine had been respited), the more fortunate were removed, as soon as the river opened, to Camp McClellan, a military prison near Davenport, Iowa. For some unknown reason, fifty of these were put into the Snelling group.[5] Pope

[2] *Report of the Secretary of the Interior,* 1862, 10, 171–72, 200, 201, 216, 217.

[3] *Ibid.,* 201. Superintendent Thompson says these were the Leech Lake and Otter-tail Lake bands, not the Pillagers as a whole.

[4] *Ibid.,* 173–74, 201. The Chippewas of Lake Superior were quiet but the Chippewas of the Red Lake and the Red River area, whom Dole and Thompson were unable to reach to treat with as mentioned above, were restless and unwill-ing to open their territory to white travel.

[5] *Report of the Secretary of the Interior,* 1863, 427–28, 436; Brown, "In Cap-tivity," 25, 27; Riggs, *Forty Years,* 193.

wanted to be rid of these Indians, and believed the Indian Bureau properly chargeable for them. But no word on their final disposition ever came from the War Department. Halleck, woefully uninformed, advised Pope on April 14 that their fate was in the hands of the cabinet while the Bureau of Indian Affairs had been engaged in their transfer since April 7.[6]

Sioux removal was necessary, partly to protect them from public vengeance, but also because an act of Congress deprived them of their treaty, which in turn left them without its benefits, including a home. The Winnebagos reaped part of the whirlwind as Congress provided for their peaceful exodus also. A third act stipulated that the Sioux be relocated somewhere outside any state lines. The debarkation of the two tribes by river to a new reservation, called Crow Creek on the Missouri above Fort Randall, took place in the spring of 1863 under the supervision of Clark Thompson.[7]

Pope had little sympathy for the imprisoned Sioux. In November, 1862, he wrote Lincoln:

> The only distinction between the culprits is as to which of them murdered the most people or violated the most young girls. . . . It is to be noted that these horrible outrages were not committed by wild Indians, whose excuse might be found in ignorance and barbarism, but by Indians who have for years been paid annuities by the Government, and who committed these horrible crimes upon people among whom they had lived for years . . . at whose houses they had slept, and at whose tables they had been fed.[8]

Pope reflected frontier opinion. He and Sibley were agreed that the Sioux prisoners ought to be punished. That they should be disarmed and confined was apparent, since many of the white refugees would not return unless the Sioux threat definitely was

[6] *Official Records*, Series I, Vol. XXII, Part II, 117–18, 123, 127, 217; *Report of the Secretary of the Interior*, 1863, 417–19.

[7] *U. S. Statutes at Large*, Vol. 12, 652–54 (Feb. 16, 1863), 658–60 (Feb. 21, 1863), 819–20 (Mar. 3, 1863); *Report of the Secretary of the Interior*, 1863, 417, 420–27.

[8] *Official Records*, Series I, Vol. XIII, 788.

removed. For all his strong words, Pope seemed aware of the root of the problem. "There will not long be trouble," he told Halleck in October, "as soon as the Government renders it impossible for white men to make money out of the Indians." If he could not condone indiscriminate slaughter of women and children by supposedly friendly Indians, neither was he so blind, even in the weeks shortly after his arrival in Minnesota, that he did not know where to place much of the blame.

After the Sirocco campaign there was talk of peace for the first time since the outbreak. On September 16, 1863, Sibley wrote from St. Paul that

> the state of destitution in which [the Sioux] . . . found themselves [after the battles of Big Mound, Stony Lake, etc.] and their utter inability to contend with our disciplined troops in the open field have so terrified the large majority of these savages that they have expressed a fervent desire to re-establish peace with the Government at any price.

Standing Buffalo, a chieftain of the Upper Sioux who had been opposed to the hostilities, desired to deliver himself and his band to the government provided he would be given assurance that they would not be made prisoners or removed to the Crow Creek Reservation. Father André, a Catholic missionary from around St. Joseph trusted by the Sioux and half-bloods alike, brought this information to Sibley. Sibley asked permission to employ Father André "and such other competent persons as may be deemed necessary," to treat with the Indians, and offer them "such conditions of peace as you [Pope] may deem proper." For terms, Sibley suggested the Sioux either deliver up those who participated in the massacre or expel them from their midst, and resettle the redmen at a respectable distance away from the frontier so as not to alarm the white inhabitants. "If properly managed I have every reason to believe that the Indian war will soon be terminated,"[9] he said.

[9] *Official Records*, Series I, Vol. XXII, Part I, 912–13.

With this assurance from Sibley, Pope sent Hatch to Pembina to "open the communications with the Indians . . . in the manner in which he [Sibley] proposes." Pope notified Halleck of the negotiations, and expressed hope the government could make "judicious" treaties with these bands. Pope adopted Sibley's relocation proposal, and set the distance at 250 miles, on pain of renewed hostilities.[10] At almost the same time Sully intended to hold council with "the largest of the bands of the hostile Sioux," the Yanktonais, and perhaps with the Blackfeet as well. Pope recommended that no easy truce be made with these Indians until another campaign, the next season, had punished them further. If Pope believed that the mailed fist had not descended hard enough to deter them from causing future trouble, he did not say so. Halleck was overjoyed to hear any talk of Indian tranquility. He wrote, "If General Sully can make a treaty of peace this fall with the Indians, I think it had better be done. If we want war in the spring, a few traders can get one up on the shortest notice."

It was not long before Pope informed the War Department that even should Sully secure the Yanktonais, a vigorous campaign against other Sioux tribes on the upper Missouri "will be necessary and judicious in the spring," although he believed Minnesota and Dakota now relatively safe from any more serious Indian damage. If Sully spoke to the Yanktonai and Blackfoot chiefs there is no record of it. The previous July, Sully reported the Sioux and Winnebagos could not sustain themselves on the Crow Creek Reservation, and were in bad shape. The Winnebagos were determined to visit their friends, the Omahas, while the Sioux planned to join other bands of their tribe elsewhere. The poor land chosen for the reservation, drought, and lack of protection from the hostile tribes were primary reasons for this exodus. Sully made no further mention of smoking the peace pipe.[11]

In the Northwest, Sibley sent former Sioux agent Major Jo-

[10] *Ibid.*, Part II, 569–70.
[11] *Ibid.*, 642; *Report of the Secretary of the Interior*, 1863, 442–43.

seph Brown with Father André to Pembina to induce the surrender of the Sioux in that area. Hatch's Battalion killed six
hostile Sioux in December, but Hatch reported no further word
from Standing Buffalo. Sibley cautioned Hatch to make no terms
with "the murdering remnant" of the lower bands in the vicinity
of Fort Garry (British America, later, Manitoba). Sibley believed there were from 800 to 1,000 Minnesota Sioux refugees
on the British side of the boundary, dangerous because the British had no force in the area to control them. He mentioned ex-
tradition, which Pope thought impractical since the number of
"criminals" was greater than the number of settlers who would
have to make arrests. So once again Pope applied to army headquarters for allowance to send Hatch after these Indians; and no
peace was made in that quarter during the winter.[12]

Sibley blamed the half-bloods on the Red River (British subjects who hunted and traded throughout the northern plains) for
continuing the war in the North. In Sibley's words

> The Red River half-breeds have succeeded in deterring them
> [the Sioux] from submitting to the Government. . . . It is for the
> interest of these half-breeds that non-intercourse between the
> Americans and the Sioux Indians should continue, as the trade
> with the latter is thereby secured to the British settlements. . . .
> In fact . . . the hostile Indians are directly aided and abetted by
> Her Majesty's subjects to so great an extent as to require the
> prompt interposition of the Government.[13]

Without orders from his superiors, Hatch, upon hearing that the
bands might negotiate, sent officers across the border to their
camp. These agents told the Sioux that any surrender would
have to be unconditional. Three of the chiefs, Little Six, Little
Leaf, and Medicine Bottle, declined the terms. However, a few
former Minnesota Sioux, believed to have been with Little Crow
in 1862, did come down and surrender at Pembina, and others
followed, until after a short time ninety men, women, and chil-

[12] *Official Records,* Series I, Vol. XXXIV, Part II, 29, 69, 100, 539–40.
[13] *Ibid.,* 152–53.

dren had come in. By June, the number dwindled to about eighty, and on June 3 Pope ordered these sent to Camp Kearny, Davenport, Iowa. Except for Little Leaf, the chiefs remained behind only to be virtually kidnapped, by three British citizens, and delivered to Hatch at Pembina. The state of Minnesota paid two of the conspirators, John H. McKenzie and Onezime Giguire, one thousand dollars for their efforts.[14] Sioux not involved in the massacre were held in confinement at Pembina until March 1864, when they agreed to remain in peace outside of Pope's 250 mile demarcation line. Little Six and Medicine Bottle were escorted to Snelling, tried by a military commission, and subsequently hanged.[15]

Then, in August, 1864, rumors of Chippewa dissatisfaction sifted into Sibley's headquarters at St. Paul. Fort Ripley's commander pictured Hole-in-the-day attempting to unite the Chippewas in a war on the whites, although not many redmen would follow the chief. Another informant disclosed a week later "Hole-in-the-day . . . sent tobacco tied with red tape to nearly all the chiefs," which was interpreted as a message to unite for war. On August 30 an alarming report of Sioux emissaries among the Chippewas excited Sibley. A. C. Morrill, the Chippewa agent, assured the military his wards were quiet, though Hole-in-the-day was dissatisfied with the treaty. The agent added "the taking away of these Indians and selling them as substitutes in St. Paul" created distress among the redmen. "The matter," Morrill continued, "is beyond my control, it being managed through mixed-bloods and by means of whiskey," and requested Sibley to do something about the situation. Sibley tried to stop the substitute brokers by extracting a provost marshal's promise to correct the evil. In June, Brigadier General Cook toured the Lake Superior Chippewa country and calmly and concisely reported,

[14] *Ibid.,* 314–15, 626, 713; Vol. XXXIV, Part IV, 209–10. *Minnesota in the Civil and Indian Wars,* 599–600; *Executive Documents of the State of Minnesota for the Year 1867,* 533.

[15] *Official Records,* Series I, Vol. XXXIV, Part III, 599–600, 622; *Minnesota in the Civil and Indian Wars,* 600.

"I . . . assure you there is no occasion for the least alarm in that region of the country." In mid-September the commander of Fort Abercrombie recorded a wandering Sioux scalped by the Red Lake Chippewas. As usual, it was those of the Mississippi bands who were the troublemakers.[16]

On November 15 Sibley found it necessary to order forty men of the Second Minnesota Cavalry to Chengwatona, Pine County, and the remainder of the company to Princeton, Sherburne County, "in consequence of the murders committed by individual Chippewas . . . and the alarm thereby produced among the people . . . manifested by their frequent and urgent applications." The inhabitants on the east side of the St. Croix River in the district of Wisconsin were also uneasy, Sibley reported. On November 23, Augustus Gaylord, adjutant general of Wisconsin, invited Pope's attention "to the existing troubles . . . upon the upper St. Croix." Gaylord cited the murder of three lumbermen, and the "feeling of insecurity . . . engendered among the settlers." He mentioned the governor's desire that "some measures be taken as shall deter the Indians from further hostilities."[17]

Captain John C. Hanley, Second Minnesota Cavalry, reported from Princeton on December 3 that the few Indians in the vicinity seemed to be very quiet. Lieutenant Patrick S. Gardner wrote from Chengwatona the same day that since there were no Indians in his vicinity, there was no trouble. Sibley's adjutant general replied to Hanley and Gardner, on December 8, directing them to appease the apprehensions of the settlers and to discourage whisky traders by denying them military protection. He cautioned them to maintain strict discipline among the soldiers and to use no unnecessary harshness in dealing with the Indians. On December 15, Hanley mentioned intelligence that the Chippewas in the Long Lake area had been quite arrogant in the fall, but were presently quiet. Samuel S. Fifield, Jr., editor of the *Polk County* (Wisconsin) *Press,* in answer to a query of Sibley's stated

[16] *Official Records,* Series I, Vol. XXXIV, Part IV, 576; Vol. XLI, Part II, 531, 591, 662, 946, 949–50; XLI, Part III, 38, 169, 196.
[17] *Ibid.,* Vol. XLI, Part IV, 579, 661.

that the people's fears were dying down, and added that he believed the liquor traffic was being carried on by persons from Taylor's Falls, Minnesota. No new Chippewa trouble was evident through January, 1865. But, as in past years, because of the wariness of the settlers and the mere presence of the Chippewas, they remained a latent threat to peace.

In regard to the wandering Winnebagos of Wisconsin, no settlement came as expected in the spring of 1864. Governor James T. Lewis of Wisconsin inquired into the situation, and forwarded to Pope a sheriff's complaint of law-breaking by this band. Pope reminded Lewis that this was a problem for the Indian Bureau, which disclaimed responsibility for these redmen. Pope continued, "It is believed that if the Interior Department has not charge of these Indians, no other department of the Government has." In instances of group hostilities, Pope expressed willingness to act, "but with cases of mere personal violation of the law committed by single Indians . . . the State laws and State authorities must deal."[18] Neither the Wisconsin officials nor the department seemed aware that "The various wandering fragments of tribes, Winnebagos, Pottawatomies, &c., which have hitherto given much trouble in northwestern Wisconsin, have been placed under the charge of a special agent." This agent, anonymous because he was neither mentioned by name nor reported to the Commissioner of Indian Affairs, apparently thought his charges sufficiently orderly so that a report was not necessary.

Again, in 1864, there was hope of peace with the Sioux. Captain John H. Pell wrote from Fort Sully about a visit of two hundred principal men of the Uncpapa Sioux and Blackfoot tribes, who told him that "we used to think we could fight like men, but now we know we can only fight like boys when we fight the whites" and that "we are sick of the war, for we cannot fight the whites any longer, and want peace." Pell told them they must first release a white prisoner they held to prove their sincerity. The Indians then bought the distraught woman from her captor for three horses. The adjutant asked for authority to repay these redmen their loss, although he made no bargain. He also wanted

[18] *Ibid.*, Part II, 31.

permission to make an agreement with them for a treaty conference in the future, and to feast them at the fort. He believed the Minneconjou and Sans-Arc bands of Sioux would make peace after they found the Uncpapas and Blackfeet had, but expressed doubt of the Yanktonais "as they have been tampered with by the traders of the north and offered munitions of war and a city of refuge in the British Possessions." Pell concluded, "their severe punishment in life and property for the last two years is an excellent groundwork for a peace that I believe would be lasting if they could only . . . be treated with justice and humanity instead of being preyed upon by a horde of Indian traders and speculators."[19]

On receipt of this report, Sully, on November 10, asked Pope for "a few thousand dollars . . . to make a treaty. . . . General, you know the Indians well enough to know . . . they judge a man by the length of his pocket. If a permanent peace can now be made . . . I look upon it as one of our greatest achievements in our Indian troubles, and I have every reason to believe it can be made." Sully allowed Pell to pay $200 "or three unserviceable horses and a lot of rations, &c." for the woman. Sully also asked Pell to tell the Indians he would send them word when he would come and make peace, and "that though the Government is determined to fight till they either exterminate them or have no more war . . . their great father would be glad to hear he had no more trouble with his red children."[20]

In mid-November Sully left for Milwaukee to discuss the situation with Pope. On November 17 Pope informed Halleck "a treaty of peace will be made with these Indians on the sole understanding that they do not commit any acts of hostility," said treaty to end with the first such act, "and no consideration [is] to be given on either side except that the Indians shall keep their peace and that the authorities . . . shall protect them against wrong from the whites. . . . Until the action of the War Depart-

[19] *Official Records,* Series I, Vol. LIII, 599–602. The woman mentioned was Mrs. Fanny Kelly. See Chapter 5, page 91.
[20] *Ibid.,* Vol. XLI, Part IV, 514–15, 847.

ment or of Congress shall be known I shall not permit intercourse between Indian agents and these Indians."[21]

But by January 1865 Sully as yet had made no truce, and had received no authorization for money to do so. Sully then relayed reports from his frontier officers to headquarters. Pell mentioned the destitute conditions of the Minneconjou and Sans-Arc Sioux, tells of their being "very anxious to come in and make peace," and suggested Fort Rice as a suitable place for this. From Fort Rice, Colonel Charles A. R. Dimon of the First U. S. Volunteers noted that the near-by Yanktonai were eager for conciliation, but others among them along with some Minnesota Sioux and mixed bloods were trying to keep the tribes as a whole from any such act. Captain Abraham B. Moreland of the Sixth Iowa Cavalry at Fort Berthold, protested against "half-breeds and whites (English and Scotch) from the Red River country . . . visiting and trading with the various bands . . . inhabiting this region, supplying them with arms and munitions . . . and inciting them to hostilities." Moreland added that many of the hostile bands desired a cessation of war due to want of supplies, but "so long as they are allowed to be tampered with by these itinerant vagabonds . . . all the efforts . . . to subdue them [will] be futile."[22]

Again, on January 22, Sully reported some minor trouble between his soldiers on the one hand and the Sioux bands of Uncpapas and Yanktonais on the other. "I hope," he remarked, "the authorities at Washington will take some action in regard to these Indians," for he thought a permanent concord would yet be easy to make. However, "there will always be some little trouble in that country so long as there is an Indian and a white man in it and the line of the British Possessions is so near." Another letter of Colonel Dimon's dated January 24, told of mixed blood traders from north of the border who visited a large Indian camp below Fort Berthold with ten sleigh-loads of freight, gave a feast, and promised the natives more goods before the month was out, including powder and arms. "They rode into the camp

[21] *Ibid.*, 544, 599–600.
[22] *Ibid.*, Vol. XLVIII, Part I, 438–39.

with the English flag at their head," Dimon expostulated as he asked for permission to break up these trading parties "and execute summary justice upon the principals." He thought that in all of this there was "a Confederate element at work." He requested more stringent rules governing traders and mentioned that there were ten of the latter, governed by no law, near Fort Sully, and others at Berthold. Dimon believed that the consequences of such influence would be felt in the spring, and he was afraid of them. Sully and Pope endorsed this report and sent it to Halleck. Moreland confirmed it all on January 31, and added a rumor of Cheyenne and other Platte River Indians camping near the Sioux below Berthold. He also pictured Berthold in peril, with only forty-nine men in a poor stockade surrounded by hostile tribes that threatened them daily.[23] Such was the unsettled condition of the upper Missouri at the beginning of 1865.

In October, 1864, Major Joseph Brown gathered intelligence regarding the Sioux in the area between the Missouri River and the Minnesota border. He reported that twenty-four lodges from Fort Thompson had moved east of the James for hunting purposes. He concluded, "Major Balcombe, Indian agent at Fort Thompson, has also been notified that the Indians [there] . . . would not be allowed to hunt or occupy any portion of the country east of the James; yet we find them moving toward the frontier in large numbers." If prompt steps are not taken to control them "the entire camp of Sioux located at Fort Thompson will be over here before winter sets in." This communique reached Sibley through Major Robert H. Rose, commander of Fort Wadsworth. A week later another message of Rose's told of some Sioux, with the expectation of more to follow, coming into the scout's camp on the James River with peaceable inclinations. Sibley wanted to use the scouts to keep the Sioux west of the river, and to warn of raiding parties from the west or the north; so he authorized the use of friendly Sisseton for this work. That they were not successful in keeping their brethren west of the "Jim" is noted in a later report of Brown's. Some Sioux had returned to the

[23] *Ibid.*, 614, 636–38, 700, 701.

old Yellow Medicine agency, a fact also attested to by Lieutenant Colonel Pfaender, commander of Fort Ridgely, on January 12, 1865.[24]

Sibley seconded Brown's suggestion that the friendly Sioux camped on the James be allowed to locate nearer Fort Wadsworth, and to plant crops in the spring, so that the expense of their subsistence would be diminished. Pope gave Sibley a free hand in the matter; but no action had been taken by the end of January, 1865.

[24] *Ibid.*, Vol. XLI, Part IV, 293, 408–10, 592–93, 909–11; Vol. XLVIII, Part I, 580.

9

It's a Little War After All

FOR A FEW MONTHS IN 1862, northwesterners forgot there was a fiercer fight elsewhere in the United States. They can be forgiven, however, because even after the awesome outbreak was over their fears told them that painted Indians with quick tomahawks skulked in every frontier thicket and behind every frontier tree. Behind oaken desks in Washington, federal bureaucrats might shrug off the uprising, but then for them the rebel yell was closer and louder and drowned out the Sioux war whoop.

This did not lessen the madness in Minnesota any. Who would help them whip the redman? The thorny question remained until Johnny Reb laid down his smoking gun. Even before federal authorities organized a special department, officials on the frontier had to face this problem. When John Pope arrived, the only experienced troops in his command were the Third Minnesota Volunteer Infantry, who, paroled after their surrender at Murfreesboro, joined Sibley before Pope appeared at St. Paul, and also some men of the unmustered Tenth Minnesota. Portions of Company I of that regiment had served with Captain E. St. Julian Cox at New Ulm, and the "Renville Rangers," another part, had been at Ridgely with Lieutenant James Gorman. Captain E. C. Saunders's "Le Sueur Tigers" were a part of Company C. Halleck had tried to send the Twenty-Fifth Missouri Volunteers, also paroled, to Pope, but they apparently were retained by General Samuel Curtis in the Department of Missouri.[1] Pope had authority to muster in the state volunteers of Iowa for nine months, provided they did not exceed a full cavalry regiment. He evidently did not take advantage of this power, since no record

[1] *Official Records*, Series I, Vol. XIII, 640–41; Vol. XXII, 128.

141

of such a muster is in the *Official Records* or the *Adjutant General's Report* for Iowa. The state volunteers alluded to must have been the Northern Border Brigade, the muster of which into United States service was unnecessary, because they were serving on border defense anyway.

According to the order constituting the Department of the Northwest, "the troops raised, and to be raised in that department . . . are hereby . . . under the command of Major-General Pope."[2] But there was some difficulty in making this effective. On September 18, Pope directed three hundred mounted men from Iowa to report at Sioux Falls, Dakota Territory. Brigadier General John M. Schofield protested to Halleck that "Pope is detaining Iowa regiments that have been ordered here [St. Louis]." Pope firmly insisted that those forces he requisitioned move to the frontier, after which the remainder of the Iowa troops could proceed to St. Louis. However, the only Iowa regiment that responded was the Twenty-Seventh Iowa Volunteer Infantry, and it did not join him until the first week in October.[3]

Pope did not fare much better with the troops raised in Wisconsin. He "requested the Governor of Wisconsin to send forward to this place [St. Paul] immediately three or four regiments now ready for service." This was on September 16. In Wisconsin, under Lincoln's call for an additional 300,000 men, six regiments had mustered: the Twenty-First, which had left the state on September 11, the Twenty-Second, which had departed on the 16th, the Twenty-Third, which had gone on the 15th, the Twenty-Fourth, which had marched on September 5, the Twenty-Fifth, which joined Pope on September 19, and the Twenty-Sixth, which had been raised among the German population of the state especially for General Franz Sigel, and which joined that division of the Army of the Potomac on October 6.[4] Seven

[2] *Ibid.*, Series I, Vol. XIII, 618.

[3] War Department, Adjutant General's Office, *Letter Books, Department of the Northwest*, Vol. I, 66, 69, (Mereness *Calendar* cards 75, 81); *Official Records*, Series I, Vol. XIII, 650, 663; Ingersoll, *Iowa and the Rebellion*, 540.

[4] *Official Records*, Series I, Vol. XIII, 642, 668; Quiner, *Military History of Wisconsin*, 134–36; *Letter Books, Department of the Northwest*, Vol. I, 17, 20, 25, 70 (Mereness *Calendar*, cards 19, 25, 30, 85).

other regiments were also authorized, the Twenty-Seventh through the Thirty-Third, but they were not filled up in time for Pope to use in the 1862 campaign. So Pope did not get very many of "the troops raised, or to be raised" in his department. Iowa's delay in sending the Twenty-Seventh left the department with only the Twenty-Fifth Wisconsin and the Minnesota regiments.

His search for men led Pope to think of the paroled troops too. He asked that those of the Third Dragoons, quartered at Fort Wayne, Michigan, be dispatched to his department, only to learn that they already had been exchanged. Stanton, who also saw the possibility of employing paroled forces in the Northwest, informed Pope that he would send him ten thousand. The original idea of using the paroled prisoners in this manner was a largely selfish one of David Tod, the governor of Ohio. The parolees at Camp Chase, Ohio, were unorganized, unpaid, and very unruly. Major General Lew Wallace was ordered to organize them "for service against the Northern Indians." Other troops at Annapolis, Maryland, were also to be transferred to St. Paul by way of Camp Douglas, near Chicago. Brigadier General Daniel Tyler was put in charge of this movement. But these soldiers were so undisciplined that organization was nearly impossible; besides which, after being paid off, they deserted in droves.[5] Before any of the paroled troops could reach the department, discussion and interpretation of the terms of the parole were so obscured that it was thought the men could not even be used against the Indians. Once again Pope found a closed door. However, the Twenty-Fifth Wisconsin Volunteers, and the elements of the Third, Fifth, Sixth, Seventh, Eighth, Ninth, and Tenth Minnesota regiments aggregated some 5,600 troops, about 1,200 of whom were not armed.[6]

[5] *Official Records,* Series I, Vol. XIII, 664, 669, 706; *ibid.,* Series II, Vol. IV, 417, 499, 522, 542, 563, 569–71, 596, 600. Paroled troops, if captured by the Confederates, would be subject to the death penalty, but when exchanged could legally fight in the South again. Thus, while on parole they might have been candidates for service in the Northwest, where their recapture would be unlikely.
[6] *Ibid.,* Series I, Vol. XIII, 669.

Pope not only worried about how to get troops, but also about putting those he had on horseback, or else getting some who were already mounted. He felt at a distinct disadvantage in this respect, since the Sioux were "all mounted," and he had no cavalry with which to pursue them. On September 25, Sibley had only twenty-five horsemen, and these were "far from efficient." Most of the mounted militiamen were not with Sibley's task force.[7]

The 1,000 horsemen that Ramsey called into service prior to August 25 were of little help in the later campaign. The War Department authorized a regiment of mounted infantry for three months' service, or "during such war unless sooner discharged," which was raised too late for the 1862 season. Before Pope had arrived, Ramsey had called on the War Department for 500 horses, and then for a regiment of cavalry that he needed "in less than a week." Sibley complained that the "lack of mounted men will tell badly . . . should the Indians determine to escape rather than to fight."[8]

One of Pope's first actions was to try to buy 2,500 horses for mounted infantry; also, he thought that two of the four regiments he expected from Wisconsin would be horse troops. He ordered a temporary mounted force raised in Nebraska. By September 25 the department was still innocent of any additional

[7] *Minnesota in the Civil and Indian Wars,* 736, 737, 743, 762, 765, 784, 790, 795, 796, 798, 805. The horsemen were disposed as follows:

Captain Ambrose Freeman's company of horsemen, seventy-five in number, were to the north, and had been organized for the relief of Fort Abercrombie; Captain C. L. Post's company of Fillmore County Volunteer Mounted Infantry, sixty-three strong, were with Flandrau on the southern Minnesota frontier; the Red Wing Cavalry, under the command of Captain P. Vanderberg, twenty-one men, served only one month in the north; the Roscoe County Mounted Militia, with Captain Fletcher Hegler and thirty-five men, served but thirty-three days in its own county; the Blue Earth City Cavalry, captained by J. B. Wakefield, forty-three in number, were under Flandrau in the south; Captain G. W. Taylor's Hastings Rangers, thirty-eight strong, served only twelve days; the twenty-three men of the Cullen Guard returned home when they found Ridgely safe; Captain Anderson's company was badly cut up at Birch Coulie, where they lost their horses. Apparently only a few of the mounted men of Captain Calvin Potter's company and Captain J. R. Sterret's company remained with Sibley under Colonel McPhail.

[8] *Official Records,* Series I, Vol. XIII, 596, 617, 620, 638; *Minnesota, Executive Documents,* 1862, 241–42, 247–48, 249–50.

Minnesota Historical Society

LITTLE CROW

A boy survivor of the Minnesota Massacre of 1862 identifies the attackers, as depicted by *Harper's Weekly*.

mounted men. Pope complained to Halleck, "I have no cavalry and see no hope of getting any. It is impossible to follow mounted Indians on foot." Sibley echoed these words back to Pope: "a pursuit with infantry alone is out of the question." Pope finally received around 2,000 horses, mounted the Third Minnesota and two companies of the Tenth Minnesota, and organized the First Regiment of Mounted Rangers (Minnesota), a battalion of which was ready before winter set in. By January, 1863, Sibley was reported to have 1,046 cavalry in his command.[9]

Attendant to the difficulties of increasing his forces, particularly with men on horseback, was the problem of obtaining wagons and harness for the supply trains of the columns in the field. On September 23 Pope took this matter up with Stanton. "We have no transportation of any description in this department, and few, if any, country wagons can be had. We must have here at least 500 wagons . . . sent without delay." Such facilities were scarce because Colonel Crooks and Captain Strout of Sibley's expedition had been empowered "to seize by force or otherwise, all necessary transportation." The same had been true for Dole's march to Ripley; also the sheriffs of Carver, Ramsey, Scott, and Dakota counties were given the same authority to find transport, and various militia organizations were similarly commissioned by the state. Even though the market had been swept before Pope arrived, this impressed material apparently was insufficient to begin with. For this reason, Pope's appeal to the War Department for wagons was justified, even though Stanton may not have thought so. The situation was further complicated since there was no purchasing organization. Pope's dispatch continued, "Some quartermaster ought to be sent to buy mules and get in trains. I have no officers of those departments here. If these things are not furnished soon it will be necessary to draw back the troops from the frontier."[10] To Halleck, on the same day, he complained, "I am acting as vigorously as I can, but without means. There is positively nothing here. It

[9] *Official Records*, Series I, Vol. XXII, Part II, 90.
[10] *Ibid.*, Vol. XIII, 662; *Minnesota, Executive Documents, 1862*, 269–294.

has been assumed that of course there would be no trouble, and everything has been taken away. There is not a wagon, mule, or horse belonging to the United States in this department."[11] These letters to Stanton and Halleck were made necessary by Stanton's dispatch to Halleck on the same day:

> The large requisition made by Major-General Pope under the Quartermaster's Department and the Commissary and Ordnance Departments, involving . . . an immense expenditure of . . . material needed elsewhere, requires . . . some order defining the extent of [Pope's] operations . . . whatever is sent to General Pope will leave a deficiency . . . in other branches.[12]

And also by Halleck's message to Pope: "Your requisitions . . . are beyond all our expectations . . . moreover, they cannot be filled without taking supplies from other troops now in the field. The organization of a large force . . . is not approved."[13]

Pope's communications apparently contained enough information for Halleck and Stanton to send advice, if not wagons and mules, two days later:

> It will be impossible to give you all the supplies you ask for, but all that is possible will be done. Move very light and keep down transportation . . . supplies can probably be transported by contract, using the wagons and teams of the settlers who have been driven from their homes. . . . Temporary expedients will be resorted to for moving your supplies.

Pope scarcely could be blamed for his angry retort: "It is impossible to get wagons in the country. Three days have been spent in getting eleven two-horse wagons to move some companies. I have no means to keep them supplied."[14]

Sibley also agreed with Pope on the matter of wagons. From his position in the field he wrote Pope on September 27, "I must

11 *Official Records*, Series I, Vol. VIII, 664.
12 *Ibid.*, 658.
13 *Ibid.*, 663.
14 *Ibid.*, 670.

now await the arrival of a provision train . . . it may not reach us for three or four days, in which case my command will be reduced to the verge of starvation." Sibley remarked that his troops were inadequately supplied with food and had to dig potatoes from the Indian fields in order to subsist. Again on October 7 he told Pope:

> I still labor under the difficulty of lacking forage and rations. I have to use my own teams, which should be kept for active operations in the field, to transport provisions from Ridgely, and they are barely able to keep the command from actual suffering. Some speedy measures should be taken to correct this.[15]

Hope of obtaining other than local contract teams and wagons faded for the 1862 season on October 13 with the receipt of the following from Halleck: "The Secretary of War directs that no more quartermaster's and commissary stores be collected in your department than may be necessary for winter's supply. At present the demands for means of transportation elsewhere are so great as to absorb all that can possibly be procured."

Problems of arms facing the Department of the Northwest were no more acute than those encountered in almost any of the military departments, and since Pope took command when forces were already armed and in the field, this particular problem caused him less concern than the others. Appeals for weapons by the governors of the territories and of Iowa, Wisconsin, and Minnesota have already been noted. Ramsey had managed to obtain 500 Prussian muskets and 10,000 cartridges from Illinois as late as the day Pope arrived, with 492 Austrian rifled muskets and 4,500 Prussian muskets and full equipment including 375,-000 rounds of ammunition, from Ohio two days later. Wisconsin had sent 25,000 rounds of ammunition on August 25. The mustering officer at Fort Snelling turned over to Ramsey 150,000 cartridges on August 24 and 29. An adjutant general's record dated December 1, 1862, but including no acquisitions after

[15] *Ibid.,* 717.

September 25, 1862, showed the state had on hand 1,698 rifled muskets, 7,683 muskets, 1,841 rifles, and 925,000 rounds of ammunition. The Sixth, Seventh, Eighth, Ninth, and Tenth regiments were armed from this stock, and 1,924 muskets and rifles along with 60,230 rounds of ammunition and some powder and lead went out to volunteer militia and to citizens. This did not mean all units were well armed. A part of the Third Minnesota that marched to the relief of Fort Abercrombie with Captain Emil A. Burger, refused to use an obsolete lot of Belgian muskets. They took instead squirrel guns, shotguns, and even long Kentucky rifles. The weapons of Company C of the Fifth Minnesota at Ripley were described as "old Brown rifles" which had no bayonets and no suitable ammunition. But when these soldiers were alerted to possible attack by Hole-in-the-day, they worked by candlelight to manufacture cartridges. Colonel Crooks, at his first inspection of the Sixth Minnesota found them equipped with Belgian rifles without proper ammunition. He thereupon set his men to the task of "swedging the bullets to fit the rifles" in order to ready them for battle. Usually troops so ill equipped received more adequate arms, as in the case of Company A of the Sixth Minnesota. They spent the winter of 1862–63 at Fort Ripley, where their Belgian muskets were replaced with Austrian rifles, which in turn were replaced by spring with Springfield rifles. The men of Company A, Dakota Cavalry, were slightly more fortunate. They had been issued Sharps carbines at the very beginning.[16]

Ammunition was not always plentiful but usually was adequate. An exceptional case was the Renville Rangers, who, overtaken on their way to Fort Snelling by couriers bringing the alarm of the outbreak, managed to arm themselves at St. Peter with Harper's Ferry muskets, and returned to Ridgely with only three rounds apiece. The lack of arms or ammunition or both from time to time was not unique in the Northwest, and was on the whole analogous to the general situation.[17]

[16] *Minnesota in the Civil and Indian Wars*, 161, 258, 304, 386–87; *Minnesota, Executive Documents, 1862*, 526–31, 534–38, 538–39.

The Indians, on the other hand, were not merely supplied with bows, arrows, and lances. The more or less standard weapon they carried was the double-barreled shotgun which fired either buckshot or large-caliber bullets they called "traders balls." Otherwise, they used whatever arms they could find. The irony of this situation is that one branch of the government, the Indian Bureau of the Interior Department, gave the guns to the Indians under the annuity heading of their treaties, while another branch of the same government, the War Department, had the responsibility of seeing that the Indians kept the peace.[18]

The problem of ammunition supply was not as critical as that of insuring transportation of it or of assuring that the right caliber was sent to the right place. At Birch Coulie, in battle, soldiers broke out 3,000 rounds of shot only to find that it was .62-caliber, though the men were carrying .58-caliber rifles. Here, as in the case of the Sixth Minnesota, the men had to whittle the balls down. Again, at Fort Ridgely, during the attack, the troops had to resort to use of spherical case-shot and nail-rods, cut in short pieces, in order to keep firing. The nail segments made such an unusual sound when fired it was said their "dismal whistling . . . was as terrifying to the savages as were their [the Indians'] fiendish yells to the garrison."[19] The psychological advantages of this strange noise doubtless did little to substitute for the sense of security a plentiful supply of standard ammunition could have given. After the first shock of the attacks, however, the situation became less pressing. On September 15, Sibley was able to send powder and shot from his supply to Flandrau, who was in com-

---

[17] *Official Records,* Series III, Vol. I, 272, 468, 513, 533, 624; for Iowa see also Cyril B. Upham, "Arms and Equipment for Iowa Troops," *The Iowa Journal of History and Politics,* Vol. 16, No. 1 (January, 1918), 3–52; for Wisconsin and Nebraska Territory see *Official Records,* Series III, Vol. I, *passim;* for Dakota Territory, *ibid.,* Series I, Vol. XIII, esp. p. 617. For a discussion of the problem of munitions supply on a general level, see Shannon, *Organization and Administration of the Union Army,* Vol. I, 107–48.

[18] "Report of Major General Pope," p. 192; *Report of the Secretary of the Interior,* 1864, pp. 184, 430–31.

[19] *Minnesota in the Civil and Indian Wars,* 254, 308.

mand in the south. And four days later Sibley told Pope that he had enough small-arms cartridges, about eighty rounds a man.[20]

The transportation bottleneck was even more acute in foodstuffs. Ammunition for a week or two, depending upon the situation, could be carried by the soldier, but food was too bulky and spoiled rapidly. Beef was usually driven along on the hoof, wherever possible, but items like potatoes and bread generally had to be hauled in. Forage for the teams, the cavalry horses, and the beef cattle also had to be supplied after the prairie grass dried in the fall. Sibley's main problem was bread, because of scarce transport.

> I have but ten days' bread rations . . . and no supply nearer than St. Peter, nearly 50 miles distant . . . unless speedily provided for I must fall back . . . We have no means of cooking flour. Send hard bread therefore instead. . . . Forage is not to be found at Fort Ridgely, and efforts should not be spared to have oats and hay received there.[21]

This was on September 19. The ten days' supply lasted only six days, and Sibley reported,

> My troops are entirely unsupplied with sufficient rations and are necessitated to dig potatoes from Indian fields to supply the want of breadstuffs. . . . Half the command [has] . . . been two days without bread . . . [and] in three or four days my command will be without a ration of any kind.[22]

Three days later Sibley said his men

> would be in a starving state but for the potatoes found in the Indian fields. . . . A full supply of provisions and forage [must be] sent on at once. . . . The grass is already so dry as to afford insufficient nourishment to the horses and cattle. . . . This corps is

[20] *Official Records,* Series I, Vol. XIII, 638, 652.
[21] *Ibid.,* 652.
[22] *Ibid.,* 679.

absolutely at a stand for . . . the want of necessary provisions and forage.

A week later, on October 7, he was "barely able to keep the command from actual suffering."[23]

This was characteristic of Sibley's reports from the time his expedition went into the field until it returned. It was fortunate the farmer Indians put in a good crop. When he accounted for Sibley's requisitions on the Indian reservation lands, Galbraith stated:

All these [Sibley's troops, released captives, and captive Indians] remained on the reservations until the 9th day of November, in all, on an average, say fifty days.

How much all these men, women, and children, horses, oxen, and ponies consumed in these fifty days I know not. The "rank and file" I know were by no means liberally supplied with rations . . . the horses had little forage besides corn, and the Indians literally lived on corn and potatoes and beef. . . .

I state only my own conclusions when I assert that more than one-half of the actual subsistence of the . . . expedition . . . were obtained from the Indian plantings.

In justice to General Sibley I must say that . . . it was utterly impossible for him to have kept even an approximate account of the things just used. . . . I expect, every reasonable account will be given [by Pope] of the property taken possession of by the Army.[24]

Apparently Galbraith expected the War Department to pay the Interior Department, as administrators for annuity trusts, for Sibley's forage, without which any decisive move for the defeat of the Sioux would have been seriously impaired.

The ambitious plan Pope conceived, upon taking over in September, 1862, was thwarted partly because of the shortages of troops and transportation, but also because of another element— time. Sibley commented:

[23] *Ibid.*, 694, 717.
[24] *House Executive Document* No. 68, 35

151

> Your plans . . . of sending a large force to strengthen me and
> to move upon the Indians from other points at the same time are
> admirable, and I only fear they will partially fail by reason of
> the lateness of the season and the difficulty of organizing expe-
> ditions . . . with new troops before the cold weather sets in.[25]

Even had the season for the Indian warfare not been so advanced,
Pope soon found other obstacles in the way of his proposed un-
dertaking. He had to fight his battles without material interference with the needs of troops and the bulk of supplies destined
for the war in the South. On the frontier it was a little war,
after all.

It was as difficult to retain troops as to find them, because of
the unceasing demand to release soldiers for service in the South.
In mid-September Major General John M. Schofield had complained that Pope was holding back Iowa troops, and Pope had
to release them. The Secretary of War hoped Pope "will not de-
tain in your department any more troops than are absolutely
necessary . . . and that you will send the rest forward immediately." By October 4 Pope told Halleck his regiments were ready
to head south as soon as they could be relieved, and inquired
where he was to send several Wisconsin regiments. He still believed Minnesota troops would be replaced by paroled men. On
October 13 he was informed no paroled units would arrive. Even
so, the next day Pope wrote Halleck that "all troops from Wisconsin and Iowa can be at once sent" wherever Halleck wanted
them, although he believed one infantry regiment should remain
in Iowa over the winter for safety's sake, and to participate in
the spring campaigns. However Halleck ordered South all troops
"not otherwise directed." This seemed to apply to five regiments
each from Minnesota and Wisconsin, and six from Iowa. On November 1, Halleck wanted the three companies of the Fifth Minnesota, who had borne the brunt of the early fighting, sent to
rejoin their regiment. While Pope went to Washington in December, Halleck ordered Sibley to send all the troops he could

[25] *Official Records,* Series I, Vol. XIII, 652.

spare down the Mississippi. Sibley was willing to relinquish the soldiers Pope had already decided to release, but added "I cannot spare another man. The Indians of the plains are gathering for a general onslaught as soon as the weather permits."[26] After this, for the remainder of the winter, the War Department did not press the Department of the Northwest by demands for troops.

During the first winter, the Third Minnesota was reorganized, assembled at Winona on January 16, 1863, and went south again a week later. Two companies of the Fifth Minnesota joined their regiment December 12 in time for Grant's expedition into central Mississippi, and the third followed February 14. The Sixth, Seventh, Eighth, Ninth, and Tenth Minnesota were spread out over the frontier. The Renville Rangers, supposed to be a part of Company I, Tenth Regiment, held that they were state militia enlisted for only three months. One suspects that there was a personality issue involved, since the promotion of M. J. Severance, a private, to captain, solved the difficulties. All that is known of the First Minnesota Mounted Rangers is that the first battalion "was sent out to the frontier as soon as organized, and remained there all winter. . . . The remainder of the regiment was stationed . . . at various places in the state." In an organizational stage was the Third Minnesota Battery of Light Artillery. The reasons for disposing the troops in scattered bodies all along the frontier were two-fold. First, of course, was the motive of protection. Even though many of the Minnesota Sioux had been captured, those who had been scattered could not help but have a hard winter without their annuity or any supplies of their own, and could be expected to move against the settlements to get food.[27] Secondly, there was doubtless not enough room at the forts to quarter all of the regiments.

The Twenty-Fifth Wisconsin, relieved from its Minnesota duty, assembled at Winona on December 13, and moved from there

---

[26] *Official Records,* Vol. XIII, 650, 663, 668, 709, 733, 734, 737, 739, 761, 772; Vol. XXII, Part I, 880.

[27] Robinson, "History of the Sioux," 308.

to Camp Randall. They were marched South on February 17. The Thirtieth Wisconsin spent most of the winter doing odd jobs in its home state. In October the Twenty-Seventh Iowa Volunteer Infantry arrived for a month's stay at Fort Snelling, then reported to General William Tecumseh Sherman at Memphis in November. On the official return for January, 1863, there was no change in the number of troops in Cook's military district; Sibley reported nearly 1,000 fewer; Elliott noted the Thirtieth Wisconsin, the Thirty-First Wisconsin, an unidentified company at Bayfield, and a company of about sixty paroled men at Superior.[28]

Pope tried his best to keep only necessary forces on hand and to release others for the larger war. In 1863 while the Sirocco campaigners were hiking across heated prairies, Pope attempted to estimate his own needs for the following year. In a letter to Halleck on August 20 Pope proposed to send south four of the five regiments of infantry and one battery of artillery now in Minnesota. He requested authority to reenlist the First Minnesota Mounted Rangers, whose enlistments were to expire October 1. Pope thought he could secure the frontier in Minnesota with one regiment of infantry and 500 mounted men, or roughly 1,500 troops.[29]

In a confidential report to Stanton the following week, the General mentioned his plan to station the Sixth Iowa Cavalry on the upper Missouri at Forts Randall and Pierre. For Minnesota he reiterated his words to Halleck, but included Hatch's Battalion among those he did not want to release. To Sully, he commanded that "some cavalry force" be stationed for the winter in the neighborhood of Fort Pierre, and also at Randall and Sioux City and enough points east of Sioux City to secure Dakota and Iowa. To Sibley, Pope again repeated his plans and suggested this disposition of troops within the District of Minnesota: three companies of infantry and one hundred mounted men at Abercrombie, the same at Ripley, and ten companies of in-

[28] Quiner, *Military History of Wisconsin*, 735, 789–90; Ingersoll, *Iowa and the Rebellion*, 540–41.
[29] *Official Records*, Series I, Vol. XXII, Part II, 90; Quiner, *Military History of Wisconsin*, 790, 793–94; *Minnesota in the Civil and Indian Wars*, 162–63, 264.

fantry and one hundred mounted men at Ridgely. He would then divide "the other two companies of infantry" into squads of twenty and sprinkle these along the frontier. The other seven hundred mounted men he would have patrol the frontier. This would have been good distribution had there existed an eighteen-company regiment of infantry, but, be that as it may, he concluded by asking for Sibley's views.[30]

On September 12 Sibley recommended that two regiments of infantry be retained, a modest request since Pope tentatively planned to use eighteen companies. Halleck gave Pope permission to remuster the First Minnesota Mounted Rangers, and also told Pope that any men he could spare should be sent down the Mississippi to St. Louis. On September 15 both Halleck and Schofield inquired after Pope's troops. He replied the surplus would be sent as soon as possible but that all had not yet reached Snelling. Again on October 3 Halleck asked about the regiments Pope was supposed to dispatch to St. Louis. On October 11 Pope received orders to send the Eighth Iowa Cavalry, raised at Davenport during the summer, to General William S. Rosecrans. Sibley sent the Seventh Minnesota, which departed on October 7, the Ninth Minnesota, which left Snelling the next day, and the Tenth Minnesota, which departed the same day as the Seventh.[31]

The departure of these regiments left Sibley with the Sixth Minnesota, the Eighth Minnesota, the Third Minnesota Battery, and Hatch's Battalion. The First Minnesota Mounted Rangers began to muster out on October 20, and the last company was dismissed December 10. However, their remuster into an organization called the Second Minnesota Volunteer Cavalry Regiment was slow, covering a period beginning in November and lasting until mid-February. There were many new recruits and mostly all new officers. Their new colonel was Robert N. McLaren, promoted from major of the Sixth Minnesota. In De-

[30] *Official Records,* Series I, Vol. XXII, Part II, 464, 493, 496, 497.

[31] *Ibid.,* 512, 513, 516, 534, 601; Part I, p. 911; *Adjutant General's Report, Iowa, 1864,* iv, vi, 12, 104 ff; *Minnesota in the Civil and Indian Wars,* 355, 418, 461.

cember Sibley reported an aggregate of 3,011 men in his department.[32] Sully lost only the Second Nebraska, which, as the First Minnesota Rangers, had only enlisted for one year's service. A change in district lines made one district out of the state of Iowa and Dakota Territory, with Sully as the commander, relieving Roberts. The only change in the District of Wisconsin was the transfer of two companies of the Thirtieth Wisconsin to Dakota Territory.[33]

In response to Pope's order that a cavalry force be stationed in the neighborhood of Fort Pierre, Sully built a fort, unofficially bearing his name, on the east bank of the Missouri River near Farm Island. The Sixth and Seventh Iowa Cavalry, the Dakota Cavalry, and three companies of the Thirtieth Wisconsin garrisoned Forts Sully, Thompson (on the Crow Creek Reservation), and Randall, as well as Davenport, Iowa, and Yankton, Dakota Territory.[34]

In Iowa, the adjutant general of the state ordered the Northern Border Brigade disbanded as of September 26 with the exception of one company to serve "until relieved by U. S. troops" or unless sooner discharged by the governor. In late October, Sully corresponded with Iowa's adjutant general. Sully was reluctant to replace the militia, but Pope doubted if they would be accepted for United States service. Troops of the Sixth Iowa Cavalry garrisoned the Iowa frontier posts shortly before Christmas.[35]

---

[32] *Official Records,* Series I, Vol. XXII, Part II, 767; *Minnesota in the Civil and Indian Wars,* 525–42, 552–71, 708.

[33] *Official Records,* Series I, Vol. XXII, Part II, 131, 137, 730–31, 767; Vol. XXXIV, Part II, 652.

[34] *Ibid.,* Vol. XXXIV, Part II, 210–11; English, "Dakota Cavalry," p. 270 n. 94. English, in "Dakota Cavalry," is mistaken in his belief that Company K of the Sixth Iowa occupied Fort Thompson, and that a battalion of the Sixth occupied Fort Sully. The official report would have three companies of the Seventh Iowa at Sully (K, L, and M). So it must have been either Company K of the Seventh Iowa or a detachment of the same at Fort Thompson. Three companies of the Seventh Iowa Cavalry, along with two companies of the Thirtieth Wisconsin Infantry were stationed there. Fort Randall was garrisoned by one company of Dakota Cavalry, at Yankton, Dakota Territory. The Sixth Iowa Cavalry was at Sioux City. At Davenport, Iowa, one company of the Thirtieth Wisconsin was posted. One company of the Seventh Iowa relieved a detachment of the Dakota Cavalry at Fort Thompson on the Crow Creek Reservation.

Over in Minnesota Pope directed Hatch's Battalion to Pembina, as Sibley had suggested earlier. The battalion got off to a slow start October 5, and various details slowed the march. It took them ten days to reach Sauk Center. From there to Pembina, they plowed through eight to twelve inches of snow, and lost many of their animals. They arrived in mid-November. One section of the Third Minnesota Artillery Battery accompanied Hatch to Pembina.[36] The Second Minnesota Cavalry remained at Fort Snelling while in an organizational state, but "a number of the companies were ordered to garrison posts on the Minnesota frontier." The Sixth Minnesota made headquarters at St. Peter and rotated companies and parts of companies between Forts Ridgely and Snelling and the villages of Fairmont, Kingston, Lake Hanska, Big Cottonwood, Watonwan River, Camp Wilkin, Buffalo Creek, Fort Burnes, Forest City, Swan Lake, Chanyaska, Mankato, and Madelia. The Eighth Minnesota maintained the same posts it occupied the previous summer and fall, while the Third Minnesota Artillery Battery, broken into sections, was at Ripley, Ridgely, Snelling, and Pembina. A detachment of the Tenth Minnesota regiment, which had moved south in October, apparently was still at St. Cloud as late as January 31, 1864, according to Sibley's report. Smith's District of Wisconsin still included seven companies of the Thirtieth Wisconsin at Camp Washburn, Milwaukee.[37]

The matter of troops for the spring exercises brought little comment except on the part of Sibley, who quite justifiably worried about sufficient frontier protection. Probably the biggest headache that beset him was the proposal to send the newly formed Second Minnesota Volunteer Cavalry and the veteran Sixth Minnesota Volunteer Infantry south. On February 5, 1864, the adjutant general's department in Washington inquired about the state of organization of the Second Minnesota Cavalry, which

[35] *Adjutant General's Report, Iowa, 1864*, 669–73.

[36] *Official Records*, Series I, Vol. XXII, Part II, 569; *Minnesota in the Civil and Indian Wars*, 595–97.

[37] *Minnesota in the Civil and Indian Wars*, 387, 543, 672; *Official Records*, Series I, Vol. XXXIV, Part II, 211.

meant to Sibley its early removal from the state. Sibley unburdened his fears to Pope, who thought some other organization could take its place before it would be needed in the department; and the Second was ordered without delay to General Nathaniel P. Banks at New Orleans. Sibley protested that the Second "was raised to replace the First Minnesota Mounted Rangers . . . [and was] authorized expressly for frontier defense." This reminder prompted Pope to ask Halleck if there was not some mistake in ordering the Second Minnesota south, and Halleck revoked the order.[38]

This particular type of military inefficiency, characteristic even in the following years, did not plague the Sixth Minnesota, although some confusion prevailed. Its officers applied to replace the First Minnesota Volunteer Infantry, due for muster out, in the Army of the Potomac. Sibley hoped the men of the First might largely re-enlist, in which case that regiment could then change places with the Sixth. By February, 1864, Sibley was aware that there was little likelihood of many veterans of the First re-enlisting, and so withdrew the application of the Sixth to go south. Agitation for this transfer, however, continued undiminished in the local press and by Minnesotans in Washington. On March 27, Pope received a directive assigning the Sixth to the Second Corps, Army of the Potomac, and immediately asked for a suspension in the execution of the order until after the coming campaign. Sibley did not care whether or not the Sixth left, provided he had a replacement of equal strength. But on April 2 the War Department consented to the retention of the Sixth in the department until the men could safely be spared.

On May 25, a few days before the Minnesota Brigade was to leave for its Missouri River rendezvous with Sully, an urgent telegram came from Halleck: "You will immediately send the Sixth Minnesota Regiment to Helena, Ark." Pope replied the next day, "Sixth Minnesota goes this evening to Cairo by rail." His order to Sibley said "the disasters in Arkansas and Louisiana

[38] *Official Records*, Series I, Vol. XXXIV, Part II, 250, 303–304, 340, 348.

make it absolutely necessary that the Sixth Regiment go south. You will please put it in motion for Cairo by rail without delay."[39] There was no way to keep the Sixth, as there had been to keep the Second, or even to replace it before the expedition took the field. This loss nearly upset plans for the Badlands campaign. Pope began his search for more troops to strengthen the campaign army by asking Major General Samuel P. Curtis if he could spare one battalion of the Seventh Iowa Cavalry or a battalion of the Second Nebraska for the summer. He also telegraphed Halleck that he needed one of these, if Curtis could lend one, or else he would have to have Brackett's Minnesota Battalion. Curtis replied, of course, that he could not spare a man. The Second Nebraska Cavalry had been mustered out, and the Seventh Iowa Cavalry was scattered along the overland stage line. Regarding Brackett's Battalion, Halleck had asked on March 15 if Pope intended keeping it on the frontier. Pope had then indicated his desire for either Brackett or troops from General Curtis; and, after the Sixth was called south, it was no longer a question of desire but necessity. On March 21 the battalion was officially ordered to remain in the department.

From the first, Brackett's men were destined to service with Sully in lieu of other cavalry. Sully also applied to Pope, and Pope to Halleck, for two hundred frontiersmen that he might "raise by enlistment or by hire" for duty with his expedition. Halleck had not answered Pope within two weeks, so Pope telegraphed for a reply. Halleck approved such an enlistment prior to Pope's telegram.[40]

The Invalid Corps, organized by the War Department under General Order No. 105, April, 1863, controlled by the Provost Marshal General's Department, caused friction in the department, which was duly reported to Halleck in October, 1863. "In several instances," Pope wrote,

detachments of the invalid corps . . . have been stationed by

[39] *Ibid.*, pp. 348–49, 626, 744–45, 766, 805; Part III, 17, 23, 33, Part IV, 40, 56–57.
[40] *Ibid.*, Series I, Vol. XXXIV, Part II, 480–81, 608, 622, 699–700.

orders from the provost-marshal-general, at military posts occupied by troops on duty in this department. The question is, how far such detachments are under the control of the military commanders at those posts. . . . This . . . is especially troublesome at Fort Snelling . . . and Camp McClellan. . . . I . . . recommend . . . the invalid corps . . . be subject to the general authority of the post commander.

Halleck did not answer Pope; Sibley gave the impression they were under some control of his when he included them in his district returns. Sully did not report them, nor did Smith. Not until March 5, 1864, was there some clarification for Pope which, in its sweeping redefinition, modified the original orders that had given him command of all the troops "raised or to be raised" in his department. Now, by official decision of the Adjutant General's Office, he no longer had any control over "all new organizations . . . as well as recruits for odd regiments and over veteran regiments on furlough, together with detachments of the Invalid Corps." Obviously, this came as a disappointment, but it did enable Pope to withdraw the Thirtieth Wisconsin from their monotonous draft duties and other assignments to the local provost marshals and use them in the coming campaign.[41]

The sudden movement of the Sixth Minnesota to the south and the decision to use the Thirtieth Wisconsin brought the Veterans Reserve Corps (as the Invalid Corps was renamed in March, 1864) under Pope's command as of June 1. When the Sixth was ordered out of the department, Pope telegraphed for permission to replace the four companies of the Thirtieth Regiment in garrison duty with an equal number of the Veterans Reserve. The provost marshal general turned all "not absolutely required for recruiting" over to Pope, and, to the extent the department was reinforced by these units, this offset the loss in expeditionary troops.

After the Badlands campaign, the troops occupied their winter stations. Troops stationed at posts such as Fort Abercrombie

[41] *Ibid.*, Series III, Vol. III, 170–72; Series I, Vol. XXII, Part II, 683–84, 767; Vol. XXXIV, Part II, 211, 511.

Harper's Weekly sketch, "Execution of thirty-eight Indian murderers at Mankato, Minnesota."

Cavalry charge of Sully's Brigade at the Battle of White Stone Hill, September 3, 1863, from an officer's sketch in *Harper's Weekly*.

usually had detachments garrisoning near-by areas, such as Pomme de Terre and Alexandria, while the soldiers of Ridgely maintained frontier strong points both north and south of the fort, and furnished escort for supply trains to other frontier posts when needed.

Two of Pope's veteran regiments left for the South late in 1864. Part of the Thirtieth Wisconsin departed from Minnesota in October, and the rest, except for the company at Fort Union, went down the Missouri from Dakota Territory the first of November. Their destination was Atlanta. The Eighth Minnesota embarked in October also, and arrived in time to join Sherman on his march to the sea.[42] The replacements for these regiments were the former Confederates who had taken the oath of allegiance and who were recruited into the First United States Volunteers and the Connecticut Cavalry. The companies of the Veterans Reserve Corps listed on the departmental returns were intended for garrison duty to replace the other troops that took the place of the Sixth Minnesota in the Badlands expedition. Hatch's Battalion was increased by two companies in September. Actually, the increment counterbalanced the withdrawals, since the December returns showed 5,636 men compared with the lists of the preceding June, which accounted for 5,159, an aggregate gain of nearly five hundred.[43]

On October 17, Sibley sent Pope word that "through remissness or connivance of the guard nearly half of some companies of the Eighth Regiment left camp last night and have gone home." The Eighth, under orders to the South, had been on the move constantly for nearly five months, and because no furlough intervened before they were to join Sherman they took their own leave. Pope ordered the arrest and dismissal of any officers implicated, and Sibley sent his adjutant general, Captain Rollin C. Olin, to investigate. No officers were implicated. The event was planned without their knowledge. The affair shocked Sibley, who told Pope, "I need not state that the reported breach of dis-

[42] *Ibid.*, Series I, Vol. XLI, Part IV, 260, 324, 515, 996.
[43] *Ibid.*, Part III, 37, 131, 625; Part IV, 995; Vol. XXXIV, Part IV, 628.

cipline . . . has mortified me not a little and causes . . . humiliation to the officers." With nearly all absentees present, the Eighth embarked on October 26. The historian of this regiment, while seeming to apologize for their conduct, does not mention this episode. However, he does record their refusal to ride in cattle cars southward from Chicago. If not discipline, the regiment had spirit.[44]

Halleck forever seemed to be asking Pope to send forces to the South, and Pope, to his credit, complied as faithfully as he believed he could. Yet both politicians and citizens by turns clamored for more men to defend them, protested the denuding of frontier stations, urged the enrolling of pet units (such as Hatch's Battalion), complained of the department's maintaining too many troops, or demanded favorite organizations be bathed in blood in the South. An example of this last instance occurred in November, 1864, when Asabel W. Hubbard, an Iowa politician, wrote Stanton that "the expedition against the Indians is now at an end, but still some 2,000 or 3,000 men are retained . . . above this place [Sioux City]. This number . . . is not required for this service. . . . The officers and men of the Sixth Iowa Cavalry . . . desire to go south, and I request that this regiment be ordered south immediately." This letter eventually was referred back to Sully, who replied, "In regard to the letter from A. W. Hubbard . . . I have the honor to state I have nearly 2,000 men . . . not 2,000 or 3,000. . . . These men garrison posts from Fort Union to Sioux City, and from there north to the Minnesota frontier. Take from these . . . the sick" and men on other duty "and it will leave about 1,500 . . . not a very large force." There was an effort also, on behalf of the officers of the Sixth Minnesota as well as the newspapers and some citizens, to effect the transfer of that regiment south in the late winter and spring of 1863. As it happened, this regiment did leave by June, but not because of public pressure.[45]

[44] *Ibid.*, Series I, Vol. XLI, Part IV, 63, 102, 125, 260; *Minnesota in the Civil and Indian Wars*, 394–95.

[45] *Official Records,* Series I, Vol. XXXIV, Part II, 348–49, 744; Vol. XLI, Part IV, 481, 652.

Even though the Department of the Northwest and the War Department bickered over the sending or retaining of troops over the years, Halleck, in a letter to Grant, August 17, 1864, remarked "I have found him [Pope] the most ready of all the department commanders to give assistance to others when asked." To facilitate the release of some of his veteran units, replacements of several types were urged. The use of paroled troops did not materialize in any substantial way, but the use of United States Volunteers promised to solve the problem, although they created a few difficulties of their own for the department. According to one source, they were excellent soldiers; but they did not behave very well in Sibley's district. He recommended they be supervised very closely. The Veterans Reserve Corps was useful in garrison duty, and released other units for the field.[46]

Although the affair in the Northwest was a sideshow to the activity in the center ring, there can be no question that the two were intimately connected by chains of command and necessities of supply, transport, and manpower. In actuality the problems of the Department of the Northwest were not so different from, for example, the Department of Virginia. In any military action there is always the demand for more supplies, more transport, more troops. The unique feature in the Northwest was keeping troops there to carry on campaigns and watch the Indians. It is a testimony to the strength of the Union that men and material could be spared to fight on the frontier.

[46] *Ibid.*, Series I, Vol. XLI, Part IV, 292, 397; Pattee, "Dakota Cavalry," 320.

10

Politics and Prima Donnas

IT MAY HAVE BEEN A LITTLE WAR, but the blues occasionally sung on its stage drowned out the beat of the tom-toms. Pride and jealousy have little place in the military picture, but because these are human failings, military men experience them, too. Such feelings even may exist when there is but one human, and when there are many, they are multiplied geometrically. This result is also intensified when the stakes are higher, and when the men in command are so troubled, their emotions seem to surpass those of men in lesser positions. Certainly pride, perhaps even jealousy, and surely temperament, had affected Pope back in Washington. It smouldered on even after that. And Pope was not alone. Sibley had his day, too. No one can be certain what prompted Sibley's desire to be replaced, although at first it might have been local criticism over his campaign, and perhaps later the fact that under Pope, he was no longer overall commander.

As early as September 5, 1862, Sibley wrote his wife, "I have placed my commission at the disposal of Governor Ramsey . . . perhaps he may relieve me, and permit me to go home, which I am quite anxious to do." In another letter two days later he added, "for I am nearly worn out with fatigue." On September 11 he mentioned to Mrs. Sibley that he had heard of the governor's request to have the area constituted into a new military department, with a skilled Indian fighter at its head. He rejoiced to hear this, "as it would allow me to go home." Two days after this he learned of Pope's appointment, and told his wife that he would soon ask to be relieved of his command. From a letter of

September 17 it was clear that Sibley believed that Pope would actually take command in the field, which would release him.[1]

In his first dispatch to Pope, September 19, Sibley made no mention of replacement, yet after he received Pope's first message to him, Sibley sent a second note to Pope. "I would not have been displeased," he wrote, "to learn that you had selected as my successor in command some one . . . who has military qualifications." This suggestion fell on barren ground, so ten days later Sibley formally requested his release. He wrote, "I respectfully ask that you will relieve me of command of the expedition, and place at its head one of your officers. . . . A strictly military commander would be better fitted for this task than myself. Besides, my private affairs are left in utter confusion and require my presence." He repeated this the next day in sharper language. He told Flandrau that his business was being destroyed and that he needed rest. Pope ignored all three of Sibley's entreaties. On September 29, Halleck wrote Pope to inform him that "Sibley is made a brigadier-general for his judicious fight at Yellow Medicine." Halleck continued, "He should be kept in command of that column." It was not until October 7 that Sibley received the news of his promotion. On that day the officers of his command asked that he withdraw his appeal to be removed, and to use his influence to have the Minnesota regiments brigaded under him "till the end of the war." After this, Sibley did not again make a similar application, or complain of his fatigue or his business.[2] The tribute of his officers and the words of Halleck apparently bolstered his spirits.

Following the Sirocco campaign, Pope recommended both Sibley and Sully for promotion "in consideration of distinguished service . . . in the campaign of the past summer against [the] Sioux." Then in October, 1864, he requested that Sully "be brevetted major-general of volunteers for arduous and distinguished services against the . . . Sioux [in the Badlands cam-

---

[1] West, *Sibley*, 266, 267.
[2] *Official Records*, Series I, Vol. XIII, 648–49, 650–51, 680, 687, 688, 717, 719–20.

paign]," omitting at this time any reference to Sibley. In December Sibley compained to Pope, "I was no less surprised than mortified to find that . . . you had warmly urged the promotion of General Sully [and] . . . had not included me in the same recommendation," although in the report "our names appeared in the context and in juxtaposition . . . so as to make the omission of my name . . . [for promotion] the more prominent and remarkable." He hoped Pope would rectify this slight, particularly since the report had been published in the newspapers throughout the country. Sibley claimed his service was not secondary to Sully's and mentioned his successes in 1862 and 1863 before Sully took the field. "I hope you will aquit me of any desire either to make a parade of my own services, or to detract . . . from those performed by General Sully. . . . I only claim from our common superior officer . . . a like public recognition of the services and labors devolved upon me in the same field. My reputation as a citizen and an officer of the army is dear to me."[3]

Pope delayed in his reply until December 29, "in the hope that you would reconsider and recall" your letter ". . . as it embodies very grave complaints . . . I . . . shall place it, together with this reply, on the records of this office." In sequence, he took up Sibley's grievances. Sibley's activities of 1862 were rewarded by his promotion to brigadier general. "I supposed the account of 1862 to be entirely settled, and so much to your credit and in your favor that I did not imagine you would refer to it as grounds for any further claims." Regarding the 1863 campaign, Pope admonished Sibley that he had acknowledged and "sustained . . . [him] more openly and decidely than did the citizens of your own State," and went on to add that Sully also performed "equally valuable services . . . though he was detained by unexpected obstacles too long for the success of the joint operations." The commander then referred to his recommendation that both he and Sully be promoted for their 1863 service. The report Sibley took exception to, Pope remarked, was the one covering military operations for the year 1864. He

[3] *Ibid.*, Vol. XLI, Part IV, 827–28, 962.

pointed out that Sully alone was in the field, and wondered "By what process of reasoning you can persuade yourself that . . . you, remaining in St. Paul, are entitled to the same credit . . . as General Sully . . . I am utterly at loss to understand." In consolation, Pope mentioned he was both surprised and shocked at Sibley's attitude. "If I had been asked to designate an officer . . . to whom I have always shown special consideration and regard, and who could not . . . have any complaint to make of me, you . . . would certainly have been the man."[4] Whether or not Sibley was mollified is questionable, yet the logic of Pope's position is clear. At least their official relations did not seem strained by this episode.

If Sibley thought he had troubles, Pope believed his own greater. The fires of indignation and humiliation lighted in Washington those first few days in September not only smouldered but erupted into flame. Two weeks after his arrival in St. Paul, Pope wrote his friend Halleck a letter that should have been, as he himself said, left unwritten.

Pope asked, why did not Halleck, as his commanding officer and friend, back him up when others wanted to remove him from his Virginia command? Why did Halleck not "sustain me against the machinations of McClellan and his parasites?" Why, "your own declarations to me up to the last hour I remained in Washington bore testimony that I had shown every quality to command success." It might have been true that personal relations between McClellan and his officers and me were such that it would have been better to change the commanders of the armies around Washington, Pope conceded, but why advance McClellan knowing as Halleck did that his neglect of duty cost the North victory at Second Bull Run, and why banish Pope "to a remote and unimportant command?" McClellan, said Pope, was not Halleck's friend. Look out for him. "Neither he nor his clique will omit any means to destroy you." Now he would be ready to drop the whole thing, Pope continued, if the govern-

[4] *Ibid.*, 961–62; the reference is to Pope's annual report, which is in *Official Records*, Vol. XLI, Part I, 133–40.

ment did not persist in keeping silent and in retaining McClellan and his henchmen in command, but this meant that Pope would have to "urge in every way" that the court of inquiry to look into Second Bull Run be held, even though it had been suspended by "the influence of the very men charged with crimes to be investigated." Unless the government could somehow clear his reputation, Pope threatened, the investigation would be held, if not by a military court, then by Congress.[5]

Halleck did not think, conceivably, that he had done the best he could for Pope, the latter chided him. Or that Pope was satisfied to be so degraded? Why did not Halleck unite the Western Department and give Pope that? This would have been acceptable to Pope "and would at once have freed me from the odium and abuse which have so shamefully and unjustly been heaped upon me by the papers and . . . the unscrupulous military clique which have made honor and duty a by-word and reproach." As a matter of fact, Pope went on, Halleck could still give him the Western Department, which was inefficiently divided into half a dozen small commands, which would help Pope's name and reputation, if Halleck were a friend. If Halleck did not, he might be in hot water when Congress met, and as a friend, Pope said he would not want to see that happen. Also, he told Halleck, look out for "the pretorian faction in the Army of the Potomac" which seeks to get rid of "every officer . . . who is not in their interests." Besides Halleck, this meant Hooker. Hooker was a good man, said Pope, so do not let them destroy him. They were after Halleck, he reiterated, and already "the journals and people in his [McClellan's] interest are representing that he is really commander, whilst you are but a tool in his hands." Some members of the Cabinet thought this, Pope insinuated, and events since September made it seem true. For his own sake, Pope urged Halleck to show them he was the commander. One way to do this was to "do me justice and relieve me from the bitter mortification I have felt without reopening old sores."[6]

[5] *Ibid.*, Vol. XII, Part III, 816–17.
[6] *Ibid.*, 818–19.

In October Halleck answered that he did not like the threatening tone Pope assumed, and replied that both his premises and conclusions were unjust. "I have done everything for you that I could have done for a brother; but you have wished me to do for you impossibilities." He could not do what his superiors would not let him do, Halleck said. He had advised against Pope's being sent out west. When Pope fell back into the defenses of Washington, McClellan as ranking officer naturally commanded both his army and Pope's. As for the Maryland campaign, his officers felt so bitterly toward Pope, said Halleck, that he could not have commanded them. This was not Pope's fault, it was simply a fact. If the court of inquiry was suspended, it was done so because the army needed the officers in the field. A new court had been ordered. Halleck urged logically that he could not help it if Pope's report was not published: the President and the cabinet had decided that, but Pope, he said, had leaked it to Washington newspapers against orders, and that was a serious offense. If that had injured Pope, he could not blame Halleck! He could not establish, either, a united Western Department or assign a commander. This, too, was out of his hands. Halleck was aware of the hostility toward himself, that Pope mentioned, "but you very much mistake my character if you suppose I will permit my personal likes and dislikes to influence me in the performance of my public duty." If they wanted his job they could have it, should the government so decide. Halleck was still Pope's friend, he said, but he was sorry Pope did not understand the facts.[7]

Far from it, Pope replied later in October, he did not intend to threaten Halleck. He only wanted his own reputation cleared, and Halleck could not expect him to remain quiet over that. The court of inquiry should be held, and the blame for second Bull Run fixed (on McClellan), or the government should "acknowledge publically . . . my services in Virginia," or "bestow some mark of public confidence" in him. But it had done none of these things, and this inaction "has done me more injury than all else."

7 *Ibid.*, 819–20.

Well, "I will not pursue the matter. It seems plain [that I have been] . . . sacrificed for some reason yet to be explained." He asserted he would find out why, if he could, so he would know what variety of public interest meant more than his honor and reputation. If Halleck could not do what Pope asked, then, he said, he didn't really command, did he?[8]

In November, Halleck cautioned Pope to be patient. He was under fire too. But, he said, "it will all come out right in the end. If you were here you would see why silence just now is the far better course." What Halleck did not say was that McClellan was being removed! Later in November Pope noted that he would "await the action of the Government with all the patience . . . in my nature." He did not seek popularity, he said, only justice. After McClellan's victory at Antietam, he was very well received, and this, Pope said, would hurt his case. It would also embarrass the government when McClellan's career was laid bare.[9]

Pope made it to Washington for the court of inquiry. He wouldn't have missed it for the world, and the result went much as Pope hoped. He was exonerated, but it was too late for the public to restore him to their esteem. Rather unjustly, Fitz-John Porter became the whipping boy, since he was court-martialed for refusing to obey Pope's orders.[10]

The civilian interference with Pope in the Northwest reflected the political division within the North. If Sibley had no real outlet for his wounded pride, Pope at least could relieve his emotions by castigating the meddling Senators Rice and Wilkinson. Rice had schemed for Pope's job, and both legislators had tried to create within the department an independent body of troops they could control, Hatch's Battalion. In the end, the Senators had not won much of a victory. Strangely enough, Pope seemed more upset at the potential insult their activity placed upon

[8] *Ibid.,* 820–22.
[9] *Ibid.,* 823–24.
[10] Williams, *Lincoln and His Generals,* 161, 163. Williams has an excellent discussion of the relationships of Lincoln, Pope, Halleck, and McClellan, 159–63, and also a good paragraph on the Porter court-martial, 163.

Sibley. Pope felt that if he were to be replaced, Sibley was the one who deserved the job, not Rice. Pope would not have minded leaving if it would have meant a chance to fight in the South again. But the failure of that scheme did not deter Rice. The Senator had a living to make and his future career as a Democrat seemed doubtful, for re-election to his Senate seat was unlikely during the war. Sibley had also been a Democrat, and had been elected governor on the same ticket Rice had been elected senator, which made it seem odd that he should be critical of Sibley's military conduct. Rice was joined in this critical attitude by Wilkinson, the Republican senator who later bolted his party. Pope, in assigning reasons for this alliance, remarked

> Wilkinson has been discarded by his party. . . . At the certainty of falling into total obscurity . . . he has joined Rice. . . . Whilst the one has political purposes, the other has financial, and my objection to Hatch . . . is simply because Hatch is but an instrument of Rice . . . and the organization is simply to be used to promote the effects I have named. . . . The history of the Indian agents and the management of Indian affairs on the frontier . . . develop the reason for this alliance.

Colonel Stephen Miller, of the Seventh Minnesota, wrote Pope on August 24, "I am glad to see that you properly appreciate the trading, corrupt, Indian politicians of Minnesota. They are selfish and heartless as Satan." Miller was nominated by the Republicans, over Wilkinson's protest, to run for governor. "Their only hope now," he continued, "is to perpetuate their power by nominating Rice against me . . . he must in that event be beaten . . . and with his fall the whole Moccasin brood, except as they are fostered at Washington, will topple." Again, a day or so later, he wrote, "The friends of Rice and Wilkinson are as rabid as ever. They denounce the expedition and General Sibley as a failure." They boasted that there would be 2,000 Sioux on Minnesota "within a month, and, of course many honest apprehensive people believe them."[11]

[11] *Official Records*, Vol. XLI, Part IV, 494–95.

The continual distortion of fact and the deliberate attempts by Rice and Wilkinson to interfere in military affairs lend some credence to the charges of Pope and Miller.[12] Even Hole-in-the-day was dissatisfied with Rice and "the late treaty, negotiated by some of the chiefs and headmen, through Mr. Rice, at Washington. It is a bad treaty for my people" not only because the new reservation lands are poor. Rather than being further removed from the white people, with the subsequent lessening of "corrupting influences," the new situation actually increased the means of intercourse, especially from Lake Superior and north of the border. Whisky was reported among them, and given as a partial cause of tribal dissensions.[13]

Rice's connection with the Indians as a fur trader and treaty negotiator, both before 1862–63 and after, cannot be denied. But his political record, though he was independent and outspoken, does not reflect the mediocrity that might be expected of one spoken of so disparagingly by Pope, Miller, and Hole-in-the-day. However, his closeness to matters of land policy, such as Indian land cessions and railroad land grants in Minnesota (his brother, Edmund, was president of the Minnesota and Pacific Railroad Company and its successors, and was also a staunch Minnesota Democrat), leave a certain cloudiness in his particular patch of sky. On the other hand, while Pope often spoke with rancor, Miller, a respected citizen, self-made and self-educated, does not seem the kind of man to utter carelessly vindictive statements.[14]

The fall and winter of 1863 also found the political circus in Missouri again in full swing, only now, in the center ring, the lions threatened their tamer, Schofield. The radicals demanded Schofield's removal and accused him of misusing the enrolled militia and of being an imbecile. At first Lincoln stood behind Schofield, but the radicals brought so much pressure to bear that the President decided to promote Schofield out of the spot.

[12] *Ibid.,* 304, 380, 381–82, 385–86, 463–64, 494–95.
[13] *Report of the Secretary of the Interior,* 1864, 446, 447, 448, 449–50.
[14] William H. C. Folsom, *Fifty Years in the Northwest,* 558–61, 589–90.

It appeared this might bring together two Missouri factions which Lincoln thought would "go far to heal the Missouri difficulty." He suggested to Stanton that Rosecrans would have Schofield's place, since the Missouri radicals agreed to this. At this point, it seems, either Halleck or Stanton mentioned Pope for this position, and Stanton put this recommendation before the President. Actually, but unwittingly, Pope suggested this himself. In an October, 1863, letter to Halleck, Pope wrote:

> Indian hostilities and military operations against hostile Indians have been transferred by this summer's campaign so far to the northwest that neither St. Paul nor Milwaukee is a proper point from which to direct them. St. Louis is the place from which supplies . . . must be drawn . . . and it is the proper point for the headquarters of a military department conducting such operations.

Lincoln dismissed this idea by standing pat with Rosecrans, since the Missouri radicals "believe that the social influence of St. Louis would inevitably tell injuriously upon General Pope in the particular difficulty existing there." It is doubtful that Pope knew of this consideration and, fortunately for him, his Minnesota enemies were in no position to try to ease him out of the Northwest. The shuffle of generals centering about the Department of the Missouri was solved when one of Grant's generals, John G. Foster, asked to be relieved, and by Grant's approval of Schofield for commander of the Department of Ohio in Foster's place, if Schofield were promoted to major general.[15]

So it was that prima donnas sang sad songs while simultaneous webs of local and national politics were woven about the stage. Even here, the department was not wholly divorced from the effects of both national and military politics.

[15] *Official Records*, Series I, Vol. XXII, Part II, 612, 745; Vol. XXXI, Part III, 529, 571; John G. Nicolay and John Hay, eds., *Complete Works of Abraham Lincoln*, Vol. IX, 155–64, 264–66.

11

Men on the Move

THERE WERE NOT VERY MANY DULL MOMENTS in Pope's Department of the Northwest. If he did not fire paper barrages at the Indian Bureau, argue with subordinates or governors or politicians, or his superiors, or launder drenched crying towels, or if his men were not skirmishing with the challenging Sioux on torrid, dusty plains, then either he or the department's soldiers were fighting the arctic blasts of the prairie winter or cautioning eager emigrants.

In October, 1863, an expedition was assembled to take a provision train overland from Minnesota to the Crow Creek Reservation. Ordinarily, provision of an escort to accompany a train of this sort would be a routine matter, but there were elements in this situation that disturbed Pope enough to call Halleck's attention to the matter.

> Indian Superintendent Thompson . . . has applied to me for an escort for a train to haul supplies for these Indians [of the Crow Creek Reservation] from Minnesota. Why it is easier to buy in Minnesota and haul provisions over the uninhabited regions south and west of the Minnesota River to the Upper Missouri, rather than from Sioux City, or the Missouri itself, so much nearer to the reservation, I will not undertake to say, but I much doubt whether, at this season of the year, it will be possible to make such a journey . . . without great suffering to the men and the loss of . . . animals and wagons. . . . The cost to the War Department will be large.

But since he did not want a failure of the reservation attributed to the military authorities, he directed Sibley to proceed with the escort. The deplorable conditions at the reservation, mentioned earlier by Sully, prompted Pope to observe, "I have little expectation that the Indian Department will be able to maintain the Indians there through the winter."[1]

The duty for this escort fell to three companies of the Sixth Minnesota, commanded by Captain J. C. Whitney. With the onset of winter imminent, everyone viewed the overland journey across the plains with concern. The operation acquired the title "Expedition to Moscow," in anticipation of frosty weather conditions. With mild days at a premium, each delay was ominous, and several postponements intervened before the long march could begin. Men to drive the wagons were non-existent, even at $3.50 a day. When no civilians could be found at this price, soldiers were offered $1.25 a day for the same work, and enough were willing. But soldiers of the escort wanted to force the abandonment of this expedition, and some went so far as to disable about forty wagons by stealing the patent burs that held the wheels to the axles. Of an unusual design, these burs could be obtained no nearer than St. Paul. This serious situation made it necessary for Colonel Crooks to ride out and lecture the troops, and caution them that every delay very likely meant worse weather for them. The contractors increased their price to the military drivers to $2.00 a day, the patent burs were found, and the expedition started.

An abortive beginning had been made on November 6, but, with the delays and mishaps they had only reached Lake Shetek by November 20. After a three-day halt at Crow Creek they returned via Sioux City for safety's sake. Sully ordered the escort into winter quarters at Fort Randall, but Whitney, deciding he was not acting under Sully's orders, continued on to Sioux City. There Sully's officers would not issue him supplies, so, putting his men on half rations, he proceeded to lead them to Minnesota. This last leg of the trip was the worst, through snow nearly all the way, with temperatures down as much as thirty-five degrees

[1] *Official Records*, Series I, Vol. XXII, Part II, 671–72.

below zero. Whitney was court-martialed by Sully for his refusal to remain at Randall, but was acquitted.[2]

Next year Thompson again applied for an escort to take a supply train across the plains from Minnesota to the Crow Creek Reservation. Even though Pope instructed Sibley to use his judgment in the matter, Pope could not withhold comment. "It is not understood why it is that the Indian Department thus a second time applies for an escort . . . at such a season of the year, nor why they have allowed the whole spring and summer and more than half of the autumn to pass [before] . . . sending any . . . train to the Missouri." On the very same day, October 10, Sibley replied the first shipment of supplies for the reservation was lost by fire on a steamer at St. Louis, and due to low water replacements now had to be sent overland. He reminded Pope that the previous expedition had not started until November 15, and justified his escort by calling attention to the fact that they also were putting "sixty or seventy" Indians back on their reservation. This forced return of the recalcitrant Sioux was a secret matter, so that they would not hide or be rescued by their friends. Sibley issued orders for sixty men to convoy the train, "and for guarding Indian stragglers to the reservation on the Missouri." The expedition was underway by October 19, and reached Fort Thompson on November 5. But only twenty-two Indians, all women and children except for three men, went along. The escort returned to Ridgely on November 18, having made the round trip in thirty-two days.[3]

More of a problem to the department was the Indian menace to emigration across the plains. Gold was discovered in the valleys and headwaters of the Missouri, then in western Dakota Territory. Miners poured into the country from every side. The detection of gold nearly coincided with the opening of the Mullen Road (named after its builder, Captain John Mullen, Second Artillery) connecting Fort Walla Walla, Washington Territory,

[2] *Minnesota in the Civil and Indian Wars*, 318–19, also Captain Whitney's report to General Sibley, 319–20.

[3] *Official Records*, Series I, Vol. XLI, Part III, 772, 799–801; Part IV, 101, 632–34.

with Fort Benton, Dakota Territory. Also, steamboats had ascended the Missouri River as far as Benton in 1859. Gold was first found in the area in 1852, but the lode discovered ten years later on Gold Creek in Hell Gate Canyon really started the tide of migration. Bannock City and Virginia City, complete with newspapers and vigilance committees, sprang up before the close of 1863, and an estimated 13,000 whites, mostly miners, were in the area before the end of 1862. A few came from the east, but most were "Yondersiders" from California, Oregon, and Colorado.[4] From the east, Captain Fisk led two parties overland, one in 1862 and another in 1863, by way of the trail that came to be called the Northern Emigrant Route. This road ran northwest across the Yanktonai country from Abercrombie, passing north of the bend of the James River, continued on the northeastern side of the Coteau (between it and the Milk River), along the Milk River and its tributaries to the Teton River, then down its valley to Fort Benton. Fisk's expedition across the plains had been in advance of the Sioux outbreak in 1862; in 1863, he was en route, St. Cloud to Fort Benton, from June 15 to September 7, without any escort from the Department of the Northwest, and made the trip without serious incident.[5]

Emigration across the Northern Plains caused the department more concern in 1864 than previously because it then was expected to furnish escort. In 1863 the Fisk party, with only fifty-three men, followed roughly in the wake of Sibley's expedition from Abercrombie to Camp Atchison. They did, however, have a twelve-pound mountain howitzer with them. In his official report, Fisk mentioned a "mounted guard," which, according to another source, included only twenty-five men. The previous year's expedition, in 1862, had had a guard of from forty to fifty

---

[4] S. J. Coon, "Influence of the Gold Camps on the Economic Development of Western Montana," *The Journal of Political Economy*, Volume XXXVIII (October, 1930), 580–82; Thomas J. Dimsdale, *The Vigilantes of Montana* (Norman, Oklahoma, 1953), 22–25; Robert L. Housman, "The Beginnings of Journalism in Frontier Montana," *Sources of Northwest History* No. 22, 3–4.

[5] "Expedition of Captain Fisk to the Rocky Mountains," *House Executive Document* No. 45, 38 Cong., 1 Sess. (Serial 1189), 2–22, 37–39; Genevieve Murray, "Marias Pass," *Studies in Northwest History* No. 12, 36.

men; in both cases, apparently, hired especially for the job.[6] Fisk believed the 1,340 mile northern way impractical, and thought he could shorten the distance nearly 500 miles by following as closely as possible the forty-fifth parallel westward to the Yellowstone Valley and along this to the mine fields. Such a line would mean traversing the plateau between the Bad Lands of the Little Missouri and the Black Hills. Pope's plan of protection by locating a fort on the James and one on the Missouri, along with a post at Devil's Lake, was not designed to protect a route such as Fisk had in mind,[7] but circumstances aided Fisk in an attempt to use the shorter way in 1864.

The War Department did not specifically require Pope to protect emigrant trains, but strongly suggested he take military measures for their protection. In the newspapers the department published a "Notice to Emigrants by way of the Missouri River and the upper plains to the Idaho mines" on March 14, 1864. In part, this document read:

> The indications of a heavy emigration to the mines . . . during the coming season . . . render it proper . . . for this Department to publish . . . information and suggestions which emigrants will find it judicious to consider. . . . All information . . . point [sic] to a combination . . . of the Yanktonais Sioux with . . . strong bands of the Teton Sioux, south of the Missouri, to obstruct navigation . . . and to resist the passage of emigrants.

This circular warned that, until the military activities planned for late spring were completed, the area would be unsafe for emigration. It noted the proposed troop movements and suggested "emigrants . . . can avail themselves of the protection of

[6] *House Executive Document* No. 45, 3; letter of W. D. Dibb quoted in the St. *Paul* (Minnesota) *Daily Press*, July 28, 1863; letter of J. A. Russell, also quoted in the St. *Paul Daily Press*, August 6, 1863; and a letter of J. R. Tysen, in the St. *Cloud* (Minnesota) *Democrat* of October 2, 1862, along with Captain Fisk's "Official Report of the Expedition of 1862," all reprinted in *Collections of the State Historical Society of North Dakota*, Vol. II, Part II, 36, 73, 82, 83.

[7] *House Executive Document* No. 45, 34; *Official Records*, Series I, Vol. XXXIV, Part II, 257, 541.

this force, if they think it necessary."[8] No promise of escort was made, although Pope assured Halleck on March 20 that he would do all he could "with the means at my command" to oversee the safety of plains travel. Pope assumed that the emigrants, as in the past, would take steps to insure their own safety. This was clear from another passage in his circular, which read:

> Such of the emigrants . . . going . . . overland . . . are recommended to select a point of rendezvous [and] . . . assemble as large a force as possible, and . . . make some organization . . . under the direction of those members of the party most experienced in Indian warfare and travel on the plains. Not less than 300 men in a body should attempt to cross the plains at present.

In order to keep the Indians from reinforcing themselves with supplies and ammunition which would increase the danger of their attacks, Pope recommended the "Indian Department should refrain from supplying the Indians with ammunition, clothing, provisions, &c." until after the spring expedition, to make sure these items would not be used against "white emigrants or settlers."[9]

In early May, 1864, a group of emigrants held a meeting at Shakopee, Minnesota, and their chairman, G. S. Benson, wrote the department to inquire about government protection for plains travel. Pope replied on May 10 that he did not know, officially or otherwise, of any government arrangement to escort a group to Idaho Territory. He mentioned again the movements his troops would make, and reiterated they would be of "sufficient strength to protect any party who desires to avail themselves of the opportunity." Benson inquired whether or not "250 well-armed emigrants, under thorough and strict discipline," should attempt the journey unconvoyed. Pope answered, "Emphatically, no!" and went on to amend the instructions in his circular of the preceding March by adding,

[8] *Official Records*, Series I, Vol. XXXIV, Part II, 607–608, 608–609; *Collections of the State Historical Society of North Dakota*, Vol. II, Part II, 421–23.
[9] *Official Records*, Series I, Vol. XXXIV, Part II, 609, 688.

> I would advise no party less in number than 1,000 of well-equipped and reliable men to attempt a passage in advance of the expeditionary column of Brigadier-General Sully. After the enemy shall have been routed and severely punished . . . a comparatively small force will be able to traverse their country.

In closing, he mentioned that he had no information concerning Captain Fisk's intentions or movements. Two months earlier Sibley had received an inquiry from a prospective plains traveler. All Sibley could reply to H. S. Jennings, of Hastings, Minnesota, was that he knew nothing of any proposed expedition to Idaho Territory. His only advice was not to attempt the trip until after the Sioux had been pacified.[10]

Now, Pope planned to protect the northern emigrant route and the Missouri River route by locating forts along the Missouri, the James, and at Devil's Lake. But Halleck, in March, 1864, wrote Pope that

> It is represented to the War Department that the main emigration from the Western States to the Idaho mining region this spring will probably move from Fort Kearny by Fort Laramie, thence north, crossing the Powder River near the mouth of Willow Creek, striking the Yellowstone at the mouth of the Big Horn, thence up the Yellowstone.

Emigration from this quarter would need protection. Halleck proposed, notwithstanding the practical difficulties, that Pope's 1864 expedition, or a part of it, move out long the Niobrara or North Cheyenne rivers and establish posts on the Powder River and Yellowstone.[11]

There were many obstacles in the way of such a move. First of all, Pope did not have the man power. Secondly, Sully failed to establish a post on the Yellowstone because of deficiencies in supply, previously explained. In the third place, while such posts would have been impossible of winter maintenance by

10 *Ibid.*, Part II, 560; Part III, 541–42.
11 *Ibid.*, Part II, 607–608.

Pope's department, they would have been of easier maintenance by the Department of Kansas, for Fort Laramie was much more convenient to that area than any of the stations in the Department of the Northwest. In fact, the department was at a disadvantage in trying to administer even the upper Missouri from headquarters as remote and inaccessible as St. Paul or Milwaukee. From St. Louis, the valleys of the Missouri, Mississippi, and the Platte could be much more efficiently administered, with quicker and much facilitated supply. After the 1863 campaign, Pope had remarked that "military operations . . . have been transferred by this summer's campaign so far to the northwest that neither St. Paul nor Milwaukee is a proper point from which to direct them."[12]

A new reorganization of the western command situation would be a logical military step. With the command divided as it then was, access to the western parts of the Department of the Northwest was difficult since the easiest routes to the gold fields lay outside the department. Pope could do little about the Indians who were interrupting supply trains bound for Virginia City (Montana Territory) and points north, as long as most of these hostilities were out of reach of his Missouri River posts. Halleck suggested in 1864 that Pope send an officer to the mining region to raise troops for service in that area, although the same difficulties were present for their supply from the Department of the Northwest as was the establishing of forts on the Powder River and the Yellowstone. Halleck thought such regiments could be brought back to the Missouri "at Omaha during the autumn, I suppose."[13] In any event, Pope did not act on this suggestion before leaving Milwaukee in 1865.

Escorts and emigrants did not end Pope's problems. In 1864 an old adversary of Pope's, (Confederate) Major General Sterling Price, returned to the Missouri from which Pope had ejected him three years before. This put new life into southern sympathizers and partisans along the Iowa border. The adjutant

[12] *Ibid.*, 677–78; Vol. XXII, Part II, p. 612.
[13] *Ibid.*, Vol. XLI, Part II, 928.

general of Iowa telegraphed Pope on October 16 and reported Price crossed into Missouri and was advancing toward Iowa. Iowa was threatened by two guerrilla bands, one of which was then in southern Iowa. Pope, in turn, telegraphed Sully to return to Iowa as soon as possible. In a calmer tone he told Iowa to use its state militia, since there were no troops in the district except those of the Veterans Reserve Corps, not equipped for combat. "I have no idea," Pope commented, "that any considerable force from Price's army will undertake to move as far north as the Iowa line, and I think . . . a force of your militia will be sufficient to protect your borders from . . . guerrillas."[14]

John M. Hiatt, mayor of Keokuk, informed Pope on October 19 that he expected a guerrilla raid in force. He believed a mounted force was "imperiously demanded," along with "stringent application of military law" in the area. Hiatt told Pope that in his opinion "no portion of your department . . . is in more need of prompt and vigilant care" than southern Iowa. Pope's reply was not to the mayor, but to the governor, William M. Stone. He asked if the mayor's fears were justified, and suggested that if they were, the governor post a few companies of militia at Keokuk. Pope explained his lack of reserve soldiers, adding that if the governor desired, the department would send an officer of rank to Keokuk to overlook matters until Sully arrived back in the state. "General Rosecrans on the one side, and General Curtis on the other will render it impracticable for Price to send troops far north on the Missouri River without rendering it certain that they would be destroyed."[15]

Pope, unwilling to trust civilians with an estimate of a military situation, ordered Major Edward P. Ten-Broeck, in charge of the district of Iowa while Sully was in the field, to "give the matter your immediate attention, and ascertain as far as in your power lies all the facts in the case. . . . [and] keep these headquarters advised . . . as long as the present border excitement continues." On his arrival at Sioux City on October 19, Sully

14 *Ibid.*, Part IV, 24, 64, 65.
15 *Ibid.*, 124–25.

received Pope's telegram. Knowing nothing about the situation, he reflected his bewilderment in an urgent telegram to Pope: "Shall I send them [my troops] to the Iowa border? To what point in Iowa shall I go? Have telegraphed to Governor, for I know nothing." Two days later, after some of Sully's earlier correspondence had reached department headquarters, in particular his proposal to wait at Sioux City in case he should be needed to make an Indian treaty, Pope advised him to remain there as long as he thought necessary, since General Thomas C. H. Smith could be sent temporarily to southern Iowa.[16]

Pope's suspicions that the Iowa militia could handle the situation were confirmed by both Ten-Broeck and Surgeon Morse K. Taylor, commander of the hospital at Keokuk. Since Ten-Broeck's information was not first hand, he was ordered to go to Keokuk and report back from there. Once there, he revised his estimate of the situation somewhat, admitted the one company of armed militia in Keokuk was scattered and might be of little use should there be a night attack; he advised the arming of three hundred or four hundred of the convalescents at the hospital; and mentioned that the amount of private and government property would be a temptation to the guerrillas. Alexandria, a Missouri town a few miles below Keokuk, was under arms and barricaded. Ten-Broeck concluded he was satisfied "that there is no danger of any large force coming into Iowa at present, but . . . it is possible for 100 or 200 men to come down on such towns as Keokuk and do great damage . . . but if . . . 200 men were there with arms I do not think . . . any such attempt would be made." The Iowa adjutant general asked that the whole southern tier of counties be placed under martial law, and the mayor of Keokuk be appointed provost marshal. He also advised Pope to arm the convalescents and send a good commander with arms and ammunition to Keokuk. In the face of all this, Pope sent Smith to look the situation over. An unusual clause in Smith's orders supposedly allowed him to "assume command of

[16] *Ibid.*, 122, 123–24, 170.

the Iowa Militia in the southern counties of the state" if it was necessary.[17]

Brigadier General Smith arrived at Keokuk on October 28, in time to report Price's last retreat from Missouri. Smith saw the likelihood of guerrilla raids' declining, and admitted there had been a few. He concurred with the others in thinking the militia and armed convalescents would be sufficient for defense of Keokuk, but insufficient for the county generally, because infantry could not pursue mounted raiders. He asked that some horses be sent from Davenport. He further recommended that a provost marshal be appointed, one who was energetic and capable, to work with "a Saint Louis detective, acquainted as far as may be with the names and history of the men in Price's army" and other former rebels, so as to be able to ferret out rebel sympathizers and partisans "living here under the protection . . . [of] the oath of allegiance." Price's retreat, the organization of the militia, and the departure of the guerrillas, led Governor Stone on November 1 to thank Pope for his willingness to aid in protecting the state, but the danger was past for the most part, and should he need Pope's help in the future he would not hesitate to ask for it.[18]

Pope forwarded this letter to Smith, and urged him to return to his command in Wisconsin. Pope was opposed to making any military arrangements in the area, since "We may get an elephant in our possession which we will not be able to get rid of for a long time to come. I prefer to stand upon the Governor's letter." But Smith was tenacious and found an excuse to remain in Iowa a while longer. The election was to be held on November 8, and "in view of . . . the notorious complicity of the secret political societies . . . with the rebels" and anticipated trouble from that quarter, he wanted to remain. He did return to Milwaukee by November 19, but not until two detectives had been engaged. The result of their work was not recorded.[19]

[17] *Ibid.*, 170–71, 197, 244, 245, 260.
[18] *Ibid.*, 263, 303–304, 396.
[19] *Ibid.*, 422, 434, 622–23.

The Department of the Northwest did not have to worry much about Price. It would have been nearly impossible for his audacious army to have crossed all of Missouri and bring the war to Iowa. Iowa itself proved quite able to handle the guerrilla problem. Also, after the Badlands campaign, hostile Indians had been pushed so far west they could better be handled from the Missouri than the Minnesota. Emigration, too, was heavier over the central routes than the inconvenient northern one. The center of activity on the northwestern frontier was shifting ever west and south from Minnesota.

12

Total War and a New Command

ESCORTS AND EMIGRANTS seem as far removed from concepts of total war as the department that dealt with them. In themselves they might have been, but nevertheless the military in the Northwest felt the new concepts of warfare as Grant prepared to bring the tremendous weight of the Union to bear fully on the Confederacy. In order to do this, the General had to know the strength of his armies, and the military tool for this was the Inspector General. The Department of the Northwest, and the officers and enlisted men of all military organizations in United States service within it, were subject, by statute, to inspection by the Inspector General's Department. This department, given early form and substance by Frederick William von Steuben and Alexander Hamilton, had the responsibility of keeping the organization of the army standard, to superintend and enforce discipline, and to inquire generally into the condition and equipment of the army. "Armies, army corps, divisions, brigades, geographical divisions and departments, had inspectors general . . . and all parts of the army were subject to frequent inspections." Inspectors general for any unit but the department itself in Washington were usually appointed by the commanding officers of the organizations they served and, called assistant or acting inspectors general, they were members of the commander's staff, and were responsible for the organization, condition, and discipline of their respective units. The secretary of war controlled the office in Washington, and it was he who was responsible for assigning general officers to inspect armies, departments, or other large organizations.[1]

[1] Theodore F. Rodenbough and William L. Haskin, *The Army of the United States*, 14, 23, 25, 28, 29.

The first inspection by an officer of the Inspector General's Department was noted by Sergeant James T. Ramer, Company B, Seventh Minnesota Volunteer Infantry, on August 20, 1863. He wrote, "The inspecting officer of the regular army inspected our command at the second crossing of the Cheyenne," on their return from the Sirocco campaign. James H. Baker, then colonel of the Tenth Minnesota Volunteer Infantry reported the examining officer to be Colonel Randolph B. Marcy, the Inspector General himself. Baker added his regiment was "much commended for drill and discipline," especially Companies B and K.[2]

If other inspections were made of the department, there is no mention of them until June, 1864. By that time, significant events had taken place in the East. In March, Grant had been commissioned Lieutenant General, the second American officer to hold that rank permanently (George Washington had been the first, and Winfield Scott had held it as a brevet rank, but not as a permanent one). With Grant in command, and Halleck as his chief of staff, a command more nearly like the modern organization emerged. Also, with the appointment of Grant, other modern features of war appeared. War ceased to be strictly a military game and affected civilians more directly because the war was carried on at the economic level as well as the military. Desolation of the enemy countryside, practiced by Sherman and Sheridan, was designed to hurt the enemy by depriving him of his resources. Also the grand strategy changed, or at least became more effective. Grant's plan was to use all Union armies, east and west, simultaneously against the Confederacy, to use the superior man power of the North effectively to crush the South. No longer would the Confederacy be free to concentrate against isolated Union offensives and in so doing be able nearly to match Union strength. But it would take every Union soldier who could be found to accomplish this task, since not only would every army east and west have to fight, but they would also have to garrison captured areas and do the hundred bothersome man-power-consuming small tasks concerned with supply and admin-

[2] *Minnesota in the Civil and Indian Wars*, 355, 460.

istration. So Grant scoured the country for men. The hospitals were cleared of shirkers, and the frontier departments relieved of all troops not absolutely necessary for border defense.[3]

In June and July, 1864, no fewer than three inspectors general descended on the Department of the Northwest. The first of these in June was Major General Napoleon T. J. Dana. Dana was obviously sent to see if Pope was holding back troops, for Sibley remarked to his commander, "I think he [Dana] is satisfied that it will not answer further to diminish the force on this frontier." Apparently this was the official visit of the Inspector General's Department, but another inspector arrived in mid-June, Colonel William L. Duff, who was gathering information for Grant. Pope obliged him by giving out a numerical breakdown of the forces in the department, concluding, "It is impossible . . . to spare any part of this small force without exposing the whole frontier." Sibley furnished Duff with a historical account of activities in the department, and judged that it would be unsafe to reduce the already small force in the area.[4]

Detailed reports of the inspector generals have not been found; but Duff reported back to Grant in some detail. In part, he said, "From these remarks [Pope's statement in the preceding paragraph] (not made, I may here observe, in response to anything falling from me as to the purpose of the lieutenant-general) it is to be inferred that General Pope looks upon the Indian war as . . . being a serious affair." And Sibley agreed. But various citizens of Wisconsin, Iowa, and Minnesota, "and in two cases influential residents of Nebraska and Dakota . . . freely expressed, and in very strong language, that the whole thing was a humbug," and that a regiment of cavalry could handle the Indians, and a company of the same could convoy the occasional caravans (although somewhat later that year, Fisk, Duff's example, disproved this last statement). Duff did not, as ordered, inspect the expeditions in the field. His report had some influence with

---

[3] Williams, *Lincoln and His Generals*, 291–92, 298, 307, 313–14.
[4] *Official Records*, Series I, Vol. XXXIV, Part IV, 151, 170, 171, 184, 449–50; Vol. XLI, Part II, 39–40.

Grant who remarked in August that he thought Pope could send off two or three regiments without danger. Two regiments, however, would have cut Pope's strength one third, and three by one half, at least in numbers.[5]

In July another inspector was ordered to the department, ostensibly by the secretary of war. This was Brigadier General William S. Ketchum, who took reports from Pope and Sibley on the strength and disposition of troops in the department. Again, as in Dana's case, the Ketchum report has not been found, but Pope's commentary on it to Halleck is a matter of record. The only action taken by Pope was the transfer of two Veterans Reserve Corps companies from Davenport to Milwaukee. "All the effective force in this department has been ordered to the field from the War Department after several inspections of the department with that view." Ketchum's object was to garner all available forces for Sherman, because, as Halleck reported to Grant on August 13, "all troops under General Pope not actually in the Indian campaign were ordered to General Sherman, and special inspection made of his department." Five days later Halleck told Grant, "It is a very great mistake to suppose that General Pope has retained an unnecessarily large force in his department. On the contrary," Pope has been most ready to help out.[6]

Pope reacted indignantly to the three June–July inspections. He wrote Halleck on August 17, "It is to be regretted that misrepresentations from irresponsible persons . . . concerning the number of troops . . . are made to authorities by the Government. . . . [and] that such . . . should have any weight with . . . any of the military authorities in the face of official returns made from this department." By September 17, Pope demanded Halleck send him the statements or letters on which the inspections were based. Such statements, Pope thought, questioned the truth of his official returns, and since they seemed authoritative enough to justify inspection, it seemed only right to him to be able to face his accusers. "It is not believed that the War De-

[5] *Ibid.*, Vol. XLI, Part II, 29–30, 619, 987–88.
[6] *Ibid.*, 30, 627, 680, 739.

partment will take action implying so insulting a charge . . . without furnishing him . . . the statements and the names of his maligners." Official channels prudently carried no reply.[7]

Pope, whom Grant considered a good subordinate, clearly did not understand the purpose of the inspections. He did not see the big picture, he did not see, like so many others, the implications of total war. All he knew was that he had sent off as many troops as he honestly thought he could, that the incessant demands of the War Department made it difficult to plan in advance, and that the inspectors questioned his integrity. It was this hurt pride which caused him to lash out against them. Perhaps he discovered other western departments suffered to the same degree.

Then, in November, an unexpected and cryptic telegram came from Washington directing Pope to report in person to the War Department. The following day Pope telegraphed Halleck that he expected to be in Washington on Saturday, November 26. On Monday, November 28, Pope received further orders "to report in person to General Grant, at his headquarters in the field, near the Army of the Potomac." Here Grant offered Pope command of the Department of the South, but Pope declined. Grant telegraphed to Halleck, "General Pope . . . has objections to the command which I proposed for him that I think well founded, and [I] will not urge it further." At the same time Grant had an alternate plan for Pope. He proposed that the Departments of the Northwest, Missouri, and Kansas be erected into a military division under Pope.

> The importance of this change is much increased because of the inefficiency of the two commanders [Curtis and Rosecrans] of departments named. I . . . think it of very great importance that General Rosecrans should be removed. There is no fault with General Canby . . . but being at such a distance from Missouri he cannot direct affairs there. . . . With Pope in command we may secure at least two advantages we have not heretofore had, namely, subordination and intelligence of administration.[8]

[7] *Ibid.*, 680, 754; Part III, 237, 281, 373, 496.

This proposition met with Pope's approval, but red tape delayed the orders until January 30, 1865. General Orders No. 11, issued by the Adjutant General in Washington, read:

I. By direction of the President the Department of Kansas is merged into the Department of the Missouri, and Major-General Curtis is transferred to the Department of the Northwest. Headquarters of the Department of the Missouri are transferred to Fort Leavenworth, Kans. [A later section stated:]

III. Major-General Pope is appointed to command the Military Division of the Missouri, including the Department of the Missouri and the Northwest, headquarters at St. Louis.

Pope officially took command of the new division at St. Louis on February 3, but it took the rather reluctant Curtis another ten days before he reached Milwaukee.[9] With the creation of the Military Division of the Missouri, the Department of the Northwest became a subordinate entity, much as its own subdivisions were secondary to it. Even though the department existed in name for some years afterwards, it was no longer a major administrative area.

The twenty-nine months between September, 1862, and February, 1865, had been busy months for Pope and for the Department of the Northwest. For one thing, even though Pope had been virtually banished, had not been a good loser, and had a poor reputation as a result, his career was not over, and his work in the Northwest was partly responsible for that. In March, 1865, he was brevetted Major General for gallant and meritorious service in the capture of Island No. 10 three years before. Beginning October 1, 1866, he took six months' leave, after which he commanded the Third Military District (Georgia, Alabama, and Florida) in the South. In 1868 he assumed direction of the Department of the Lakes, then in 1870 he moved west again, taking over the Department of Missouri. His permanent promotion to Major General came in 1882. From 1883

[8] *Ibid.*, Part IV, 661, 672, 702, 709, 716, 717.
[9] *Ibid.*, Vol. XLVIII, Part I, 686, 694, 734, 845.

he commanded the Department of California and the Division of the Pacific until he retired at the age of 64 in March, 1886. On September 23, 1892, he died of "nervous prostration" in the home of his wife's brother-in-law, General Manning F. Force, governor of the Ohio Soldiers' and Sailors' Home.[10]

The influence of the Civil War on the American thinking has been so great that it still seems real and near to us even though one hundred years have elapsed since it began. In its own time it was really the first American struggle that brought home to all the people of the United States the significance of war. It was felt in every section, North, South, and West. There was probably no living American whom it did not touch in some way, either through news, taxes, the prosperity it brought, the effort to escape it, service in the army, politics, or death. The northwestern frontier felt the war in all these ways, and in an additional one, through the Sioux uprising and the campaigns against the redmen in succeeding years. The onset of the Civil War caused a weakening of the frontier which the Indians were not unaware of, and this weakened condition added to the terror the "accidental outrage" caused. The Department of the Northwest was a military administrative area run by the same War Department that conducted the main show, the officers were of the same army that fought the big war (many of them were veterans of it), and the main event precipitated many of the problems Pope had to face while running the sideshow.

No one can deny, in the face of troop shortages caused by the war in the South, the important contributions of the local areas, especially the new state of Minnesota, toward ousting the Sioux from settled areas. These contributions of men and supplies were as necessary there as their volunteers, foodstuffs, manufactures, and moral support were to the ultimate defeat of the Confederacy. If at first the Second Battle of Bull Run clouded the extent of the Sioux outbreak in Minnesota and drowned out the screams from the frightened frontier, the Union did move to

[10] Cullum, *Biographical Register*, Vol. II, 49–50; *Appleton's Cyclopedia of American Biography*, Vol. V, 68–69.

protect its troubled western brothers by creating the department, and Pope acted as expeditiously as he could, in the face of many obstacles, to remove the menace.

The military problems of the department were of a curious nature, compared with those of departments not on the frontier. First of all, the department was an orphan in many respects. Initially, Pope was the department, without staff or experienced aides. His job was first to quell the Indian uprising, and then to protect the settlements, emigration, and mails from hostile Sioux. The furious war between the sections occupying the main theater intensified problems of supply and man power. In the first few weeks after the department was created it was clear Pope would have to get along as best he could with local resources and leftover materials of war. The greatest difficulty, and perhaps the most annoying, was the problem of keeping troops in the department. Although he was given command of all in his area, he was successful in procuring only one of the five Iowa regiments that mustered into United States service in September, 1862, and that one arrived too late to be useful in the campaign. The experience with Wisconsin troops was similar, but here he was even less successful, retaining only one regiment of six, which he was able to keep until December. In Minnesota, where the immediate danger was greatest, he found five regiments, in various stages of organization, either already in the field or preparing to move thither. The civilian volunteers and militia of Minnesota, Iowa, and Dakota were useful and necessary in the absence of other troops, and supplied garrisons, particularly during the winter of 1862–63, at posts that otherwise could not have been maintained.[11]

Pope was an unusual commander in several ways, although not spectacular, unless one considers his vivid temper and fierce pride. He was a man responsive to civil rights, unlike Burnside and Butler, and civil affairs were generally rather well handled. He was a man who genuinely wanted to solve the Indian prob-

[11] *Report of the Adjutant General of Iowa,* 1863, 850–1013; Quiner, *Military History of Wisconsin,* 135–36, 735.

lem, and even though his proposed solutions were unique (removal of the Indians *east* of the frontier) and controversial (the military should control them if they remain out west), and even impractical, there was honesty in the attempt. In other ways Pope was simply another soldier, given to bursts of indignant bombast that were far from average. When civilians tried to interfere, he handled them roughly; subordinates who stepped out of line got the same treatment; superiors whom he imagined wronged him also came in for their share. He was pompous, arrogant, boastful, proud, and sensitive, but he was not afraid to fight, as he proved in Missouri and Virginia (although he had no average adversary in Virginia), he could take orders like the soldier he was, and even though he believed he had been victimized by the "McClellan clique," he did his best in the Northwest. Perhaps he was just human.

There is one more consideration: since it is difficult to separate the action on the frontier from the Civil War, so too is it impossible to separate the Indian problem during the war years from the same enigma in the decades following. For the Sioux, this was just a beginning. After the war they remained troublesome; other soldiers fought them later. If this story is one chapter of the War of the Rebellion, then so too is it one chapter of many on the Sioux.

Appendices

DISPOSITION OF THE TROOPS ON THE NORTHWESTERN
FRONTIER, JANUARY 1, 1861

Fort Abercrombie, Dakota Territory
Second Infantry, Companies A, D, I.
Fort Ripley, Minnesota
Second Infantry, Companies C, K.
Fort Ridgely, Minnesota
Second Artillery, Battery I.
Third Artillery, Battery E.
Fourth Artillery, Batteries F, K.
Fort Randall, Dakota Territory
Fourth Artillery, Batteries E, G, H, I, M.

APPENDIX 2

DISPOSITION OF THE TROOPS ON THE NORTHWESTERN
FRONTIER, AUGUST 1, 1862

Fort Abercrombie, Dakota Territory
Fifth Minnesota, Company D.
Fort Ripley, Minnesota
Fifth Minnesota, Company C.
Fort Ridgely, Minnesota
Fifth Minnesota, Company B.
Fort Randall, Dakota Territory
Fourteenth Iowa, Companies A, B, C.
Yankton, Elk Point, Vermillion, etc., Dakota Territory
Dakota Cavalry, Company A.

Fort Snelling, Minnesota
Sixth Minnesota*
Seventh Minnesota*
Eighth Minnesota*
Ninth Minnesota*
Tenth Minnesota*
Eleventh Minnesota**

* In the process of mustering, no regiment complete.
** Disbanded to complete organization of the Tenth Minnesota.

APPENDIX 3

DISPOSITION OF THE TROOPS ON THE NORTHWESTERN FRONTIER, AUGUST 30, 1862

Fort Abercrombie, Dakota Territory
Fifth Minnesota, Company D.
Volunteer Citizens, 1 Company.
Fort Ripley, Minnesota
Fifth Minnesota, one-third of Company C.
Seventh Minnesota, Companies C, G.
Fort Ridgely, Minnesota
Fifth Minnesota, two-fifths of Company B, two-thirds of Company C.
Sixth Minnesota, Companies B, C, D, E, F, G, H, I, K.
Minnesota Militia, Cullen Guard (Mounted), two-thirds.
Minnesota Militia, Renville Rangers.
Volunteer Citizens, about 25.
Birch Coulie, Minnesota
Sixth Minnesota, Company A, plus 18 volunteers from the other companies.
Minnesota Militia, Cullen Guard, one-third.
South Bend, Minnesota
Minnesota Militia, Mankato Company.
New Ulm, Minnesota
Minnesota Militia, two Companies.
Eighth Minnesota, Company F.
Crisp's Farm, Minnesota
Ninth Minnesota, Company E.

Garden City, Madelia, and along the Blue Earth River, Minnesota
Minnesota Militia, three Companies.
Winnebago Agency, Minnesota
Tenth Minnesota, Company B.
Forest City, Glencoe, and Hutchinson, Minnesota
Ninth Minnesota, Companies B, F, H.
Volunteer Citizens, about 46.
Minnesota Militia, Sibley Guards.
Minnesota Militia, Hutchinson Guards.
Fort Randall, Dakota Territory
Fourteenth Iowa, Companies A, B, C.
Yankton, Elk Point, Vermillion, Dakota Territory
Dakota Cavalry, Company A.
Spirit Lake, Iowa
Sioux City Cavalry, Detachment.
Sioux City, Iowa
Sioux City Cavalry, Detachment.

ADDED BY SEPTEMBER 15, 1862

Estherville and Iowa Lake, Iowa
Northern Border Brigade, Companies A, B.
Peterson, Cherokee, Correctionville, Ocheyedan, Ida, Sac City, West
   Fort, Little Sioux, and Melbourne, Iowa
Northern Border Brigade, Companies C, D, E, in detachments.

APPENDIX 4

CONSOLIDATED FIELD RETURN OF TROOPS OPERATING AGAINST THE SIOUX
Commanded by Colonel H. H. Sibley, for the Month of September,
1862, at Camp Release, Minnesota.*

Garrison	Present for Duty		By Authority		Without Authority		Present & Absent		All	Aggregate Present for Duty		
	Off.	E.M.	Off.	E.M.	Off.	E.M.	Off.	E.M.		Inf.	Art.	Cav.
Brigade, Field & Staff												
Officers	10						10		10			
Artillery	3	13					3	13	16		16	

Cavalry 3rd	4	24				4	24	28			28
Minn. 6th	1	229	12	135	229	2	603	605	230		
Minn. 9th	33	684	2	80	8	35	809	844	715		
Minn. 7th	3	75		9	1	3	88	91	78		
Minn. Renville	21	483	2	31		19	525	548	507		
Rangers 5th	1	37		2		1	37	38	38		
Minn.		8					8	8	8		
Totals	76	1553	16	247	238	76	2112	2118	1575	16	28

* Abstract of Return from Minnesota, *Executive Documents*, 1862, 308–309.

APPENDIX 5

ABSTRACT OF RETURNS OF THE DEPARTMENT OF THE NORTHWEST . . . FOR THE MONTH OF JUNE, 1864*

District of Iowa
   Northwestern Indian Expedition (Brigadier General Alfred Sully)
      Eighth Minnesota Volunteer Infantry
      Thirtieth Wisconsin Volunteer Infantry, Companies A, C, H, I
      Dakota Cavalry, Companies A, B
      Sixth Iowa Volunteer Cavalry, eleven companies
      Seventh Iowa Volunteer Cavalry, Companies K, L, M
      Second Minnesota Volunteer Cavalry, six companies
      Independent Battalion Minnesota Cavalry (Brackett's Battalion)
      Indian Scouts, one company
      Third Battery, Minnesota Light Artillery, two sections
      Prairie Battery
   Farm Island, Dakota Territory (Fort Sully)
      Thirtieth Wisconsin Volunteer Infantry, Companies D, F
      Seventh Iowa Volunteer Cavalry, detachments of Companies K, L, M
   Fort Randall, Dakota Territory
      Sixth Iowa Volunteer Cavalry, Company K

Appendices

Davenport, Iowa
  United States Veteran Reserve Corps, two companies
Keokuk, Iowa
  United States Veteran Reserve Corps, one company
Sioux City, Iowa
  Seventh Iowa Volunteer Cavalry, Company I
District of Minnesota (Brigadier General Henry H. Sibley)
  Fort Ridgely, Minnesota
    Second Minnesota Volunteer Cavalry, four companies
    Thirtieth Wisconsin Volunteer Infantry, Company G
    Detachment of Rebel Deserters
  Fort Snelling, Minnesota
    Second Minnesota Volunteer Cavalry, Co. K
    Third Battery, Minnesota Light Artillery, one section
    United States Veteran Reserve Corps, two companies
  Fort Wadsworth, Dakota Territory
    Second Minnesota Volunteer Cavalry, Company M
    Thirtieth Wisconsin Volunteer Infantry, Companies B, E, K
    Third Battery, Minnesota Light Artillery, one section
  Fort Abercrombie, Dakota Territory
    Independent Battalion Minnesota Cavalry (Hatch's Battalion)
  Fort Ripley, Minnesota
    Eighth Minnesota Volunteer Infantry, detachment
District of Wisconsin (Brigadier General Thomas C. H. Smith)
  Madison, Wisconsin
    United States Veteran Reserve Corps, one company
  Milwaukee, Wisconsin
    United States Veteran Reserve Corps, two companies
  * *Official Records,* Series I, Vol. XXXIV, Part IV, 628–29.

APPENDIX 6

ORGANIZATION OF TROOPS IN THE DEPARTMENT OF THE
NORTHWEST ... DECEMBER 31, 1864*

District of Iowa. Brigadier General Alfred Sully
  Fort Berthold, Iowa, [sic] Sixth Iowa Cavalry (one company)
  Crow Creek, Iowa, [sic] Sixth Iowa Cavalry (one company)
  Davenport, Iowa, Fourth U. S. Veterans Reserve Corps, Company K

172nd Company, Second Battalion, U.S. Veterans Reserve Corps

Keokuk, Iowa, 169th Company, Second Battalion, U.S. Veterans Reserve Corps

Fort Randall, Dakota Territory, Sixth Iowa Cavalry (five companies)

Fort Rice, Dakota Territory, First U.S. Volunteers (six companies)

Fort Sully, Dakota Territory, Sixth Iowa Cavalry (three companies)

Sioux City, Iowa, Sixth Iowa Cavalry (one company)
   Seventh Iowa Cavalry (two companies)

Spirit Lake, Iowa, Seventh Iowa Cavalry, Company K

Fort Union, Dakota Territory, Thirtieth Wisconsin, Company I

Vermillion, Dakota Territory, Dakota Cavalry, Company A

Yankton Agency, Dakota Territory, Dakota Cavalry, Company B

Yankton, Dakota Territory, Sixth Iowa Cavalry (one company)

District of Minnesota. Brigadier General Henry H. Sibley

Chengwatona, Minnesota, Second Minnesota Cavalry, Company M (detachment)

Princeton, Minnesota, Second Minnesota Cavalry, Company M (detachment)

Fort Ripley, Minnesota, First U.S. Volunteers, Company G
   Second Minnesota Cavalry, Company K
   Hatch's Battalion Minnesota Cavalry, Company E
   Minnesota Light Artillery, Third Battery (section)

Fort Snelling, Minnesota, Second Minnesota Cavalry, Companies A, D, H, L
   Twenty-third U.S. Veterans Reserve Corps, Company K
   Hatch's Battalion Minnesota Cavalry, Company F

Sauk Centre, Minnesota, Second Minnesota Cavalry, Company E

Fort Abercrombie, Dakota Territory, First U.S. Volunteers, Company A
   Hatch's Battalion Minnesota Cavalry (four companies)

Fort Ridgely, Minnesota, Brackett's Battalion Minnesota Cavalry (four companies)
   First Connecticut Cavalry, Company G
   Second Minnesota Cavalry, Company F
   First U.S. Volunteers, Company I
   Minnesota Light Artillery, Third Battery (section)

Appendices

Fort Wadsworth, Dakota Territory, Second Minnesota Cavalry,
    Companies B, C, D
    First U.S. Volunteers, Company F
    Minnesota Light Artillery, Third Battery (section)
District of Wisconsin
    [Milwaukee, Wis.] Fourth U.S. Veterans Reserve Corps (two com-
    panies)
    Twenty-third U.S. Veterans Reserve Corps (two companies)

* *Official Records,* Series I, Vol. XLI, Part IV, 995–97.

Bibliography

Note on the Sources

THE MAJOR SOURCE FOR this account is the *Official Records*, buttressed and supplemented by various other government documents. The Mereness *Calendar* of the *Letter Books, Department of the Northwest* was used to supplement the *Official Records*, which are more selective in the early volumes, but more complete in the later ones. Considerable reliance also was placed upon *Minnesota in the Civil and Indian Wars*, a compilation of regimental histories and statistics, written by members of the organizations included, and also comprising military reports and records not otherwise available. The notations of other contemporaries are taken into account, such as Buell, English, Ingham, Kingsbury, Pattee, Renville, Riggs, Sweet, and Whipple. Heard's *History of the Sioux War* includes much firsthand observation and a document or two. Adrian J. Ebell happened to be on the scene making stereoscopic pictures when the war broke out. Rodenbough and Haskin edited a volume with sections written by members of the organizations included, and the book contains considerable material from various files not elsewhere reproduced, if not always first hand. Valuable because they, too, contain unique information are Ingersoll's *Iowa and the Rebellion,* and Quiner's *Military History of Wisconsin,* a work heavily drawn upon by other writers. Both expand the adjutant general's reports of their states.

With few exceptions, all items in the bibliography also appear in footnotes. The *Reports of the Secretary of War* for the years 1860, 1861, 1863, 1864, 1865, and 1866 were valuable as supplements to, and as checks upon, the *Official Records,* although they do not appear in the following lists. *The Sessional Papers of the Province of Canada* were also consulted from time to time, as were numerous monographs and articles that did not find their way into the notes of the final draft.

Bibliography

I. Government and Legal Documents, Manuscripts, Registers, and Treaties

Benet, S. V. *A Treatise on Military Law and the Practice of Courts-Martial.* Fifth Edition. New York, D. Van Nostrand, 1866.

Commissioners, The Board of. *Minnesota in the Civil and Indian Wars, 1861–1865.* Second Edition. St. Paul, The Pioneer Press Company, 1891.

Cullum, George W. *Biographical Register of the Officers and Graduates of the U. S. Military Academy at West Point, N. Y., from . . . 1802 to . . . 1866–67.* 2 vols. New York, D. Van Nostrand, 1868.

Executive Documents of the State of Minnesota for the Year 1862. St. Paul, William R. Marshall, 1863.

Executive Documents of the State of Minnesota for the Year 1863. St. Paul, Frederick Driscoll, State Printer, 1864.

Executive Documents of the State of Minnesota for the Year 1867. St. Paul, Press Printing Company, 1868.

Halleck, Henry W. *Elements of Military Art and Science.* New York, D. Appleton and Company, 1863.

———. *International Law, or Rules Regulating the Intercourse of States in Peace and War.* Philadelphia, J. B. Lippincott and Company, 1866.

Heitman, Francis B. *Historical Register and Dictionary of the United States Army, 1789–1903.* 2 vols. Washington, Government Printing Office, 1903.

House Executive Document No. 4, 29 Cong., 2 Sess. (Serial 479.) Washington, Ritchie and Heiss, 1846.

House Executive Document No. 8, 30 Cong., 1 Sess. (Serial 515.) Washington, Wendell and Van Benthuysen, 1848.

House Executive Document No. 68, 37 Cong., 3 Sess. (Serial 1163.) Washington, Government Printing Office, 1863.

House Executive Document No. 80, 37 Cong., 3 Sess. (Serial 1164.) Washington, Government Printing Office, 1863.

House Executive Document No. 45, 38 Cong., 1 Sess., "Expedition of Captain Fisk to the Rocky Mountains" (Serial 1189). Washington, Government Printing Office, 1864.

House Executive Document No. 58, 38 Cong., 1 Sess. (Serial 1189.) Washington, Government Printing Office, 1864.

Joint Committee on the Conduct of the War. *Supplemental Report* of the Joint Committee on the Conduct of the War, Vol. II, "Report of Major General John Pope." Washington, Government Printing Office, 1866.

Kappler, Charles J. *Indian Affairs, Laws, and Treaties* 2 vols., *Senate Executive Document* No. 452, 57 Cong., 1 Sess. (Serial 4253–4254.) Washington, Government Printing Office, 1884.

Kennedy, Joseph C. G., comp. *Agriculture in the United States in 1860, Compiled from the Original Returns of the Eighth Census.* Washington, Government Printing Office, 1864.

———. *Population of the United States in 1860, Compiled from the Original Returns of the Eighth Census.* Washington, Government Printing Office, 1864.

Messages of the Governor . . . Together with Annual Reports of the Officers of the State . . . 1864. Madison, Wisconsin. Atwood and Rubles, State Printers, 1865.

Nicolay, John G., and John Hay, eds. *Complete Works of Abraham Lincoln* (12 vols.) New York, Francis D. Tandy Company, 1905.

Phisterer, Frederick. *Statistical Record of the Armies of the United States.* New York, Charles Scribner's Sons, 1907.

Report of the Adjutant General and Acting Quartermaster General of Iowa, 1862. Des Moines, F. W. Palmer, State Printer, 1863.

Report of the Adjutant General and Acting Quartermaster General of the State of Iowa, 1863. Des Moines, F. W. Palmer, State Printer, 1864.

Report of the Adjutant General and Acting Quartermaster General of the State of Iowa, 1864. Des Moines, F. W. Palmer, State Printer, 1865.

Report of the Secretary of the Interior, 1862 (House Executive Document No. 1, Vol. 2, 37 Cong., 3 Sess., Serial 1157). Washington, Government Printing Office, 1863.

Report of the Secretary of the Interior, 1863 (House Executive Document No. 1, Vol. 3, 38 Cong., 1 Sess., Serial 1182). Washington, Government Printing Office, 1864.

Revised Regulations for the Army of the United States, 1861. Philadelphia, J. B. Lippincott and Company, 1861.

Richardson, James D., comp. *A Compilation of the Messages and Papers of the Presidents, 1789–1897* (10 vols.). Vol. VI. Washington, Government Printing Office, 1896–1899.

Scott, Robert N. *An Analytical Digest of the Military Laws of the United States.* Philadelphia, J. B. Lippincott and Company, 1873.

Senate Executive Document No. 7, 37 Cong., 3 Sess. (Serial 1149.) Washington, Government Printing Office, 1863.

Senate Miscellaneous Document No. 28, 56 Cong., 2 Sess., Brown, Samuel J., "In Captivity: The Experience, Privations, and Dangers of Samuel J. Brown and Others while Prisoners of the . . . Sioux During the . . . War of 1862 . . ." (Serial 4029.) Washington, Government Printing Office, 1900.

Senate Miscellaneous Document No. 241, 58 Cong., 2 Sess. (Serial 4591.) 1904.

Senate Report No. 1362, 54 Cong., 2 Sess. (Serial 3475.) n.d.

State Department of History. "Official Correspondence Pertaining to the War of the Outbreak, 1862–1865," *South Dakota Historical Collections,* Vol. 8. Pierre, S. D., 1916.

Statistical Atlas of the United States, 1924. Washington, Government Printing Office, 1925.

Thwaites, Reuben Gold, ed. *Civil War Messages and Proclamations of Wisconsin War Governors.* Wisconsin History Commission, 1912.

United States Statutes at Large. Vol. XII. Boston, Little Brown and Company, 1863.

Walker, Francis A., comp. *The Statistics of the Population of the United States . . . The Ninth Census.* Washington, Government Printing Office, 1874.

War Department, Adjutant General's Office, *Letter Books, Department of the Northwest.* Mereness *Calendar,* Illinois Historical Survey, Urbana, Illinois.

The War of the Rebellion: A Compilation of the Official Records of the Union and Confederate Armies. 74 vols. in 132. Washington, Government Printing Office, 1885–1901. Series I, vols. XIII, XXII, XXXIV, XLI, XLVIII, LIII, Series II, Vols. I–VII, Series III, Vols. I–V, Index, and Atlas.

Winthrop, William, ed. *Digest of Opinions of the Judge Advocate of the Army . . . Between September, 1862, and July, 1867.* Third Edition. Washington, Government Printing Office, 1868.

Winthrop, William. *Military Law and Precedents.* 2 vols., 2 edn. Boston, Little, Brown and Company, 1896.

II. Biographical Studies, General Histories, and Monographs

Ambrose, D. Leib. *History of the Seventh Regiment Illinois Volunteer Infantry.* Springfield, Ill., Illinois Journal Company, 1868.

Berghold, Alexander. *The Indians' Revenge; or Days of Horror, Some Appaling Events in the History of the Sioux.* San Francisco, P. J. Thomas, Printer, 1891.

Catton, Bruce. *Mr. Lincoln's Army.* New York, Doubleday and Company, Inc., 1951.

Coues, Elliott, ed. *Forty Years a Fur Trader on the Upper Missouri: The Personal Narrative of Charles Larpenteur, 1833–1872.* 2 vols. New York, Francis P. Harper, 1898.

Cox, Jacob D. *Military Reminiscences of the Civil War.* 2 vols. New York, Charles Scribner's Sons, 1900.

Dimsdale, Thomas J. *The Vigilantes of Montana.* Norman, Oklahoma, University of Oklahoma Press, 1953.

Donaldson, Thomas. *The Public Domain.* Washington, Government Printing Office, 1884.

Dupuy, R. Ernest and Trevor N. Dupuy. *Military Heritage of America.* New York, McGraw-Hill, 1956.

Farrow, Edward S. *Farrow's Military Encyclopedia.* 3 vols. New York, Published by the Author, 1885.

Folsom, William H. C. *Fifty Years in the Northwest.* St. Paul, Pioneer Press Company, 1888.

Folwell, William Watts. *A History of Minnesota.* 4 vols. St. Paul, Minnesota Historical Society, 1911.

Gordon, George H. *History of the Campaign of The Army of Virginia.* Boston, Houghton, Osgood, and Company, 1880.

Gue, Benjamin F. *History of Iowa.* 4 vols. New York, The Century History Company, 1903.

Hanson, Joseph Mills. *The Conquest of the Missouri.* Chicago, A. C. McClurg and Company, 1916.

Heard, Isaac V. D. *History of the Sioux War and Massacres of 1862 and 1863.* New York, Harper and Brothers, Publishers, 1864.

Hubbard, Lucius F., and Return I. Holcombe. *Minnesota in Three Centuries.* 4 vols. The Publishing Society of Minnesota, 1908.

Ingersoll, Lurton Dunham. *Iowa and the Rebellion.* 2nd edn. Philadelphia, J. B. Lippincott and Company, 1866.

Leach, Jack Franklin. *Conscription in the United States: Historical*

Background. Rutland, Vt., Tokyo, Japan, Charles E. Tuttle Publishing Company, 1952.

Leech, Margaret. *Reveille in Washington.* New York, Universal Library, 1941.

Oehler, C. M. *The Great Sioux Uprising.* New York, Oxford University Press, 1959.

Paxson, Frederic Logan. *The Last American Frontier.* New York, The Macmillan Company, 1922.

Quiner, E. B. *The Military History of Wisconsin . . . A Record of the Civil and Military Patriotism of the State, in the War for the Union . . .* Chicago, Clarke and Company, Publishers, 1866.

Randall, James G. *The Civil War and Reconstruction.* Boston, D. C. Heath and Company, 1937.

Riggs, (Reverend) Stephen Return. *Mary and I, Forty Years with the Sioux.* Chicago, W. G. Holmes, 1880.

———. *Tah-koo Wah-kan, or, The Gospel Among the Dakotas.* Boston, Congregational Publishing Society, 1869.

Rodenbough, Theodore F., and William L. Haskin. *The Army of the United States.* New York, Maynard, Merrill, and Company, 1896.

Ropes, John C. *The Army Under Pope.* New York, Charles Scribner's Sons, 1881.

Schafer, Joseph. *Four Wisconsin Counties, Prairie and Forest.* Madison, Wisconsin, State Historical Society, 1927.

Shannon, Fred Albert. *The Organization and Administration of the Union Army 1861–1865.* 2 vols. Cleveland, The Arthur H. Clark Company, 1928.

Shortridge, Wilson P. *The Transition of a Typical Frontier.* Menasha, Wisconsin, George Banta Publishing Company, n.d.

West, Nathaniel. *The Ancestry, Life, and Times of Hon. Henry Hastings Sibley, LL.D.* St. Paul, Pioneer Press Publishing Company, 1889.

Williams, Kenneth P. *Lincoln Finds a General.* 4 vols. New York, The Macmillan Company, 1949.

Williams, T. Harry. *Lincoln and His Generals.* New York, Grosset & Dunlap, 1952.

Wilshin, Francis F. *Manassas.* Washington, Government Printing Office, 1953.

Whipple, Henry Benjamin. *Lights and Shadows of a Long Episcopate.* New York, The Macmillan Company, 1912.

Wilson, James Grant, and John Fiske, eds. *Appleton's Cyclopedia of American Biography*. New York, D. Appleton and Company, 1888, Vol. V.

III. Articles

Bryant, Charles S. "History of the Sioux Massacre of 1862," in Edward D. Neill, *History of the Minnesota Valley*. Minneapolis, North Star Publishing Company, 1882.

Buell, Salmon A. "Judge Flandrau in the Defense of New Ulm During the Sioux Outbreak of 1862," *Collections of the Minnesota Historical Society*, Vol. 10. St. Paul, Published by the Society, 1905. Part II, 783–818.

"Chief Big Eagle's Story of the Sioux Outbreak of 1862," *Collections of the Minnesota Historical Society*, Vol. 6. St. Paul, The Pioneer Press Company, 1894. pp. 382–400.

Clark, Dan Elbert. "Frontier Defense in Iowa 1850–1865," *Iowa Journal of History and Politics*, Vol. XVI (July, 1918), 315–86.

Coon, S. J. "Influence of the Gold Camps on the Economic Development of Western Montana," *The Journal of Political Economy*, Vol. XXXVIII (October, 1930), 580–99.

Ebell, Adrian J. "Indian Massacre and War of 1862," *Harper's New Monthly Magazine*, Vol. XXVII (June, 1863), 1–24.

English, A[bner] M. "Dakota's First Soldiers," *South Dakota Historical Collections*, Vol. IX (1918), 241–307.

Fisk, (Captain) James L. "Official Report of the Expedition of 1862," *Collections of the State Historical Society of North Dakota*, Vol. II. Bismarck, North Dakota, Tribune, State Printers and Binders, 1908. Part II, 34–72.

Housman, Robert L. "The Beginnings of Journalism in Frontier Montana," *Sources of Northwest History*, No. 22. Missoula, Montana State University, n.d.

Humphrey, John Ames. "Boyhood Remembrances of Life Among the Dakotas and the Massacre of 1862," *Collections of the Minnesota Historical Society*, Vol. 15, 337–48. St. Paul, Published by the Society, 1915.

Ingham, (Captain) William H. "The Northern Border Brigade of 1862–3," *Annals of Iowa*, 3rd Series, Vol. 5 (October, 1902), 481–527.

Bibliography

Jones, Robert Huhn. "The Northwestern Frontier and the Impact of the Sioux War, 1862," *Mid-America,* Vol. 41, No. 3 (July, 1959), 131–53.

Kingsbury, (Lieutenant) David L. "Sully's Expedition Against the Sioux in 1864," *Collections of the Minnesota Historical Society,* Vol. 8. St. Paul, Published by the Society, 1898.

Marshall, William R. "Henry Mower Rice," *Collections of the Minnesota Historical Society,* Vol. 9. St. Paul, Published by the Society, 1901.

Murray, Genevieve. "Marias Pass," *Studies in Northwest History,* No. 12. Missoula, State University of Montana, n.d.

Nicolay, John G. "The Sioux War," *The Continental Monthly,* Vol. III (January, 1863), 195–204.

Pattee, John. "Dakota Campaigns," *South Dakota Historical Collections,* Vol. V. Pierre, S. D., State Publishing Company, 1910.

Renville, Gabriel. "A Sioux Narrative of the Outbreak in 1862, and of Sibley's Expedition in 1863," *Collections of the Minnesota Historical Society,* Vol. 10. St. Paul, Published by the Society, 1905.

Robinson, Doane. "A History of the Dakota or Sioux Indians," *South Dakota Historical Collections,* Vol. 2. Aberdeen, S. D., News Printing Company, 1904.

Sweet, George W. "Incidents of the Threatened Outbreak of Hole-in-the-day and Other Ojibways at the Time of the Sioux Massacre of 1862," *Collections of the Minnesota Historical Society,* Vol. 6. St. Paul, The Pioneer Press Company, 1894.

Upham, Cyril B. "Arms and Equipment for Iowa Troops," *Iowa Journal of History and Politics,* Vol. XVI (January, 1918), 3–52.

Index

Index

Coteau des Prairies: 52, 68, 76, 80, 93, 177; Re Iphan (head of), 78

Cox, E. St. Julian: 44, 141

Craig, James: 33

Crook, George: 15

Crooks, William: 35, 145, 148, 175

Cullen, William J.: 34

Culver, Norman K.: 39

Curtis, Samuel P.: 107, 141, 159, 182, 190, 191

Custer, George A.: 15

Dakota Indians: *see* Sioux Indians

Dakota, soldiers in: militia, 32, 56, 193; cavalry, 25, 27, 32, 53 ff., 67, 70, 84 f., 90, 148, 156

Dakota, Territory of: xi, 15, 18, 28, 29, 30, 31, 45, 46, 53, 60, 69, 70, 76, 81, 84, 92, 93, 94, 118, 132, 154, 156, 176, 188; Bad Lands, 85, 87, 178; Big Mound, battle of, 65; Black Hills, 178; Bon Homme, 31; Camp Atchison, 64, 66, 177; Camp Hayes, 63; Camp Peoria, 67 ff.; Sioux Indian Reservation at Crow Creek, 67, 130 f., 174, 175; Dead Buffalo Lake, battle of, 65; Devil's Lake, 61, 64, 78 f., 90, 93, 116, 124, 178, 180; Elk Point, 31; Hell Gate Canyon, gold in, 177; Killdeer Mountain, battle of, 85; Pembina, 78, 81, 115, 132 f., 157; Primeau's Trading Post, 51; Richland, 31; Sioux Falls, 29, 31 f., 50, 54, 142; Stony Lake, battle of, 65; Vermillion, 31 f., 54; White Stone Hill, battle of, 69; Yankton, 24, 31 f., 53, 92, 156; Yankton Indian Agency, 29

Dana, Charles A.: 118

Dana, Napoleon T. J.: 188 f.

Dandy (Indian chief): 72

Dearborn, Abraham F.: 53

Deserters, Confederate: 82, 93

De Smet, Peter J. (Missionary): 23

Dill, Daniel J.: 85, 90

Dimon, Charles A. R.: 138

Disloyalty, treatment of: 97

Dodd, William B.: 43

Dole, William P.: 28, 35, 40, 60, 125, 128, 136, 145

Donnelly, Ignatius: 28

Downing, Jacob: 123

Draft: 96, 102, 104 ff., 107; draft dodgers, 90, 106; draft rioters, 103

Duff, William L.: 188

Duncan, Thomas: 105, 107

Dustin, Amos: 73

Edwards, Newton: 84, 117 f.

Elliott, Washington L.: 55, 103, 154

Emigration west: 176, 177, 179 f., 185

English, Abner M.: 53

Ewell, Richard S.: 10 f.

Ex parte Merryman, Milligan, Vallandigham: 97

Expedition to Moscow: 175

Feilner, John: 84

Fifield, Samuel S.: 135

Fisk, James L.: 23, 83, 90–93, 177 f., 180, 188

Flandrau, Charles E.: 35, 42, 47, 55, 98, 149, 164

Fobes, Frank B.: 41

Force, Manning F.: 192

Forts: Abercrombie (Dakota Territory), 24 f., 30, 40, 42 f., 45 f., 52 f., 61, 63, 67, 76, 78, 81, 93 ff., 135, 148, 154, 160, 177; Benton (Dakota Territory), 60, 177; Berthold (Dakota Territory), 57 f., 60, 75, 81, 89 f., 90, 94, 119, 138 f.; Garry (British America), 133; Hayes (projected), 80; Kearny (Nebraska Territory), 33, 180; Laramie (Nebraska Territory), 33, 91, 180 f.; Leavenworth (Kansas), 191; Mims (Mississippi Territory), 37; Pierre (Dakota Territory), 51, 54 f., 57, 60, 67 ff., 78, 82, 154, 156; Randall (Dakota Territory), 24 f., 27, 29, 32, 42, 51, 54 f., 60, 62, 68, 70, 76, 80, 93, 130, 154, 156, 175; Rice (Dakota Territory), 80, 82, 85, 89, 91 f., 119, 138; Ridgely (Minnesota), 16, 24 ff., 28, 30, 38 ff., 42 f., 43, 45 f., 67, 90, 92 f., 95, 140 f., 147 ff., 150, 155, 157, 161, 176; Ripley (Minnesota), 24 ff., 38, 41 f., 45, 61, 67, 94 f., 128, 134, 145, 148, 154, 157; Snelling (Minnesota), 26 f., 34 ff., 39, 42, 52, 67, 92 f., 99, 129, 134, 147 f., 154 f., 157, 160; Stevenson (projected), 80; Sully (Dakota Territory), 76

211

Index

Pemmell, Richard Bickerton, Earl Lyons: 62
Pfaender, Colonel: 95, 140
Pollock, Samuel M.: 84
Ponca Indians: 58
Pope, John: xvi, 3–10, 15, 37, 54, 60 ff., 68, 71, 75–82, 84, 90 f., 95, 98, 101–37, 139–93
Pope, Nathaniel: 84
Porter, Fitz-John: 8, 11, 170
Potawatomi Indians: 72, 136
Potomac, Army of: xiii, 98, 142, 158, 168, 190
Price, Sterling: 8, 109, 181, 184

Ramer, James T.: 187
Ramsey, Alexander: 27, 34 ff., 42 ff., 71, 102, 129, 144, 147, 164
Red Buttes, battles of the: 91
Red Iron: 50
Refugees: 38 f., 130
Renville, Gabriel: 76
Reynolds, John F.: 4, 8
Rice, Edmund: 172
Rice, Henry M.: 111 ff., 170 ff.
Ricketts, James B.: 8
Riggs, Stephen R.: 16, 21, 99, 122
Roberts, Benjamin S.: 108, 113, 156
Robinson, Charles: 29
Rogers, Henry C.: 83
Rose, Robert H.: 139
Rosecrans, William S.: 155, 173, 182, 190

Salomon, Edward: 34, 71, 102 f.
Saunders, E. C.: 141
Sawyer, James A.: 31
Scarlet Plume: 64
Schofield, John M.: 142, 152, 155, 172 f.
Scott, Winfield: 187
Severance, M. J.: 153
Seward, William: 97
Shannon, Fred A.: xiii
Sheehan, Timothy J.: 38 f., 41
Sheridan, Phil: 187
Sherman, William T.: 127, 154, 161, 187, 189
Shoshone Indians: 22
Sibley, Henry H.: 15, 34 f., 38, 44–52, 55–57, 60–70, 75–82, 91, 94–101, 105 f., 112, 114 ff., 119, 129–35, 139–46, 151–67, 170 f.,

174, 176, 180, 188 f.
Sigel, Franz: 142
Sioux Indians: 23, 64, 80 f., 84 ff., 88, 90, 92, 94 f., 100 f., 114 f., 121, 124, 128, 132 ff., 136 ff., 144, 149–53, 176, 193; brutality of, 98, 102, 123 f., 129 f., 130, 134; raids of, 70, 76; refugees, 133; relocation, 130, 132; sentenced by military commission, 99; surrender to Sibley, 98; treaties, 18 ff., 116; war, xv, 12, 15–36, 37–56, 57, 192, 194
Sioux tribes: Blood, 58; Brulé, 31, 33, 58; Cut-Head, 69; Dakota, see Yanktonai; Devil's Lake, 118; Gros Ventre, 58, 89; Mandan, 89; Minneconjou, 57, 87, 137 f.; Minnesota Sioux, 18, 23, 29, 45 ff., 51, 53 ff., 58, 67, 69, 74, 76, 87, 98, 128, 131, 133, 138, 153; Mdewakanton band, Minnesota Sioux, 16, 48, 51; Sisseton band, Minnesota Sioux, 16, 48, 64, 139; Wahpekuta band, Minnesota Sioux, 16; Wahpeton band, Minnesota Sioux, 16, 48, 51, 64; Missouri Sioux (see also Teton), 23, 58, 118, 125, 132; Oglala, 85; Piegan, 58; Sans Arc, 57, 87, 137 f.; Santee (see also Minnesota Sioux), 58; Teton, 64, 66, 75, 178; Two Kettles, 57; Uncpapa, 57, 69, 87, 136, 138; Yanktonai, 18, 26, 29, 31, 33, 45, 57, 64, 69, 75, 87, 128, 132, 137 f., 178
Sirocco Campaigns: 57–74, 75, 105, 131, 154, 165, 187
Sitting Bull: 15
Sleepy Eyes: 51, 60, 94
Smith, B. F.: 94 ff.
Smith, Caleb B.: 22, 27, 33
Smith, DeWitt C.: 90
Smith, T. D.: 43
Smith, Thomas C. H: 72, 157, 160, 183 f.
South, Department of: 190
Standing Buffalo: 50, 52, 64, 131, 133
Stanton, Edwin M., 12, 14, 29, 33–36, 112, 115, 120 f., 126, 143, 145 ff., 152, 154, 162, 173, 186, 189
Steamers, river: 68, 80, 89.
Stevens, Isaac: 4
Stone, William M.: 109 f., 182 ff.

215

DATE DUE

JAN 2 4 '64			
DEC 10 65			
DEC 3 '69			
MAY 6 '70			
NOV 1 8 '70			
DEC			
DEC 3 '70			
MAR 1 8 '71			
DEC 6 '71			
MAR 1 3 '72			
MAY 3 '72			
MAR 27 '73			
GAYLORD			PRINTED IN U.S.A.